A Life in
the Balance

A Life in the Balance

The Memoirs of Stanley J. Winkelman

Stanley J. Winkelman

With a Foreword by

Philip P. Mason

Wayne State University Press

Detroit

Great Lakes Books

*A complete listing of the books in this series can be found
at the back of this volume.*

Philip P. Mason, Editor
Department of History, Wayne State University

Dr. Charles K. Hyde, Associate Editor
Department of History, Wayne State University

Copyright © 2000 by Wayne State University Press, Detroit,
Michigan 48201. All rights are reserved. No part of this book
may be reproduced without formal permission.
Manufactured in the United States of America.

04 03 02 01 00   5 4 3 2 1

Library of Congress Cataloging-in-Publication Data

Winkelman, Stanley J., 1922–1999
A life in the balance : the memoirs of Stanley J. Winkelman /
Stanley J. Winkelman ; with a foreword by Philip P. Mason.
p. cm.—(Great Lakes books)
Includes index.
ISBN 0-8143-2942-x (alk. paper)
1. Winkelman, Stanley J., 1922–1999
2. Businessmen—United States—Biography.   3. Clothing
trade—Michigan—Detroit—History.   I. Title.   II. Series.
HD9940.U6 W6 2000
338.7'687'092—dc21
00-010468

To Peggy Winkelman,
my loving bride of fifty-six years and
partner in all that I have done

Contents

Foreword

In 1992 Stanley J. Winkelman donated the first installment of his personal and business papers to the Archives of Labor and Urban Affairs at Wayne State University where I was director at the time. I had known Stanley for many years as one of our community's leaders and because of his service on the Executive Committee of the Archives. But it was not until I had an opportunity to review his voluminous collection of records, and have many conversations with him about them, that I learned what a remarkable man he was and how much he had contributed to the city of Detroit.

Of special interest were the detailed records Stanley kept of all aspects of his life, including an account of his childhood in the Upper Peninsula of Michigan. He had to adjust quickly to urban life when he moved to Detroit, where he witnessed the impact of the Great Depression that left nearly half the city's workforce unemployed and destitute. Stanley's records include descriptions of this experience and of his observations on Detroit's leaders at the time, including Henry Ford, Father Charles Coughlin, Walter Reuther, and many others. The rise of Nazi Germany and the persecution of German Jews also received his attention.

Stanley thoroughly documented his lifelong association with Winkelman Stores, Inc. He covered both the early years of his association with the company—beginning in 1935 when he started working there part-time, learning each of the various aspects of the business—and the later years, during which he provided innovative leadership to the family business.

A second installment of his papers revealed his active interest in the community life of Detroit and his deep commitment to the civil rights movement, social welfare, health education, and consumer affairs. Stanley was a key figure in New Detroit, the nation's first urban coalition, established following the riot in Detroit in 1967.

When I wanted to learn more about Stanley and his career, I began a systematic search of the histories and publications about Detroit and its leaders. To my surprise, I found practically nothing about him, except for a few scattered news clippings. Unfortunately, this oversight is true for many of Detroit's men and women who have made significant contributions to the city and its quality of life; only our political leaders have received the attention of our historians.

As a result of this unsuccessful search, I urged Stanley to prepare his memoirs to fill this void and ensure that he receive the recognition he deserved. More importantly, such a work would provide a firsthand account on this important period of Detroit's history that would be available to scholars and others. I was delighted when Stanley agreed, and during the next few years he set about this task.

He spent weeks reviewing his records and checking newspapers and other sources. With the help and support of his wife Peggy, who shared most of his life with him, he was able to recall key episodes of his lifetime. He carefully described his years at the University of Michigan, his work with Linus Pauling at Cal Tech, and his career in the U.S. Navy in the Pacific Theater. He discussed in great detail his return to Detroit to begin a long association with Winkelman's stores, focusing especially on the important innovations he introduced in the management of the company that enabled it to adapt successfully to a rapidly changing business environment.

Stanley's attention to recent Detroit history—in which he describes his work with New Detroit and other social, political, and religious organizations that struggled to overcome the impact of the riots and the flight to the suburbs that followed—provides a rich account of this volatile period. Throughout the memoir, Stanley's lifelong struggle to develop a philosophy of life that would encompass family, business, religion, politics, and society is evident.

In the fall of 1998, Stanley suffered a serious illness that left him hospitalized for a number of months. Despite considerable pain and discomfort, he continued to diligently write and rewrite his memoirs. He spent days going through the thousands of photographs he had accumulated in order to select just the right ones for his memoirs. Finally, in August 1999, he presented his completed manuscript to the Wayne State University Press. Tragically, within a month of having finished his years-long project, he died.

Although Stanley did not live to see the final publication, *A Life in the Balance: The Memoirs of Stanley J. Winkelman* will leave a lasting legacy for future generations.

Philip P. Mason
Distinguished Professor of History
Wayne State University
Detroit, Michigan

Preface

*The Twentieth-Century
Balancing Act*

With the accelerated pace of life that exists as we approach the new millennium, it is important to pause for a look back over developments of the twentieth century, to gain a perspective on the past that will help us—and our children and grandchildren—face the future.

Many of the most profound changes I have witnessed during my own lifetime have been brought about by the invention of new technologies. The century's technological changes have been overwhelming in their breadth and impact. Think of them—from cyclotrons and satellites to pantyhose and Tylenol, from electron microscopes and the Hubble Space Telescope to compact discs and air conditioning, from computer clones to cellular phones, from heart transplants to polyester pants. How these inventions have affected the quality of our lives deserves great scrutiny.

I have been blessed with a life full of activity and opportunity. But it has not been easy—indeed, it is not easy for anyone—to balance all of the factors of family, business, religion, community, and politics, even with clearly established objectives in each area.

When I sailed on a landing ship tank—an LST—in the Pacific during World War II, I first became determined to attempt such a balance in my life. And I feel that I have been quite successful in that attempt.

I have had an enthusiastic partner. My bride of fifty-six years has contributed significantly of her own time and substance to the cultural institutions of our city and state, and she has been a strong participant in and supporter of my various endeavors.

As activists, Peggy and I believe that life should be lived to the fullest. We value the development and cultivation of human relationships. Yes, family is primary, and earning a living is essential; yet, without involvement in the larger society, something is missing.

Our children—Andra Soble, Margi Epstein, and Roger Winkelman—probably will never forgive us for some of the time we committed to others at their expense. But we believe that they are better for the experiences they enjoyed with us along the way, and they do respect us for feeling that we have an obligation to participate in the larger society.

In the twilight of the twentieth century, I can look back at my beginnings in a small town in the Upper Peninsula of Michigan and then forward to my life today, three-quarters of a century later, in a metropolis of 4.5 million people and with access to the world. From this vantage point, I can assess my own successes and failures, as well as the successes and failures of society as it has spawned and then adapted to technological change.

Indeed, the true balancing act of this century—for society and for individuals—has been between technology and humanity. This memoir offers one view of twentieth-century life, reflections on one man's efforts to strike that balance.

Acknowledgments

Without the encouragement and support of Peggy Winkelman, there is no way that I could have or would have spent three years in writing this memoir.

Phil Mason encouraged me to continue writing after I showed him my first very crude draft. His continuing support has been a source of great inspiration to me.

Roger Winkelman helped me analyze and assisted in handling some of the sensitive material. He has been extremely helpful in refining my thinking.

Wendy Warren Keebler did a superb job of reorganizing my writing without changing the content. Her responsiveness to our discussions was outstanding.

A Life
in the Balance

1

Early Years and
Family Life

A Boy Grows

My seventy-five years have been full
of contrasts. Even my earliest childhood was a study in opposites. Take, for
example, my family's move in 1928, when I was just five, from the small town
of Sault Ste. Marie—population ten thousand—in the Upper Peninsula of
Michigan to the large industrial city of Detroit.

The Soo (the nickname was derived from the "Sault" of "Sault Ste.
Marie") was a quiet town on the St. Marys River where the famous Soo
Locks connect Lake Michigan on the west with Lakes Huron and Michigan
on the south. The Canadian Soo, now joined with the American city by a
bridge, lies just across the river. In the spring, the extreme quiet cold of
winter gave way to the excitement of ships that passed through the locks
during the warm months.

My father, Leon ("L.W."), had opened a dress shop on Main Street
not far from the present site of the Ojibway Hotel. Leon Winkelman was
born in Manistique, a town some eighty miles to the west. My mother,
Josephine Rosenblum Winkelman, hailed from Gladstone, fifty miles west
of Manistique on Little Bay de Noc.

Both of my grandfathers immigrated to the United States from Europe just before the end of the nineteenth century. With the booming
lumber business of the day, each man was able to make enough money
selling supplies to lumberjacks to open department stores—Rosenblum's
and Winkelman's—that catered to the needs of their respective bustling
communities. Henry Rosenblum's reputation for honesty was so well known
that people often came to him for advice as well as merchandise. The
defining contrast in my grandfathers' lives was the oppression they had
faced in their countries of birth and the freedom they found in the United

Stanley, at age two, with Uncle Isadore Winkelman at the Soo, 1924.

States. In this country, my grandfathers created their own businesses and forged social acceptance in communities where there were few, if any, Jewish families. While public schools were relied on for basic education, there was an almost complete absence of religious education. Mose Winkelman maintained traditional Jewish rituals and managed some Hebrew teaching for his four boys. Henry Rosenblum was less religious and more assimilated into the social life of Gladstone. Several Jewish families lived in Escanaba, just seven miles away, and there were some joint holiday celebrations.

Many of the contrasts in my life have resulted from changes in technology over the decades, changes that have revolutionized how we get around, how we communicate—indeed, how we live.

Getting Around

There were occasional car trips from the Soo to Manistique and to Gladstone on gravel roads, which more often than not caused me to be carsick. The car would stop, and my father and I would get out to throw stones and get my mind off my stomach. Winter travel was extremely difficult because of heavy snow, scarcity and slowness of snowplows, and inadequate heating systems in the automobiles of the day. This was all quite a contrast to the marvelous limited-access highways and climate-controlled automobiles of today.

Road maps often relied solely on landmarks, with, for instance, an indication that the driver should turn right at the little red schoolhouse. If the school had burned down, the driver was lost. Compare this to the latest satellite navigation systems that let drivers see their exact location and the best route to their destination displayed on a monitor in the car.

Stanley's grandparents Henry and Rose Rosenblum and Hattie and Mose Winkelman
on the day Josephine Rosenblum and Leon Winkelman became engaged, 1920.

One day, when I was four years old, I was playing with the door handle in the back seat of a 1927 Buick as it drove slowly along Main Street in the Soo. I fell out onto the street when the door opened accidentally. Fortunately, the small Upper Peninsula town was so quiet that there were no other cars to run over me. I was left with a broken collar bone and a vivid memory. Today, of course, such accidents are much less likely in cars with child seats and child-safety locks.

It was a great thrill for me, at the tender age of four, to ride the train from the Soo to Gladstone, with stops at Trout Lake and Engadine. I always found the steam locomotive and its whistle greatly exciting.

My grandfather Henry Rosenblum—an exceptionally warm man who took a great interest in me—would take me on the interurban train from Gladstone to Escanaba. In Escanaba, we would visit the Fair Store and members of the Gessner family who operated it. On the way to Escanaba, the train followed the bluff along Bay de Noc, and we could see the iron ore carriers at the loading docks.

Trains today have been relegated to carrying containers of freight, with passenger trains—the epitome of luxury travel through the 1950s—limited mainly to the most heavily traveled corridors. But high-speed, 200-m.p.h. trains have been successful in Japan and in Europe, and there is still a chance that they will be developed in this country.

One winter, when I was very small, a group of ski-equipped, single-engine, open-cockpit planes flew in from Selfridge Air National Guard Base and circled over the locks. This frightened me, since I could not understand why they would not fall out of the sky right onto me. It was all the more frightening because the previous summer, we had heard the noise of a plane stop suddenly overhead, and the plane crashed nearby, killing the pilot.

Today, by contrast, supersonic Concorde and other intercontinental jets are remarkable developments that have made the world a much smaller place, with all nations closely connected. How else could Peggy and I have visited Europe one hundred times in the last forty years and the Orient ten times since 1963? Although my visits to the European markets did begin in 1957 before the Jet Age, the development of Winkelman's import program and its international fashion emphasis would have been impossible without jet travel.

All of these remarkable transportation advances seem pale in comparison, however, with the development of space travel. Only Jules Verne or the creator of Buck Rogers could have imagined such technological miracles. The very idea of a man *on* the moon—as opposed to the man *in* the moon—is mind-blowing.

Stanley, age four, with his parents and Uncle Isadore at the Soo.

Conveniences and Communication

Back in Gladstone, ice from Bay de Noc was cut in the winter, stored in an ice house, and covered with sawdust to make it last through the summer. I remember riding along on the horse-drawn ice wagon, watching the ice man carry big blocks hanging from large tongs into each home along the way.

It is hard now to imagine life without refrigeration or indoor plumbing. Two of the great labor-saving inventions over the years have been the refrigerator and the freezer.

Telephones back in my boyhood days were of the hand-cranked variety, with a long hand-held receiver connected by wire to a separate mouthpiece mounted on the wall or standing on a table. Party lines, which allowed neighbors to listen and gain fodder for gossip, were normal in those days. Today, my personal cellular phone can go with me wherever I go. The elaborate, labor-intensive switchboards of large organizations have become dinosaurs with the advent of direct dialing and electronic switching. (To get the effect of a party line, one can use the modern version: an Internet chat room.)

In the spring of 1928 came a very important telephone call. It was from my uncle, Isadore ("I.W.") Winkelman, who was operating a men's apparel store on Woodward Avenue at Milwaukee Street, near the General Motors Building in Detroit. He wanted to know if my father would be interested in going into business with him in Detroit. The answer from my father was, "Yes, as long as it is the ladies' ready-to-wear business." That "yes" marked the beginning of the Winkelman Brothers Apparel Store chain of ladies' fashion specialty stores. Much later, the name would be changed to Winkelman Stores, Inc.

In Detroit, station WWJ already had begun commercial radio broadcasting. How well I remember Rudy Valee and his "My Time Is Your Time," and also the voice of the then young groaner, Bing Crosby.

The multitude of AM radio stations and the later mushrooming of FM radio offered quantity, quality, and variety that were a far cry from the days of almost unintelligible reception in the Soo.

And what became of the typewriter of my youth? Now we have the computer! How did I get through school and my early business life without it? The incredible and almost incomprehensible computer makes difficult computations quickly and provides the basis for word processing, financial information, and access by on-line connections to vast information sources via the Internet. We have scanners, digital cameras, and inexpensive color printers to expand the possibilities of home publishing.

We take for granted that accurate calculations can be made easily on our pocket calculators. Compare the calculator with the hand-cranked adding machines of the 1920s, and even the slide rule, which was my own method of competing with those quick accounting minds that were so facile with arithmetic calculations.

Early in the nineteenth century, Samuel Morse invented the electromagnetic telegraph using wires to transmit signals. Morse's invention made it possible to send dots and dashes from coast to coast at the speed of light. In the late nineteenth century, Guglielmo Marconi discovered wireless telegraphy; he sent long-wave signals over a mile in 1895 and established the first transnational signals in 1901. Next came the telex with typed text transmitted by telephone. These new communication devices shrank the size of the world, which became even smaller with telephone cables under the ocean connecting the continents. And now, suddenly, we have clear satellite communications and fax machines, to say nothing of email, that enable us to communicate instantaneously with someone anywhere in the world, even in our own handwriting if we so choose. It's somewhat sad that modern telecommunications have replaced the sort of handwritten letters that I sent to my parents while I was at the University of Michigan and to my beloved Peggy while I was aboard ship as a naval officer.

Medical Miracles and Quality of Life

We were all vulnerable to childhood diseases such as scarlet fever, measles, and chicken pox, to say nothing of the near hysteria related to polio in the 1930s or all of the flu epidemics. First came vaccines, and then came sulfa drugs, to be followed by penicillin and other antibiotics—all merely a prelude to the newest genetic approaches to controlling and eliminating disease.

Has the quality of our lives undergone the same exponential improvement over the course of this century as have the ways we move about, how we communicate, our means of protecting our health? My answer to that would have to be no.

And why not? This is a troubling question to which we must have answers sooner rather than later. Much of this book is devoted to my personal views regarding this very question. If we truly want a better society and a better world for our children and our children's children, we must address this issue and our way of life in philosophical terms.

The name of the game is change. From the time we are born until the time we die, we experience continuous change in our bodies, in our lives, and in our environment. There is no such thing as the status quo or keeping things as they are at any particular time. The challenge in life is to adapt to change, to accept its inevitability, and to capitalize on the opportunities that change brings for us along the way.

My childhood in the late 1920s and early 1930s was marked by the beginning of the Great Depression and its devastating effect on Detroit. My own life was fortunately not directly touched by it. I continue, however, to feel the tragedy of the Depression and its human consequences as I think of the general complacency and materialistic emphasis of life today.

Early Schooling and a Move

I spent the summer of 1928 in Gladstone as my parents conducted the move from Spruce Street in the Soo to the Wilshire Apartments in Detroit. I was brought down by train in time to enter the first grade at Doty School, just before my sixth birthday.

While the Soo was now part of my past, I continued to spend wonderful summers in Gladstone until 1933, when I would go to camp with my cousin Howard near Hayward, Wisconsin.

My paternal grandparents moved to Detroit around 1930. We would go to their flat on Philadelphia Avenue for Sabbath dinners on Friday night and for the traditional Seder on the Passover. The 1932 photograph shows the four brothers standing with Heiman on the right, my father Leon to his left, then Isadore (the youngest), and finally Alvin (the oldest). My cousin Howard is standing on the left of the photograph while I am standing at the right. Rosalind is sitting below Heiman with my cousins Eugene and Stuart. My mother Josephine is sitting in front of Alvin with my twin brothers, Jack and Fred. On the end is Roulene with Robert on her lap. My grandmother, Hattie, and my grandfather, Mose, are in the center.

I enjoyed going through grades one, two, and three at Doty School and did well despite the contrast with my kindergarten experiences in the Soo.

On May 14, 1929, my father informed me that my mother had given birth to twins, my brothers Jack and Fred. "Hot dog!" was my enthusiastic response. But I had to keep my distance from the babies because I was recovering from chicken pox at the time.

My father drove daily to the store at Fort Street and Junction, which was growing slowly. My mother did not like to drive. She did her shopping over on Hamilton, just a block away from home. I was often sent to buy grocery items at the C. F. Smith Store.

In the summer of 1931, in order to accommodate our growing family, my father rented a home on Fullerton near Livernois in Russell Woods. This meant my transfer to Winterhalter School, where I was to receive my education for the next three years. Classes were large, but the teaching was of high quality and the subjects were interesting to me. My major problem was handwriting; my coordination was not the best.

I developed my first real friendships with John Anger, the boy next door; Bob Feinberg, who lived three doors to the east; Jim Topoloski, a student at St. Cecelia; and Jane Buck, a girl about a year older than I was and the person who first described for me the facts of life.

The Mose Winkelman family, around 1930.

My twin brothers were a real handful. Our parents hired an English nurse to provide much of their care. When she wasn't around, I was often assigned to supervise them. This was not a simple task with three-year-old twins. I can vividly remember chasing after them in our backyard—with a shovel.

By then, at age ten, I could take the Dexter bus alone, to Temple Beth El on Woodward at Gladstone and then to the dentist afterward in the Stroh Building downtown. I could also go by bus to the Fisher YMCA at Dexter and Grand Boulevard. Being so independent at such a young age was a great experience for me. Today, such travel is much too risky for children, a sad commentary on the quality of contemporary life and a severe limitation on developing a sense of independence in the young.

One summer, I sold newspapers at the corner of Livernois and Fullerton. The prices of the *Detroit News*, the *Detroit Times*, and the *Detroit Free Press* were three cents for each daily paper and ten cents on Sunday. I could keep a penny for each daily paper I sold. But I was not cut out to sell papers. Instead, I used to go into the cleaning establishment on the same corner to talk with the proprietor, a man named Schiff, who had also come from the Upper Peninsula.

Gladstone Summers

I spent the summers from 1929 to 1931 in Gladstone at my grandparents' home, enjoying the beach and my friends Naomi Staple, who lived next door, and Morris Riley, who lived about two blocks away.

Naomi and I made it our business to annoy my aunt, June Rosenblum, who was just seven years our senior. We also enjoyed riding in the rumble seat of a Chevrolet coupe with my aunt's friend on trips to Escanaba.

My grandfather, Henry Rosenblum, died of a heart attack in 1932. This was my first experience of a loss in my family, and it left an emptiness in my life that became less over time but has never fully disappeared.

Walter Ericson, the owner of the local pharmacy, would take me fishing for perch in Bay de Noc. Later, he would also take my son, Roger, and me fishing with him. That was in 1959, when four-year-old Roger caught his first fish.

My grandmother was a great cook. I particularly enjoyed watching her make kreplach soup.

The dining room of that marvelous house was always a place for wonderful meals and conversation. The house, where my mother grew up, was always open to friends coming and going. It stood on the corner of Seventh Street and Michigan Avenue. Huge oak trees adorned the grounds. The

Stanley, age seven, with girlfriend Naomi Staple and Grandpa
Rosenblum in front of his grandfather's home in Gladstone.

exterior was painted wood siding, and the interior was beautiful varnished wood floors, high ceilings, and papered walls.

My Uncle Herb and Aunt Anita visited in Gladstone along with my Aunt June during at least a part of each summer. They would play the banjo and the piano, attempting to reproduce the popular music of the day. Herb and Anita had graduated from the University of Michigan, as my mother— having studied sociology—had done before them, and June would do a few years later.

There were picnics at Pioneer Trail Park, about halfway between Gladstone and Escanaba. There we would meet other families for fun and games along with fabulous dinners.

By 1932, Rosenblum's Department Store had closed, and the building was leased to J. C. Penney through the efforts of my father. It was the end of an era, although family members continued to occupy the home in Gladstone until 1980. In 1957, Peggy and I drove through the Upper Peninsula with Roger as we visited the Soo, Manistique, Gladstone, and Escanaba. We continued going to Gladstone periodically until my Aunt Anita Lewis died in 1980.

In the fall of 1932, I was moved ahead half a grade to 4A because of overcrowding at Winterhalter School. I also became active as a member of the safety patrol.

And then came the move to Fairfield, just north of Six Mile Road and half a block from the University of Detroit. My father purchased the house for $10,500 in March 1933. In the depths of the Great Depression, that price was remarkably low for a home in the "golf club district."

This was right at the time of the Roosevelt Bank Holiday. Fortunately, my father and uncle had their money in the Detroit Bank at that time. The Detroit Bank reopened almost immediately, and they lost no access to their deposits.

Winkelman's was growing despite the Depression, with newer stores at Jefferson and Chalmers and at Grand River and Grand Boulevard. In addition, there was a leased ladies' apparel department in the Demery Department Store at Woodward and Milwaukee.

At about this same time, a central office was established in the Charlevoix Building on Park Avenue, near Grand Circus Park in downtown Detroit. The space would become too small, and about five years later, the office and warehouse were moved to 2210 Park Avenue, remaining there until 1944, when Winkelman's purchased the building at Parsons and Woodward, across Parsons Street from the empty Orchestra Hall. That building became the hub of the company's growth and expansion throughout my career and until my retirement in 1984.

Middle School Years

With the move to Fairfield came my transfer to Hampton School, which offered kindergarten through eighth grade. This permitted me to stay in the same school building until my graduation to Cooley High School in 1935. I entered Hampton in grade 5A in the fall of 1933 and managed to graduate in June 1935, having been pushed ahead again, this time from 6A to 7A, because I was excelling academically and also because of overcrowding.

Rhoda Montgomery, the assistant principal at Winterhalter, was now the principal at Hampton, and a very good one. My grades continued strong with all 1's and 2's (they would be A's and B's today). I also continued my "career" with the safety patrol and eventually became captain; it was my first leadership position.

There were boy-girl parties in those days, and spin-the-bottle was a favorite game. Being a year ahead of normal grade progression, I was less advanced both physically and socially than my classmates. Following in my father's footsteps (Leon Winkelman played in one of John Philip Sousa's bands as a navy seaman first class in World War I), I learned to play the trumpet, which I enjoyed, although my lip was relatively soft.

My friends in those days included Bob Feinberg, whose family had moved from Fullerton to Oak Drive just a few blocks away. From my Hampton class were Dick Hascall, whose father was a Chrysler executive, and Arnold Wigle, whose family was in the plumbing and heating business. And then there were my Catholic friends, who attended Gesu Elementary School and later University of Detroit High School. Chuck Steiner (a nephew of Father Celestin Steiner, president of the University of Detroit) was my closest friend. We played baseball together in the summer, touch football in the fall, and ping-pong in the winter. Through Chuck, I met Jack Ewald, Hilary Leger, and Jim Coyle (the son of M. E. Coyle, then general manager of Chevrolet).

On Saturday mornings, I would take the bus to Temple Beth El and afterward to the dentist to have my braces adjusted. The Fisher YMCA was too far away from my home then, but there was always plenty of activity in the neighborhood.

We were all Detroit Tigers baseball fans and very excited by the arrival of Mickey Cochrane as the playing manager. Cochrane purchased a home a few blocks from us, and we would get a kick out of riding past his house on our bicycles. This was the beginning of the 1934 and 1935 pennant-winning teams, with Hank Greenberg at first base, Charlie Gehringer at second, Billy Rogel at shortstop, and Marv Owen at third. Jo White played center field and was marvelous to watch stealing bases. Hal Newhouser, Tommy Bridges, and Elden Auker were the pitching stars. Goose Goslin

Stanley, age sixteen, with brothers Jack and Fred, age eleven, and Hank, age five.

batted in the run that won the 1935 World Series in the ninth inning of the seventh game with the St. Louis Cardinals. What a thrill it was to see a World Series game in person or to hear Ty Tyson describe the scene on WWJ. (There was no television in those days.)

For football, we focused on the University of Michigan Wolverines and on the Detroit Lions, who started playing in the University of Detroit Stadium just half a block from our house. Potsy Clark was the great Lions coach of the day, with Earl "Dutch" Clark the spectacular quarterback who would drop kick for extra points.

Joe Louis, the Brown Bomber, was another great Detroit sports success of the 1930s, with an incredible record of early knockouts of the best heavyweights from around the world. On the radio, we would listen to his thrilling championship fights. And what an embarrassment it was to Adolf Hitler when Louis knocked out Max Schmelling.

Finally, there were the Detroit Red Wings, many-time winners of the Stanley Cup, with that unforgettable front line of Ted Lindsay, Sid Abel, and Gordie Howe.

Detroit was truly a city of champions in those days, and what a sense of pride we had in it, despite the Depression—and despite the fact that the unemployed were selling apples on the street for a nickel each. We did recognize that there was human tragedy all around us.

The recovery programs of Franklin Roosevelt, who had been inaugurated as president on March 4, 1933, were beginning to take hold. The National Recovery Act (NRA), the Civilian Conservation Corps (CCC), the Works Progress Administration (WPA), the Federal Reserve Act, and the Social Security Act were ingenious efforts to bring the United States out of the Depression by providing employment (unemployment was running about 11 percent), stabilizing the banking system, and providing for long-term security of the American people.

This was a time for remarkable changes and renewed optimism regarding the future. This was also the time of Hitler's rise to power in the aftermath of World War I and a reassertion of German nationalism along with the persecution of German Jews as scapegoats for Germany's problems.

Countering fascism on the right of the political spectrum was the growth of communism in the Soviet Union, under the iron hand of Joseph Stalin, on the left. Our system of government found itself under attack by dictatorships on both ends of the political spectrum, raising questions in the environment of the Great Depression about the ultimate viability of American democracy.

The newspapers of the day were of a better quality than today, with emphasis on news and frequent extra editions when developments warranted. Radio newscasts did not assume great importance until the beginning of

World War II, and, of course, television did not exist. President Roosevelt did communicate with great success in his fireside chats on radio. I remember that his speeches usually began with the phrase "My friends," and I was struck by his warmth and directness.

High School and Summer Work

I graduated from the eighth grade at Hampton School and, in 1935, began traveling to Cooley High School each day by bus. I began my preparation for college as one of a class of a thousand students.

Bud Krohn and I were the only Jews in the class. At the same time, there was no observable anti-Semitism.

Stanley's high school graduation photograph, 1939.

This was at the time when Father Charles Coughlin, pastor of the Church of the Little Flower in Royal Oak, began his diatribes against Jews. He was not alone. Henry Ford, through his newspaper *The Dearborn Independent,* and Charles Lindbergh, whose only claims to fame were his precedent-setting solo flight to Paris in 1929 and the tragic kidnap-murder of his small son in 1934, joined Coughlin in Jew-baiting and praise of Hitler as World War II approached.

At Cooley, I began to develop some social life and learned debating, and in my senior year I managed the campaign for class president of a friend of mine, Don Robinson, a star halfback on the football team—but we lost.

Academically, I was doing well, with four years of math, four years of Latin, and three years of science. My chemistry teacher, a Mr. Gordon, came from Gladstone in the Upper Peninsula. He had been a victim of mustard gas in France during World War I. His influence inspired me to think of chemistry as a focus for my college education as I sought to become independent of my father and Winkelman's.

For our senior prom, we rented a Boblo Boat and band for a moonlight cruise down the Detroit River. It was a marvelous, romantic experience.

In those days, we could drive at the age of fourteen. Of course, there was much less traffic in 1936. My driver training was conducted primarily by Aunt June or Uncle Herb in Gladstone during the summer or on the uninhabited streets off Outer Drive west of Livernois in Detroit. Learning to shift gears, especially while making left turns, was the most difficult part. (The contrasting ease of automatic gear shifting was just in its infancy in the mid-1930s.)

I had great affection for Uncle Herb, with whom I felt a sense of camaraderie. He taught me to play chess. I suspect that his relationship with me carried him back to his own youth in Gladstone. It was Uncle Herb who would give me my first audio recordings when I turned sixteen and headed for Ann Arbor and the University of Michigan—Glenn Miller's "In the Mood" and "Moonlight Serenade," along with Artie Shaw's "Begin the Beguine" and "Frenesi," on breakable 78-rpm disks, so different from the CDs of today. (And the music so different then, too!)

My religious education was moving along at Temple Beth El, where I was confirmed in 1936. Confirmation was a moving experience, but much more moving would be the sixtieth anniversary of that event in June 1996, a reunion at which those of us in attendance conducted the service and were blessed individually, as in the original ceremony, by the rabbi.

There was no teaching of Hebrew and no bar mitzvah in those days, as Reform Judaism, and especially Beth El, headed toward assimilation in conducting Sunday morning services and rejecting Zionism. These major errors in direction would be brought to light by Nazi Germany through its persecution of German Jews who thought that they had been assimilated into German society.

One valuable experience from my years at Temple Beth El was a course on comparative religion that included visits to various churches and study of their religious philosophies.

In June 1939, I graduated from Cooley High School and from Temple Beth El. That summer found me at work in the blueprint room of the Chrysler plant in Highland Park, where Bob Janeway, a Chrysler engineer, had arranged for his son, Cornell, and me to work. "Heat up" was the order of the day as we produced blueprints for the 1940 cars in an environment of extreme heat that required us to consume salt pills. The blueprints were made using a wet process, long since made obsolete by dry methods.

After eight weeks of hot work, Cornell and I took off on a long bus trip to New York for the 1939 World's Fair. This was the fair at which General Motors provided a breathtaking view of the highway system of tomorrow, with limited-access superhighways and very smooth traffic flow that is still the ideal today.

From New York, we traveled to Atlantic City and then to Washington, D.C., before cutting cross-country to Louisville, Kentucky, where we stayed a few days with the Switow family before heading home. (Marge Switow later became Mrs. Max Fisher.)

Later that summer, I paid a visit to my cousin Howard Winkelman in Chicago, where we attended another All-Star football game. Howard was about to enter the University of Chicago to study chemistry.

It was on Labor Day, while I was driving by the Indiana dunes on my way back to Detroit, that tragedy struck in Europe as the German army invaded Poland to set off World War II.

2

Science and War

A Young Man's Journey

On Labor Day 1939, the bad news came that the Nazis had invaded Poland and that France and Britain were declaring war on Germany. Appeasement of Adolf Hitler had come to a sudden end, with belated recognition that he would violate any agreement when he felt it advantageous in order to take over neighboring countries in his quest for *Lebensraum* for Germany.

As war broke out, I was planning to head for Ann Arbor to begin orientation before the start of my freshman year. The draft posed no immediate threat, but there was always the looming possibility that the war would disrupt my education. The United States was technically a neutral power, although the president arranged the transfer of forty World War I destroyers to the British to help them protect supply shipments.

Since I had already selected chemistry as my college major, the first year would be somewhat routine. Entering the University of Michigan very young—I was still only fifteen—I accepted fraternity rushing but missed the deadline for deciding that I wanted to pledge Zeta Beta Tau. The dean of students did permit me to become a pledge, however. According to our class song, we were "seventeen strong from '43 and the best you've ever seen," to the tune of "I'm a Rambling Wreck from Georgia Tech."

Long-term Romance

It was in December of 1939 that I met Peggy Jayne Wallace at a tea dance at the home of a mutual friend during Christmas vacation. This was the beginning of a beautiful and loving relationship that has grown and flourished for close to sixty years. Peggy was a junior at Central High School in Detroit at the time.

I spent the summer of 1940 working in stores and spending weekends at Gratiot Beach. One weekend, I gave a party at the family cottage near

Port Huron for a number of my friends, with Peggy as my date. That was the best party experience I have ever had. With the swimming, the moonlit beach, and great picnic food, it was a weekend to be remembered.

Peggy and I had a marvelous time that whole summer, dancing to the best of the big bands of the day, outdoors at Eastwood Park, where we could have a great evening for not much more than a dollar. Tommy Dorsey, Jimmy Dorsey, Kay Kayser, and Benny Goodman were among the orchestra leaders providing the best of swing music. Canoeing at Belle Isle was another outstanding adventure.

Fraternity life turned out to be a growing experience but an uncomfortable one, as I was much less sophisticated than my brethren. Living in a dormitory was fine during my freshman year, and even walking up to my fourth-floor room didn't bother me. There were no telephones to distract us in those days. There were some communists around to cause us to think in political terms, although this was not something I wanted to do. The courses at Michigan were challenging, and my roommate, Bud Krohn, and I took part in intramural debating.

Tragedy struck in the fall of our sophomore year, when we lived in the fraternity house at 2006 Washtenaw. On one of the fall weekends when there was no football game in Ann Arbor, Arnie Schiff, a classmate, was killed in an automobile accident while driving back to Ann Arbor from his home in Columbus, Ohio.

The shock of Arnie's death was devastating to us. This was my first funeral of someone near my age and a very emotional experience. I was shocked at details of the graveside service, as the dirt was shoveled onto the plain pine coffin during the Orthodox service with all of the accompanying shrieking by the grief-stricken family. The upsetting scene left a lasting impact on me.

The football seasons were a highlight each year, with Tom Harmon, one of the greatest of all-Americans, playing tailback for Michigan and generating so many incredible touchdowns for the home team during my first three years. Our seats were in the end zone or close to it until our senior year, but that did not dampen our enthusiasm in any way.

With chemistry, physics, and math, I kept very busy. I learned two important practical lessons in time management while taking multiple laboratory courses each semester. Moving from one laboratory to another and scheduling my activities to make sure that each experiment was properly executed, day or night, taught me the art of intricate scheduling. By working through these timing problems, I acquired the ability to shift focus with ease from one activity to another on very short notice.

By the spring of 1941, as I was finishing my sophomore year, the war situation in Europe had worsened, with Germany in control of the continent, carrying the war into the Soviet Union to the east while bombing Great Britain heavily on the west.

By this time, the Army and Navy ROTC programs were attracting many students, as was the Navy V-7 program that permitted university students to avoid the draft and complete their education if they committed themselves to naval officer training immediately afterward. So far, my draft status as a student was "deferred," because I was training for essential war work as a civilian.

The highlight of fall 1941 was the arrival of Peggy Wallace on campus. I asked her to keep one weekend night for me each week, which was all I could afford in both money and time away from study. I would have preferred that we be together continuously, but that was not feasible. We did meet frequently during the week for study together or to have a Coke. This was the best of all worlds for me, although the war in Europe was getting worse and the war in North Africa was reaching a critical point.

Pearl Harbor

Then came the afternoon of Sunday, December 7, 1941, and the radio report of the Japanese attack on Pearl Harbor. Peggy and I were in our respective homes just a mile apart in Detroit when the story broke, just before we were to go back to Ann Arbor together.

As in the rest of the country, life for everyone on campus changed dramatically with Franklin Roosevelt's announcement the next day that a state of war existed between the United States and Japan.

What had been a deliberate pace of preparing to participate in the war effort now reached fever pitch following the huge loss of life and crippling blow to our navy. We all, in our own ways, felt a patriotic commitment to defeating the Axis powers of Germany, Italy, and Japan.

Our J-Hop, the junior-year formal dance, in January of 1942 was nevertheless an exhilarating event, with Tommy Dorsey supplying the music for this white-tie occasion. Peggy and I had a marvelous time. But then it was back to thinking about the war. I decided to attend the full summer session, an opportunity the university provided so that we could complete our education before going to war.

Summer of '42

Peggy decided on summer school, too. We took a class in Shakespeare together and one in psychology. These were wonderful learning experiences for us as our romance was blossoming into true love. I took a course in modern physics that was, in fact, nuclear physics. This is where I learned about the theory of atomic energy and the atomic bomb, the development of which was moving along rapidly with momentous initial success, when the graphite pile with rods of U-235 under the squash court at the University of Chicago went critical on December 2, 1942.

In fact, the summer of '42 was, for Peggy and me, a series of unforgettable experiences. We walked in the Arboretum. We went canoeing on the Huron River and enjoyed picnics. In general, we had a fabulous summer on the relatively quiet Ann Arbor campus.

By fall, I was looking for a position in chemistry but, hindered by the prevalent anti-Semitism of the time in industry, could find none. I was fortunate that Professor Bartell, a physical chemist, advised me of a position available in an OSRD (Office of Scientific Research and Development) project at the California Institute of Technology in Pasadena. I applied and was accepted, and was scheduled to report as soon as possible.

During that fall semester, I gave Peggy my fraternity pin. This called for my being thrown, fully clothed, into a cold shower by my fraternity brothers. The event surprised no one, since our show of mutual affection was obvious to everyone we knew and many we didn't know.

The Senior Ball was moved up into the fall, because of the war, and the Glenn Miller Band played for that spectacular white-tie event.

During the Christmas holiday, we spent an evening with my parents. I told my mother and father that Peggy and I planned to be married. My father wanted to know if we thought we were old enough. (I had turned twenty, three months earlier.) We replied that of course we were old enough. He then asked me to get out the bottle of champagne that he had put on ice for the occasion.

I did not wait around for the January commencement, which Peggy and my parents did attend in my absence. At the end of December, I took the train from Ann Arbor, where Peggy bid me a loving but tearful goodbye. In Chicago, I changed stations and boarded the Santa Fe Chief for California.

In a strange stroke of luck, sitting across from me on the train was Linus Pauling, professor of chemistry at Cal Tech, who was destined years later to receive two Nobel prizes, one in chemistry and the other a Nobel Peace Prize.

When Linus Pauling learned that I was headed to Cal Tech, he began a nonstop lecture on two subjects that consumed most of the two-day trip. He would alternate between the history and background of Cal Tech on the one hand and the geology of the country we were passing through on the other.

Life and Work in Pasadena

I arrived in Pasadena on New Year's Day in a driving rainstorm. It's a good thing the Rose Bowl game had been canceled because of the war, since it would have been a washout. I dragged my suitcase across the tracks to a hotel and spent the night contemplating the task of finding a place to live. The next day arrived with improved weather, and I was able to find a room for rent in a nice flat about two blocks from the campus and a reasonable boardinghouse for my meals not too far away.

Life in the Gates-Crellin Laboratory Building was fascinating, especially my developing relationship with the project leader, Don M. Yost, a professor of inorganic chemistry.

We were involved in a project dealing with measurements of poison gas concentrations under various micro-meteorology conditions. This meant developing sensitive instruments to measure wind and temperature gradients at relatively close distances to the ground—for example, determining readings on a continuing basis at three feet and six feet above the ground. The purpose was to predict gas concentrations needed to break gas masks under different meteorological conditions.

The gas we were to use in hundred-pound bomb field tests was to be sulfur dioxide. We therefore needed a device for measuring gas concentrations at these same levels above the ground. We had a good machine called "Egbert" that would take in a slug of water and then a slug of gas and measure the electrical conductivity of the gas so inhaled.

It was my task, working in a room where I could control the temperature, to develop a graph to translate Egbert's readings into gas concentrations at various temperatures. This work led to my one and only patent.

When we were ready, our field tests were set on the site of an abandoned silver mine near Victorville, California, in the Mojave Desert. We slept in sleeping bags under the stars. Shoes were put on with care to make sure no scorpions had crawled in during the night. Bombs were fired and data collected on Esterline Angus continuous recorders and the data taken back to the lab for analysis.

There were two PhDs on the project, Lindsay Helmholz and Dick Dodson. Everyone was cordial, and we worked well together. But I was very lonesome. One day, while we were working in an athletic field across the street from the lab, I asked Don Yost if it would be possible for me to fly home for a weekend to be married.

With his affirmative reply in hand, I wired Peggy: "Can you be prepared for a late March wedding?" Telephone calls were too expensive, and letter writing was still the custom, except for special or urgent occasions when Western Union was used.

Plans were set by Peggy's mother for a March 27 wedding at the Statler Hotel in downtown Detroit. I would fly out from and return to the Los Angeles Airport at Burbank, located at the site of the Lockheed plant in the San Fernando Valley. A friend of mine agreed to take me to the airport and pick us up on our return.

There was only one major problem. Since I had no travel priority, there was no way to be absolutely sure I'd get to Detroit in time for the wedding—or get back in time for work on Monday morning.

I left on a Thursday evening and arrived at Chicago's Midway Airport early Friday morning with time enough between planes to go to a barbershop for my first commercial shave.

As the tired and nervous bridegroom, I got myself cut and scraped a bit by the barber but still arrived in Detroit in relatively good condition to be reunited with my bride-to-be before the dinner for out-of-town guests given that evening by my Uncle Isadore and Aunt Marion.

The wedding itself was a beautiful but subdued black-tie affair for about eighty people. Some of Peggy's sorority sisters were there, as were a half dozen or so of my fraternity brothers who had not left campus early to go to war. They provided a spark with their singing and joking. It was welcome, since all of us were concerned about Peggy's beloved grandmother, who was gravely ill at that time.

My twelve-year-old twin brothers, Jack and Fred, got tipsy from consuming the champagne that was left in many glasses. As Peggy and I got ready to take off for our flight to Chicago, the twins were tended to at the airport by my Port Huron cousin, Eugene, who would later become a doctor and chief of internal medicine at the Cleveland Clinic. My seven-year-old brother, Hank, handled himself with great circumspection, as did Peggy's sister, Barbara, who was about thirteen.

After a six-hour honeymoon in Chicago's Palmer House, where rice was falling out of Peggy's hair as we checked in at midnight, we taxied to Midway for the three-stop journey to L.A. The flight was very rough; DC-3s flew at about 180 miles per hour at low altitudes. Both newlyweds became airsick.

It got worse after our first stop in Omaha. By the time we arrived in Denver, Peggy had to be taken to the stewardesses' quarters, and I to the pilots' quarters, to lie down while the plane was refueled. Salt Lake City was next, and we were feeling a little better; it now appeared that we would get to L.A. on time and that we would not be bumped for priority military personnel.

We arrived at the Burbank Airport in L.A. at about four in the morning and were met by my friend, Alan Grossberg, who took us to the apartment I had rented for fifty-five dollars a month at 61 North Allen in Pasadena.

We recovered quickly and settled into married life. I had to teach Peggy how to cook. I was earning thirty-five dollars a week at the time. We had no telephone and no automobile. But we did not mind. We particularly enjoyed going to the Huntington Library on weekends.

There was good grocery shopping, a drugstore, a Bank of America branch, and even a public telephone about half a block away on Colorado Boulevard. Peggy took easily to household responsibilities. I left each day at about eight in the morning and returned each evening at about six.

I traveled by bus to the lab, but often Linus Pauling, who lived in Altadena, would stop and pick me up at the bus stop in his old—even for that time—black Model-A Ford. I found Pauling to be alert, wiry, and somewhat eccentric.

Robert Milliken was the president of Cal Tech at that time. He became famous as the first scientist to measure the charge on an electron. Robert Oppenheimer was a Cal Tech professor of physics and already in charge of the top secret Los Alamos nuclear facility, where the first atomic bomb was assembled before being exploded at Alamogordo, New Mexico, in July 1945.

Both Dodson and Helmholz went to Los Alamos in the summer of 1943. I, not having a PhD, was transferred to the University of California at Berkeley. Louis Stang, who joined our project a month or two after I did, went off to work on the first atomic pile in the squash court at the University of Chicago, which had gone critical with the first self-sustaining atomic reaction using U-235 in December of 1942.

During his short tenure in Pasadena, Louis married Don Yost's secretary. I served as usher at the wedding, which took place at Woodlawn Cemetery in Glendale. It seemed strange to us that the wedding ceremony was held in a cemetery, but Woodlawn—"burial place of the stars"—is no ordinary cemetery.

Don Yost was an outstanding project leader, a colorful, rather short and wiry mustached man with an interest in everything. Peggy and I developed a friendship with Don and his wife, Marguerite, that endured until his death in the late 1970s. Over the years, we would compare notes on science, retailing, and the urgent problems of society. (Many of Don's letters can be found in my archives at the Walter Reuther Library at Wayne State University.)

Back in Pasadena, our first dinner party just missed disaster on three counts. Peggy managed to spill a bottle of nail polish all over the bathtub. The Jell-O spent too little time in the refrigerator. And finally, we forgot to have cigarettes in the house for Don, who was a chain smoker. (He nevertheless lived in a healthy state until age ninety.)

The one thing that Don, and almost everyone else involved in scientific work, detested was the "top secret" designation of the projects and the

Stanley on a bicycle in Pasadena, 1943.

restrictions on communication that were reluctantly followed to the letter. On the plus side was the corresponding priority we had available for purchasing and transportation.

All of the scientists I met felt that none of the research and development we were doing was really secret in the ultimate sense, since most of the concepts, including those for the development of the atomic bomb, were available before the war began in readily accessible publications.

Peggy and I took many weekend trips by Pacific Electric to L.A., and then by bus to Hollywood and Beverly Hills. Each month, my father provided one hundred dollars and my father-in-law gave us fifty to be used for our social life.

One Saturday, we went to Romanoff's in Beverly Hills where the prince himself gave us the best table in the house, for no other reason except that he liked young people and liked the way we looked.

On another occasion, we went to Earl Carroll's Vanities; we also saw Mae West at another nightclub. We went to radio broadcasts at the new NBC studios at Sunset and Vine and afterward to the Brown Derby restaurant at Hollywood and Vine. Those were exciting times, despite the difficulty of getting around the area on the Pacific Electric and buses.

The Rat House in Berkeley

Toward the end of September 1943, we moved to Berkeley where I was to work on another OSRD project. This one was led in the field by Sam Rubin, the man who did the original carbon-14 tracer work in examining the process of photosynthesis.

Wendell Latimer was the head of the chemistry department and author of the analytical chemistry text I had used at the University of Michigan. He was the titular head of the project. Years later Latimer provided some very negative testimony at the Oppenheimer congressional hearings, the stress of which led to his death from a heart attack.

Ken Pitzer, the discoverer of plutonium, was an adviser to the project. Ken would occasionally show up at the lab or at the site of our field work. He played a significant role in the development of the atomic bomb and years later served an important role on the Atomic Energy Commission.

I would also see E. O. Lawrence from time to time, although he was not a part of our project. Lawrence won a Nobel prize for his invention of the cyclotron in 1939. The cyclotron, which played a key part in developing the physics and chemistry for the A-bomb, still sits on the side of a hill just a few hundred yards from where the "Rat House" stood while I was at the University of California.

The Rat House was our scene of action, an old chemistry building at the center of the campus. Our assignment was to break gas masks. Instead of using actual poison gases in our field work, we used butane, which had similar flow characteristics. All field work would have to be verified using the real thing in the laboratory and eventually at the Dugway Proving Ground, an army chemical warfare installation near Salt Lake City.

Peggy and I were living in an apartment loaned to us by one of the PhDs on the project, Tom Norris. (We eventually found a place of our own, on Telegraph a few blocks from Sather Gate.) Norris and his wife were on location at the foot of Mount Shasta, a huge extinct volcano about two hundred miles north of San Francisco.

Peggy went with me on a trip to Mount Shasta. We slept in a double sleeping bag in a tent set atop six inches of lava dust that penetrated every pore. I remember sitting around after meals in our mess tent and discussing all sorts of fascinating subjects with the other couples.

Bill Gwinn assisted Sam Rubin in managing the project, and more often than not, he would be our leader in the field. Tom and Faith Norris were a very interesting couple with whom we developed a cordial social relationship.

Besides me, there were two other men who had not earned graduate degrees: Muddy Ruhl and John Thomas. Ruhl was an unusual man, a great storyteller who had been educated in China. Thomas was at Shasta with his wife, Mitzi, a schoolteacher. John would later complete his doctoral work and go on to become the president of Chevron Research. We became good friends and have stayed in touch over the years. At this writing, he and Mitzi continue to ski in the Sierra Mountains.

At Shasta, we would be up at four in the morning, ready to fire hundred-pound bombs of butane at the height of the temperature inversion (temperatures close to the ground were much lower than those a few feet above the ground), which ensured a maximum concentration of gas where it was most desired.

Our measuring instrument for the butane was a hot wire, hooked up to an amplifier. The resistance of the wire would vary with the gas concentration, and the resulting flow of current would be recorded on a moving graph meter. A small amount of vile-smelling ethyl mercaptan was added to the butane as a safety measure. The concept was simpler than that of Egbert at Cal Tech, but it required a rather complicated amplifier and circuitry.

Tragedy struck when Sam Rubin drove off the road one night on his way back to Berkeley. He broke his arm in the accident and then made the fatal mistake of working with phosgene in the lab the next day without benefit of a gas mask. With his injured arm causing some awkwardness, he was transferring the liquid gas into an evacuated system, the standard technique, when a container cracked and the phosgene gas boiled up all over him.

We were all shocked by Sam's death. We attended the funeral, a strange nonreligious affair as compared with the Orthodox funeral of my classmate Arnie Schiff in Columbus, Ohio, four years earlier.

Bill Gwinn replaced Sam as our field commander, and soon afterward we shifted our field work to Stinson Beach, which was just north of the Golden Gate Bridge on the Pacific Ocean in Marin County. Butane, in hundred-pound bombs, remained our method of choice for determining gas flow with onshore and offshore winds.

I suspect John Thomas and I could have gone to jail for carrying blasting caps and bomb explosives through the Walnut Creek Tunnel and over the Bay Bridge and the Golden Gate without permits or perhaps a police escort.

Peggy remained in Berkeley, where she was continuing her education at the University of California. But since the distances were short, we were not apart for more than a day or two at a time.

Work in the Rat House was like that of plumbers, glass blowers, and electricians. Real chemistry was in the background. One of my roles was to take a panel truck from the motor pool to secure the electrical and glass supplies from wholesalers in San Francisco. Armed with our AA-l priority, I would drive along the bay to the Bay Bridge and then on into the city. The views were incredible.

Peggy and Stanley in San Francisco, 1943.

Peggy and I would take "the train" to the city for dinner or to spend the day on weekends. We loved Fisherman's Wharf and enjoyed restaurants such as Don the Beachcomber and Trader Vic's. Nearby, on the Berkeley waterfront, was an excellent seafood restaurant, Spenger's. For sundaes and chocolate sodas, there was Edy's over on Shattuck Avenue.

The Camp family, friends of my family, operated leased millinery departments in department stores across the country and were often our hosts. Two years later, in 1946, it would be Herman Camp with whom I would talk philosophy on my return from naval officer duty in the Pacific.

The Florida Jungle

Just as everything was moving along smoothly, the U.S. government decided that we would do field work with real poison gas with the army's chemical warfare unit in the swamp adjacent to the Withlacoochee River near Bushnell in central Florida. Our objective was to work in near-jungle conditions and test our results with real toxic gases. Our group left Berkeley just after Thanksgiving in a three-vehicle caravan for the three-thousand-mile drive.

It took almost a week to reach our destination. John Thomas and I shared a room in Bushnell. It was pleasant enough, with only an occasional cockroach. But it was very difficult work lugging equipment into the junglelike environment. We used goats hooked up to breathing machines for monitoring gas mask effectiveness.

My Uncle Isadore and I met in Orlando during the Florida field tests. It was good to see him, and I enjoyed his company as I always had in my youth. He broached the subject of my postwar future and indicated that both he and my father would like me to join Winkelman's. I made no decision at that time, for I was still in the process of learning that I could make it on my own.

Finally, in early January 1944, we headed for home via the southern route through New Orleans, Texas, and Arizona, to arrive just in time for Peggy's birthday and a great reunion. Shortly thereafter, Thomas and I were sent to the Dugway Proving Ground near Salt Lake City to relate our butane test results in field tests to the genuine product. This time, we traveled by train and were gone for a little less than a week.

We would fire bombs of butane and bombs of phosgene and then don gas masks to go into the gassed area briefly to check our instruments. A problem developed with a change of wind when John Thomas had taken off his mask too soon and began to choke. I stayed on an extra day with him while he was in a Salt Lake hospital. Fortunately, John had no lasting effect from the incident, and we returned to Berkeley together the next day.

The Dugway incident caused me to ask for a transfer from the project when I learned that the next venue for the poison gas show would be the real jungles of Panama with the U.S. Army. Unlike army personnel, we had no training for the jungle, and I was not about to risk my life and my beautiful marriage in that situation.

USC and Los Angeles

The result of my request was a transfer to still another OSRD project, this time at the University of Southern California (USC) under Professor Anton B. Burg, the head of the chemistry department. The transfer took place toward the end of February 1944, and, once again, Peggy and I found ourselves looking for an apartment.

Luck was on our side as an army officer and fraternity brother of mine, with an apartment at Wilshire and Fairfax, was being transferred, and there was time to run on the lease. Chick and Nori Zolla were happy to see us and even happier to know that we could use the Cathay Apartments space. It was with Chick and Nori that we went to the Cuckoo Nut Groove nightclub to hear the song "Who Slapped Annie in the Fanny with the Flounder."

We celebrated our first anniversary in L.A., and a few days later, I wrote to my father for his forty-ninth birthday on March 31 that I hoped to make him a grandfather by his fiftieth. Peggy was somewhat concerned by my comment but did not challenge it.

The project I was working on this time—besides fatherhood—was surveillance of a new plant making cyanogen chloride, a new poison gas, in Azusa, between Pasadena and San Bernardino. We would periodically go to the plant to obtain samples then bring them back to the lab, where we would run tests to be sure that the product, being manufactured by American Cyanamid, was according to specifications. We wore gas masks and worked inside a ventilated hood when doing the testing.

While Peggy and I lived in Los Angeles, we made some interesting friends. There was Vera Lasserson, a concert pianist who played with the Los Angeles Philharmonic, and her English parents. Sadly, Vera died a year or two later, at a very early age, during childbirth. There was also Allen Rosenstein, a young professor of electrical engineering from UCLA who belonged to a group associated with the American Friends of the Hebrew University in Jerusalem. Allen remains a close friend. We visit with him and his wife, Betty, in Palm Springs or L.A. every year.

At around this time, our poor religious education became apparent. We would be asked our views on Zionism—a word never mentioned at Temple Beth El. The temple had been led by Rabbi Leo M. Franklin and a group of anti-Zionists who were members of the American Council for Judaism (soon to be discredited).

The Fourth of July weekend of 1944 found us with a group at the cottage of Irky Goldenberg, a member of the Friends of the Hebrew University, at Lake Arrowhead. It was here that we believe our daughter Andra was conceived.

A few weeks earlier, after D-Day in Normandy, it became clear to me that the younger scientists would be forced out and into the army, with the prospect of being sent over for the battle of Japan. This prospect prompted me to take two tests for the navy. The first was the test for radio operator as an enlisted man. I passed and would be eligible for training. The second test was to qualify for a direct commission. It took place on a Saturday at Hollywood High School. I was soon invited to accept a commission as an ensign in the U.S. Navy. It didn't take much time for me to decide which avenue to pursue. I accepted the commission and was ordered to arrive at the gymnasium of the University of Arizona in Tucson for eight weeks of indoctrination.

Anchors Aweigh

About mid-July 1944, Peggy and I closed out what proved to be a remarkable honeymoon time in California and returned to Detroit as I prepared to go to war. There were many pleasant reunions and a trip to Chicago, from which I departed for Tucson. While in Chicago, we spent time with my cousin Howard Winkelman, who was also wearing the uniform of a naval officer.

The gym at the University of Arizona was not at all bad as a place to sleep during our training. The daytime temperature was around 105 degrees. But that did not hinder our physical conditioning or slow down our marching on the nearby athletic field.

A man from Charlevoix, Michigan, was in the class just ahead of me, and it turned out that he was the manager of the band. With his guidance, I joined the band as a drummer and set myself up to succeed him as band manager three weeks later when he had completed his indoctrination.

As band manager and drummer, I wouldn't need to stand watches as everyone else had to do. My more flexible schedule would enable Peggy to join me. She arrived for the second month of my indoctrination and took a room in a home not far away. She was not feeling well early in her pregnancy, but we were both happy that she was there. We were able to see each other at five o'clock each evening in the bleachers at the athletic field, but regulations prevented us from even holding hands. My band duty did permit me to spend the weekends with her.

We shared some wonderful times with friends of Allen and Betty Rosenstein by the name of Rosenbaum. They had a simple but effective air-conditioning system: a fan blowing air across wet cloths.

Meantime, we officers and gentlemen, by act of Congress, were in training to be effective leaders and knowledgeable about ships and armaments.
Indeed, our education was well conceived and executed.

By the middle of October, my indoctrination was completed. I was
ordered to report for advanced indoctrination training at the Hollywood
Beach Hotel in Hollywood, Florida, the best of all possible assignments at
that time.

Peggy and I arrived together in Hollywood and were able to get a small
apartment about a block from the hotel where I was to be stationed for the
next two months.

As an officer in advanced training, I had much more freedom to be
with Peggy in the evenings and on the weekends. She was feeling much
better, and the temperatures in November and December were much more
comfortable than we had experienced in Tucson.

Saul Salon, husband of my Aunt Fanny's sister Bertie, was pretty well
retired from the Salon Jewelry store in downtown Detroit. The Salons had a
home about a half-mile from the beach. They were very hospitable, inviting
us over for dinner and, on occasion, to the newly opened Gulfstream Race
Track, where Saul was a fanatic about betting on the horses.

Emil and Shirley Rose, owners of Rose's Jewelry Stores and friends of my
parents, also had a home in the area. They, too, provided warm hospitality
to us while we were in Hollywood.

And then there was my Uncle Isadore, who showed up in Miami Beach.
One weekend we visited him and had the memorable experience of eating
at Joe's Stonecrab.

As our advanced indoctrination training was drawing to a close in December, it appeared that most of us would be assigned to the amphibious
forces. My orders were to Fort Pierce, Florida, for small-boat training, the
worst of all possibilities. However, after the short train trip to Fort Pierce,
my orders were changed, and I was directed to report to the amphibious
base at Little Creek, Virginia.

Peggy and I took an apartment on the beach at nearby Virginia Beach
from which I would commute daily for the next six weeks. At Little Creek,
I was assigned to the company commanded by George Ceithaml, the all-
American quarterback who had played with Tom Harmon at Michigan.
George and I had known each other on campus and had taken a scientific
German course (a study of the German words related to the science of
chemistry) together.

Within a couple of weeks of my arrival at Little Creek, I was ordered
to report as a supernumerary to the LST-384 berthed at the Norfolk
Navy Yard. The 384 had been rebuilt after being buzz-bombed in London.

Immediate orders were to take her on a shakedown cruise in Chesapeake Bay and to prepare to ship out.

I was assigned to the supply function as a deck officer and spent my off-watch hours working with the chief commissary steward, Bill Adney, to ensure that the proper complement of supplies was brought aboard and that we were as well prepared as possible for the long trip across the Pacific that was all too likely in the near future.

Adney had been at sea for many years and knew that taking up valuable refrigerator space with fresh stuff was a mistake. Instead, he wanted to load

Ensign Stanley Winkelman with Uncle Isadore in Florida, 1944.

LST-384, with Ensign Stanley Winkelman on
board as line officer and in charge of supplies.

as much meat, butter, and eggs as our cold storage facility could handle.
This we did.

I felt that our morale would be helped by having certain equipment that
was not normally found on an LST. To that end, we went to various supply
facilities on the Norfolk naval base and were successful in acquiring an
ice cream machine, a Coke machine, and a 35-mm movie projector. We
also loaded the officers' mess with canned tuna and pimentos for snacks.
One attractive feature of the navy, as opposed to the other services, was the
officers' mess, where we had tablecloths, silver, and china along with a mess
steward to handle food preparation and service.

The result of all this activity on my part was a permanent assignment
as supply officer when the shakedown was completed, while other super-
numeraries were put ashore. In trying to protect myself and the crew of
the 384, I had earned myself a place on the ship and would be shipping out
sooner rather than later. In retrospect, I survived very well. Who knows
what my fate would have been if I had not been so conscientious?

At this point, our parents came over to Virginia Beach to bid me adieu,
and Peggy prepared to return to Detroit for the duration. It was a very sad
occasion for me to be leaving her with our baby alive in her womb and not
knowing when or if I would return. Indeed, parting was such sweet sorrow.

The 384 departed near the end of January 1945 and headed south on
rough seas for Guantánamo Bay, Cuba, at the snail's pace of seven knots. It
did not take long for me to learn that I would be standing watch high up
on the conning tower with a bucket—I became seasick every time we left

port. I would be fine after about three days, but in the meantime I would take quite a ribbing from the real sailors on board.

To prepare for exposure to the weather in Chesapeake Bay, I acquired the materials necessary for the chief boatswain's mate to build a steel-pipe-framed enclosure for the conning tower with sliding plastic windows. This protected us from much of the snow, sleet, and rain, although it did nothing to alleviate the extreme cold of the midwinter North Atlantic. But then, in a few days, we were in a much warmer climate.

On this first leg of the long journey to the other side of the Pacific, as we would do on all the other legs, we literally rolled along, swinging from

Peggy, carrying Andra, with Stanley at Virgina Beach.

Ensign Stanley Winkelman at Virginia Beach
just prior to his departure on LST-384, 1944.

side to side on our round bottom thirty-two degrees in each direction every thirty seconds. I stood watch with a senior officer, learning the ropes as we kept a sharp lookout for submarines.

From Guantánamo, we headed south to Panama and a trip through that amazing canal. Out in the Pacific, we traveled up the coast of Mexico, at one point in sight of Acapulco, as we moved toward our destination of San Diego.

We remained in San Diego for about ten days. Peggy and I had several anxious telephone conversations as her due date drew near. I could not discuss where we were or where we were going, because of censorship. But Peggy did have a good idea of where I was headed.

The last time I talked with Peggy was on March 31, just as she was going into labor and the 384 was leaving for Pearl Harbor. Andra was born on Easter Sunday, April l, when the ship was about two hundred miles out on the very slow trip to Pearl.

My first knowledge of Andra's birth came in a letter from my mother, closely followed by a telegram from the navy and a letter from Peggy. What a relief! All was well; Peggy and Andra were fine. I learned for the first time through my mother's letter that Andra had been born on my father's fiftieth birthday and that the comment in my letter one year earlier had been prophetic after all. (It seems his mother had said that his birthday was March 31, when in fact it was April l. She would not admit to an April Fool's son.)

The Tour of the Pacific

The reality of Pearl Harbor sank in quickly as we moved through the antisubmarine net at the entrance to our anchorage near Ford Island. The sight of the U.S.S. *Arizona* on its side and the presence of two battered

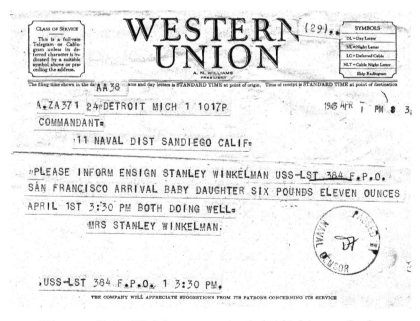

Telegram to Ensign Winkelman announcing Andra's birth in 1945. Stanley received the telegram on April 10, when his ship arrived in Pearl Harbor.

aircraft carriers under urgent repair completed the awesome picture. And so began six weeks of preparation.

During our stay in Honolulu, Franklin Roosevelt died and Harry Truman became president. And then, on June 6, 1945, came VE-Day, victory in Europe, a joyous occasion. Executive officer Bob Cressor, gunnery officer Bill Gillam, engineering officer Stuart Goodhale, and I were at Waikiki Beach when we read the headline in the *Honolulu Star Bulletin* and were photographed holding it.

The officers' club at the Hotel Moana was a place of celebration that day, although we all knew that many of us would not be coming back from the pending Battle of Japan.

The 384 made a shakedown trip to Kauai, where we shot up the beaches with our 20-mm antiaircraft guns and the five-inch gun on our stern. We then participated in antiaircraft gunnery practice with targets trailed by a fighter plane.

Back at Pearl Harbor, an LCT (landing craft tank) was loaded onto a cradle on the top deck and secured with chains. There was also a trigger so that it could be launched without help. We then took on a load of building material that would be used to build a permanent airstrip on the island of Kwajalein.

Since our departure from San Diego, I was qualified to stand watch on my own. On the trip to Pearl Harbor, it had been four hours on and eight hours off—quite a rigorous schedule. But now, on leaving Pearl Harbor, with three additional officers from the LCT aboard, it would be four hours on and twelve or sixteen off. This gave us time for reading and for bridge, which we played every day.

The toughest watch was the mid-watch—from midnight to four in the morning—after sleeping for just a few hours and then getting up and needing to be fully alert. For twenty minutes, I would wear red goggles in order to adapt to the darkness; then I would go out into the night in command of the ship for the next four hours.

As we traveled in a small convoy, our primary task was to maintain station, keeping our assigned position. This meant that we needed to keep the distance between ships on both sides and in front and back at the distance specified by the senior officer present, who was automatically the convoy commander and the person charged with the responsibility of getting the convoy to its destination.

Besides being responsible for the ships in the convoy, the convoy commander was in command of the navy ships that were escorting the convoy. He set the course and speed of the convoy, which was, of course, geared to the slowest ship, usually the LST-384. This meant continuous changes in speed and adjustment in course direction, communicated down a voice tube to the wheelhouse. "Come right to two-four-zero" or "All engines ahead two-thirds" are examples of those direction commands. When the rudder would fail, which was not infrequent, we would shift to a steersman below decks at the stern of the ship and regain our station while the rudder was being repaired.

At night, we traveled without running lights but usually could see quite well. We used our radar, with its ability to give us precise distances to the ships around us, as the primary tool in maintaining our position. Radio silence was not imperative at night. We were able to talk to the other ships by radio when necessary, although Morse code by signal light was the preferred method. Convoy orders usually were communicated during daylight hours by signal flags from the command ship.

The ten-day "cruise" to Kwajalein was uneventful. The bay where we anchored was quite desolate, although the color of the water over the coral bottom was a beautiful azure blue. The atoll itself had some palm trees and low bushes, providing lush color against the white coral. Ashore were the airstrip and a few Quonset huts.

The mail was the first thing on our minds, and an LCVP—a small landing craft that hung on the davits when not in use—was sent ashore to pick it up. The letters from Peggy were warm and loving as we continued our long-distance love affair. It was wonderful to hear from her and to be assured that all was as well as it could be at home.

At about this time, I asked Peggy to send me a wedding band (we had not been married in a double-ring ceremony), as I was getting more and more lonesome. I also asked her to send me a supply of novels; I would be doing more reading on the 384 than I had done at any time before or have done since.

We did some swimming out of the bow doors with the ramp down, and we even did a little fishing without success. Within a few days, we beached the ship and disgorged our cargo over that same ramp.

There was usually a supply ship in each anchorage if no supply facility was available ashore. This meant that Chief Adney and I would take a working party over to the ship in an LCVP and compare the list of what was available with a list of our needs. We would stock up on all of the fresh fruit and vegetables we could carry topside and as much beef, chicken, butter, and eggs as we could carry in our freezers and refrigerators. We also filled supply needs for other items, such as paper goods, soap, and so on.

The Australian lamb (or possibly goat) that came as part of the "meat package" was usually thrown over the side because no one would eat it. We wanted to keep our meager freezer facilities packed with the most desirable products that were available.

Orders came from the Port Authority to depart for Saipan in the

Marianas, the scene of fairly recent heavy fighting. This time we traveled alone, without benefit of a convoy's escort vessels and without running lights. Instead, we had to rely on our own vigilance. At first it was a little scary, especially when the silhouette of a ship was spotted coming toward us on the horizon at night. But there was no enemy contact, and we moved slowly toward our destination.

Saipan was a more interesting island than the coral atolls of Kwajalein or Eniwetok. There was much more tropical vegetation and a real sand beach. At the same time, we had to be vigilant when we were beached or ashore because there were still some Japanese soldiers hiding in the jungle.

So far, we had not seen liberty in the six weeks since we left port. Saipan had very limited facilities except for beer drinking. In any event, it was a good respite after our long journey to the western Pacific.

While we were in Saipan, I received the wedding band that I had requested along with several novels. I put on the beautiful gold band and have never removed it in the more than fifty years since.

From Saipan, we were ordered to Noumea, New Caledonia, where we were slated to pick up a load of army troops presumably headed for the Battle of Japan. The trip was uneventful, although we were now headed into the general area of the earliest hard-fought victories of our marines and the scene of some of the greatest naval battles of the war in the South Pacific and the Coral Sea.

For the first time, we crossed the equator into the land of the Southern Cross, always a brilliant landmark in the southern night sky. It was the highlight in the sky at dusk and dawn as the navigator or one of the other officers would take the sextant sightings on two planets above the horizon to calculate our position, using published tables, and determine a new course setting for the next twelve hours.

Of course, there were initiations into the appropriate societies as we crossed the dateline and moved immediately into tomorrow, and again when we crossed the equator into the southern hemisphere. These were exciting experiences for the entire crew, and a lot of fun for all of us.

As we seemed prepared to head for the war zone, I yearned more and more for my family. It was about this time that I discovered the inscription on the inside of my wedding band: "Never apart, Eternally yours, Peggy." I was thrilled by my discovery but nevertheless became more and more introspective as I contemplated going into enemy fire and wondering: *Why am I here? What can I do to help prevent war in the future?*

Reading and playing bridge in the ward room helped pass the time of night and day. Using the stores I had purchased in San Diego for the officers' mess, we would eat canned tuna mixed with pimentos and stuffed green olives, which I usually prepared. There were enough officers aboard so that we were able to have our OD (officer of the day) duty four hours on and sixteen hours off.

We docked in Noumea on July 13, 1945, just in time for the Bastille Day celebration. We had not visited a liberty port in the two months since we had left Pearl Harbor. The whorehouse ashore did a land-office business, and the bars did likewise. About two-thirds of the crew could go ashore each day. The officer of the day would be on duty for twenty-four hours when we were in port and would be at the gangway wearing sidearms as the crew left and returned.

It was often smart for the OD to stay in the background when the sailors returned after drinking too much. This avoided unnecessary confrontations and permitted the petty officer on duty to assign other crew members to take the boisterous men below decks and settle them down for the night. Occasionally, there would be a captain's mast to mete out punishment for minor infractions, and in one case an enlisted man was sent to the brig for a couple of days. But, generally, the crew did not require stern disciplinary measures.

After the holiday, we loaded our National Guard troops and got under way in the direction of the tip of Australia. We passed in sight of Port Moresby and proceeded north toward Guadalcanal, the scene of the first victory of the marines as the advance of the Japanese was stopped and our counteroffensive began.

Guadalcanal is a typical tropical island with a multitude of coconut trees and an abundance of betel nut, which the natives would chew for the kick it provided even though it would make their lips and mouths red. The vegetation had mostly grown back, and there was little obvious visual evidence of the terrible battle that had taken place after the marines landed.

After a couple of days, we headed slightly northwest toward the Solomon Islands, where another great battle had taken place. It was here that we took on ballast on one side of the ship at a time and dropped the pontoons that we had carried from Pearl Harbor. About two days later, near the end of July, the 384 weighed anchor and headed north across the equator to that huge anchorage, Ulithi. Ulithi was surrounded by tiny coral islands that produced a very calm "harbor" in the middle of nowhere. This was the staging area for the coming Battle of Japan.

While we always had a relatively cool breeze in tropical climates when we were underway, there was no such breeze when we were at anchor and the temperature was close to 100 degrees Fahrenheit. It was so hot that I had a fan installed at the foot of my bunk. This helped tremendously unless some joker would come in during my siesta and turn it off. In that case, I would wake up almost immediately in a pool of perspiration.

There were many supply ships in the anchorage, so we were able to restock our refrigerators and our supplies for the first time since we left Saipan, more than a month before. There were shore parties, such as they were, to consume beer on the barren coral atolls. But then, on August 6, a B-29 dropped the first atomic bomb on Hiroshima and shortly thereafter a second atomic bomb on Nagasaki.

The news was unbelievable and the implications not understood by anyone on the ship but me. My course in atomic physics during the summer of 1942 and my experiences and knowledge of the University of Chicago atomic pile, as well as a sense of what was happening at Hanford, Washington, and in Tennessee and Los Alamos, qualified me to give a background lecture on the development of atomic energy and the theory of atomic explosion, even though I had no knowledge of how the bombs were assembled and triggered.

Within a few days, we were ordered to Okinawa, where kamikaze attacks on U.S. ships were continuing in high gear despite the pending VJ-Day, which was set for early September. We arrived at the beaches of Okinawa on VJ-Day, at which time all fighting stopped. On that day, a good friend and naval pilot, Eugene Mandeberg, was shot down and killed. A few days before that, another boyhood friend, Jack O'Hara, and the great war correspondent Ernie Pyle were killed.

Suddenly, the life-and-death pressure of the war was behind us, and thinking began to develop about how and when we might get back to the States and resume our lives.

But there were more urgent problems, such as resupplying the ship and having to leave Okinawa on three occasions during September and early October to avoid typhoons. We would leave port suddenly and ride out the storm on the edge of the Yellow Sea. The first two hurricanes found me standing watch according to schedule and seasick most of the time. The third time, I was ashore with a working party picking up supplies when the 384 was ordered out to sea urgently. We spent the next three days in a Quonset hut on the beach, with winds howling outside, waiting for the 384 to return.

On Rosh Hashanah that year, several of us held a service, which I conducted, on the ship. For Yom Kippur, we were able to go ashore to attend more formal services with a chaplain.

Then came the call from the harbormaster advising our skipper that we would be assigned to the first convoy headed for Inchon, the port for Seoul, Korea. We were ordered to put ashore the National Guard troops we had been carrying since Noumea. In addition, we would unload the LCT that we had been carrying topside since Pearl Harbor.

The convoy departed with the battle cruiser USS *Alaska* in command and steamed northwest across the Yellow Sea toward Korea. The trip was made eventful by the mines floating on the surface of the water, which we exploded by shooting at them with our 20-mm guns. Also floating were a number of Asian soldiers' bodies—Korean or Japanese, we could not be sure.

We arrived at the harbor in Inchon and dropped anchor, awaiting further orders. The tides ran between twenty-five and thirty feet, and particular vigilance was necessary to maintain our anchorage. Within a day or two we put ashore the National Guard troops and waited for orders to launch the LCT. I decided to requisition a jeep for a bumpy ride to Seoul with two of my fellow officers. Our visit to that city was incredible, for the place was in ruins. Almost no buildings were left standing.

My next visit to Seoul would come nineteen years later, in 1964, when I would find the city chaotic, with a massive building program taking place and apparel manufacturing becoming an important part of the economy. Peggy and I would feel very much at home as we entered our room at the Chosen Hotel, for on the radio, over the Armed Forces Radio Network, was our good friend Karl Haas conducting his daily classical music program from New York.

By 1986, on our most recent visit, forty-one years after my first visit and twenty-two years after the second, Seoul had become a magnificent city preparing itself to host the Olympics.

Turning back to my navy days, I remember we returned from Seoul in mid-afternoon, arriving at the Inchon landing to board an LCVP and return to our ship. Much to our surprise, we could see that the 384 was listing sharply to starboard and that the LCT had not been launched from her deck. We were ordered to stand by and wait for the trigger to be cut, even though by then the tide was rushing out.

In a few minutes, the LCT was launched and slid gracefully into the water, where it was supposed to come to rest next to our ship. But the lines that were to hold it in place parted, and the LCT took off on the current through the anchorage with no one aboard and us in hot pursuit. One of the LCT officers was with us, but the engine on the LCT had not yet been hooked up to run.

A number of ships witnessed our plight and sent small boats to help us tame the runaway. We did finally gain control and slowly guided the recalcitrant LCT back to the side of the 384. It was a harrowing and embarrassing experience, especially for the skipper, since the incident took place in sight of the battle cruiser USS *Alaska* with the convoy commander aboard.

Everything worked out well except that the skipper received an official reprimand on his record, which would not be a big problem since the war was over.

We carried a load of Japanese prisoners back to Okinawa, then headed south to the Philippines where we beached for several days at Manila. We then left for the Leyte Gulf naval base for a short rest and resupply. It was here that Stuart Goodhale and his chief engineering mate discovered a crack in the flywheel of one of the engines, which posed the potential danger of splitting and throwing off pieces of metal. The crack in the flywheel would become our ticket to San Francisco, since no one in authority was willing to take the responsibility for sending us on to new assignments and no facilities on that side of Pearl Harbor could supply and install a new flywheel.

Meanwhile, I was ordered ashore to a new assignment that, but for the grace of God and Stuart Goodhale, would have kept me in the western Pacific.

In November 1945, the number of points one had accumulated toward getting back to civilian life was all-important. Goodhale had more than enough points to get out immediately; I had more time to serve because I had entered the navy later. Instead of leaving the ship immediately and flying home, Stu agreed to stay aboard if the powers that be would permit me to go back with the ship.

The 384 was ordered back to San Francisco via Iwo Jima and Pearl Harbor. Iwo Jima is the volcano rock where thousands of U.S. Marines died storming the black volcanic lava beaches and raising the American flag, a scene memorialized by incredible photography and the famous statue. The airstrip there was essential for our bombers and fighters, since it was a short hop from Iwo Jima to Tokyo.

After being beached for a few days on the desolate island, we finally headed east. We happened to cross the dateline on New Year's Day 1946, giving us two New Year's Eves to celebrate as we made our way toward the United States for decommissioning. At our top speed of seven knots, it took three weeks to make the journey, with a two-day stop at Pearl Harbor en route to the Golden Gate.

What a marvelous sight it was as we entered San Francisco Bay and tied up at the Oakland Navy Yard just south of the Bay Bridge. After a few days of getting reaccustomed to life in a big city, we were ordered to an anchorage near San Quentin prison, where we would decommission the 384.

Reunion and First Meeting

Peggy came to meet me, and we had a joyous reunion at the Claremont Hotel in the hills near Berkeley. She even spent a night with me aboard the 384 in a rather daring and exciting episode that involved being picked up by an LCVP at San Quentin and climbing the Jacob's ladder from the small boat to the deck of the 384 at a height of twenty feet above the water.

Leon Winkelman with his granddaughters Andra and Margi at
the wedding of Sharon Robinson and Jack Winkelman, 1955.

I flew to Detroit on leave for about ten days and met my beautiful
daughter, Andra, who was eleven and a half months old by that time. It
was marvelous, though I created a crisis by accidentally knocking her over
onto the floor just as we were getting acquainted. She must have been
wondering, "Who is this huge man, and why has he come to spoil my life?"

Back at San Quentin, I took part in stripping the ship and preparing it
to be mothballed. I was now the executive officer, because the more senior
officers had all been ordered ashore. When I last saw the 384, she was
swinging on her hook, empty but proud—the second-oldest LST in the
fleet, she had seen service in both the European Theater and the western
Pacific.

My souvenirs of navy life are a small piece of volcanic rock from Iwo
Jima, a pair of high-powered British World War I field glasses that had
been left aboard the ship, and a few photographs, including one of the 384
as we sailed under the Golden Gate.

Reflections on the War

Of all the technological advances during World War II, radar was the most
important to us in the amphibious forces on a day-to-day basis. The most
spectacular development, of course, was the atomic bomb, to which I believe
we who were in the American armed forces owe our lives.

More recently, the development of satellite navigation of delivery systems for guided missiles, tactical nuclear weapons, and the hydrogen bomb has revolutionized warfare, even though the latter two have not been used.

While there has been debate about Harry Truman's decision to use the atomic bomb on Hiroshima and Nagasaki, for those of us in the service at that time, it was a matter of thousands of American soldiers' lives versus thousands of Japanese lives.

For those of us who survived the war in one piece, the experience was a priceless education and exposure that would be of tremendous value in our future lives—and not only in terms of technical knowledge and skills but in human terms as well. As for me, I learned to get along with all kinds of people and to manage a diverse group under trying circumstances. The management skills I developed and the self-confidence I felt were significant factors in my decision to return to the family business after the war, despite my earlier efforts to get away from the dominance of my father.

3

A Merchant's Life

The Story of Winkelman's

With my postwar return to Detroit, I began a new family life and a new business life. Within a few months, Peggy, Andra, and I moved into our own home on Roselawn, just two blocks from the University of Detroit High School in a lovely neighborhood of homes built on thirty-five-foot lots.

With the houses so close together, there was a great deal of neighborliness and the development of friendships that lasted for many years. Our

Stanley, holding one-year-old Andra, with his brother Henry,
their mother Josephine Winkelman, and Aunt June Dover.

daughter Marjory ("Margi") was born in June 1948, a wonderful addition to our family.

By 1950, Andra had started public school, to be followed three years later by Margi. Public schools in the area at that time were of good quality, and we believed then, as we do now, that a strong public school system with English as the one required language is essential to the maintenance of a strong democratic society. On the other hand, it is important for young people to learn other languages in order to communicate with people in other countries in what is becoming an ever smaller world.

In the late 1940s, I was attempting to develop an overall philosophy of life that would encompass family, business, religion, politics, and society.

Conceptually that task was not too difficult, but it took about seven years for all of the pieces to fall into place. The much more difficult challenge was to achieve a desirable balance on a month-to-month or even year-to-year basis.

While my objectives in relation to family and business fell into place rather easily at the beginning, even this relatively simple balance was not easy to achieve. To be successful in the retail business required a huge time commitment on a continuing basis.

The amount of detailed information that I felt it necessary to absorb in order to manage effectively, and the time required to follow the competition closely and observe the status of our own store stocks and merchandise presentation, detracted from my family commitment. More and more often, the work week involved all seven days, and evenings as well.

By 1954, I had become an officer of Winkelman's and a director of the United Foundation (which later became the United Way). That was also a banner family year, with the birth of our son, Roger, preceded by our move into the home built by Peggy's parents in Sherwood Forest in the beautiful Palmer Park area of Detroit. In addition, 1954 was the year of my initial involvement and participation in Temple Beth El leadership roles.

While Peggy and I were married in 1943, the first of my brothers to be married twelve years later—in 1955—was Jack. Our father L.W. lived to see Jack married but not Fred or Hank.

A Retail Apprenticeship

Beginning at age ten, I spent my summers working in the family business. In 1934, at the age of twelve, I worked as a porter in the Fort Street store. Washing windows, vacuuming floors, and folding box cartons for merchandise were important activities.

The following year, I went to camp at Hayward, Wisconsin, with my cousin Howard, who lived in Chicago. Camping was a great experience for me; I especially enjoyed horseback riding and learning to fire a .22-caliber rifle at a target. On our return to Chicago after eight weeks of camp, Howie and I spent time at the Century of Progress World's Fair on the current site of Miegs Field airport. We would go alone to the fair on the Illinois Central train. We also attended the annual All-Star football game, which was the brainchild of Arch Ward, the dynamic sports editor of the *Chicago Tribune*. Those were exciting days.

From 1935 to 1938, I worked summers in various capacities in the Winkelman's warehouse downtown on Park Avenue. It was here that I learned about handling incoming merchandise, checking shipments, making distributions to the stores, and sending shipments back to the manufacturers. As a sideline, I learned to play checkers during lunch hour.

From the warehouse, it was on to the display department where I was involved in the process of pulling merchandise from the warehouse stock, developing the plan for each store, and physically distributing the merchandise to the rolling racks for each week's new window presentations in the individual stores. The store display windows were trimmed by a group led by Julian Oribello, a remarkable man and a good friend.

One summer, I used a handwritten pass to ride by bus and streetcar to check the Winkelman's advertising placards on those vehicles.

My retailing career started in earnest after the war, when I was assistant store manager for the first year after my separation from the navy. It was stimulating to have so much customer contact and to work directly with the manager and others in the retail sales organization.

I worked with the management team of Zaphyr, Zeimer, and Zubrin at the Oakman Boulevard/Grand River Winkelman's store for several months. Polly Zaphyr was a delightful, dynamic selling personality. Willard Zeimer would become supervisor of the growing group of stores in Cleveland about ten years later.

This was an auspicious beginning in store management for me and an excellent entry into the world of retailing, which did not relate directly to my scientific background or to my experience in the navy. By this time, I knew I did not want to be cooped up in a laboratory, and I was confident that I had something to contribute to the family business.

At the same time, I was learning that the principles of management were not essentially different in science, the military, and retailing. It took a little more time to realize that the scientific method could, indeed, be utilized in approaching retail management problems, in developing alternative solutions, and in testing new approaches.

In my next store management assignment, I had the good fortune to work for Florence Large, probably the best manager in the fourteen Winkelman's stores operating at that time. She was the inspirational leader of the

Andra and Margi, holding Brownie, with Stanley and his twin
brothers Jack and Fred at the house in Roselawn, 1953.

Highland Park store, which had the largest sales volume of any Winkelman's
store in 1946. Sales were $1 million in a store that occupied a space of forty
feet by one hundred fifty feet, or $150 per square foot.

From Miss Large, I learned the advantages of an enthusiastic approach to
selling, the importance of highly disciplined management, and the benefits
of daily meetings with the sales staff to review advertised and window
merchandise as well as prepare for new merchandise arriving in stock.

I was taught to do as directed with layout and signs for the store and to
conduct meetings on sales techniques and merchandise information. This
included suggested additional items for a customer's wardrobe, especially
hats from the millinery department.

Multiple sales were extremely important and carefully monitored on the
simple theory that it is easier and more productive to sell an additional piece
of merchandise to a customer who has already made one or more purchases
than it is to sell to a new customer.

As management, we were responsible for selling from a stock of dresses,
coats, and suits that was hidden from the public. We controlled the ready-
to-wear selling floor by using a notepad to keep tabs on the salespersons
and their effect on the customers, as well as the garments shown them, after
we had placed a customer in a fitting room and assigned a salesperson to
assist her.

We would know which three garments were brought to the customer at one time and could provide direct assistance in selling when appropriate.

The intensity of selling and supervision in some cases crossed the border into overselling. Some years later, I was to find that our best salespeople were not always our brightest salespeople but rather those who sold as we prescribed and at the same time avoided the pitfalls of overselling.

After a year of store management experience, I was assigned in 1947 to work in the main office with Ken Board, the dress department manager. There I learned the unit control system and the approach to merchandising and budgeting that would be so important to me in the years ahead.

I was present for, and gradually participated in, the weekly advertising and window meetings, which under my father's direction were rather free-wheeling and at the same time filled with the tension that derived from free-for-all discussions and frequent changes in plans.

My bent for analysis and a scientific approach to tracking enabled me to interpret some trends, such as the success of our advertising and window displays, that resulted in moving our price structure somewhat higher. I had been able to construct a graph that showed price-line selling each week. When we ran an ad, it was easy to see a bulge in sales at the particular price points that had been advertised.

In the weekly dress meetings with my father, Ken Board, and the general merchandise manager, Jerry Morton, we reviewed sales and ending stock for the previous weeks by type and price range. Reorders were determined from a handwritten selling sheet listing the manufacturer and style number for each garment with unit sales and ending stock for each color. Planning was extended out a week at a time by type and price based on the sales trend, seasonal timing, and feedback from the market. These planning discussions, in which the budget was developed preliminarily by type and price for the next month, were remarkable for their level of detail and their development of consensus.

Winkelman's Past

My father L.W. and my uncle I.W. were the founding principals of the business in 1928. L.W. was the merchant and I.W. the operator as the first store opened at Fort and Junction in Detroit.

There is a 1928 photograph of that location showing Winkelman's along with Rose's Jewelry and Cunningham's Drugs in a situation that was to be repeated many times during the expansion of the business between 1929 and 1953 as Winkelman's grew from one to twenty stores, all in the Detroit area.

With L.W. specializing in merchandising and I.W. specializing in the selling and other nonselling functions, they avoided an organizational problem that jeopardized many young retail companies.

Merchants did the merchandise planning and buying, with buyers executing the merchandise orders from the manufacturers. The merchants planned the supporting advertising assisted by the advertising and publicity department. They arranged for timely distribution of merchandise and provided promotional information to the stores.

Selling was the responsibility of store management. Store managers, with guidance from district managers or supervisors, hired and trained the salespeople and supervised the selling on the sales floor. They also set up the store to support the promotional programs, held meetings with salespeople to familiarize them with the merchandise, and controlled the cost of selling. Their bonuses were tied to their results.

More often than not, in other small retail chains, two partners would split the merchandising function and other functions of their business. The result, all too often, was a fragmented and incoherent merchandising approach.

The first Winkelman's store opened in 1928 at Fort Street and
Junction, nestled between Rose's Jewelry and Cunningham's Drugs.

While the management concept of Winkelman's was sound from the beginning, there were many emotional arguments between L.W. and I.W. These were brought on, in many cases, by store managers viewing the merchants as spies when they visited the stores and by the merchants viewing store management as insufficiently attuned to the merchandise. This situation was somewhat exacerbated by a personal relationship between I.W. and Vera Regati, the manager of the Jefferson Avenue store.

With the second store open at Jefferson Avenue and Chalmers Street in 1931 and the third store at Grand River Avenue and Grand Boulevard in 1932, the chain was developing. There was a brief deviation when a leased ready-to-wear department was opened in the Demery Department Store at Milwaukee Street and Woodward Avenue near the General Motors Building.

Thus, by 1932, Winkelman's had grown significantly. With the opening of the second store, L.W. made an unusual decision for a small retail operation by hiring a full-time dress buyer in New York. Elsie Jacobs occupied space inside Kirby, Block, and Fisher (hereafter referred to as Kirby Block), Winkelman's resident buying office at 128 West 31st Street. She devoted full effort to the market, but there was an obvious gap in her knowledge of what was happening in the stores, which she never visited.

As Winkelman's grew, the merchants and buyers took the train. (A few years later, they would fly on a DC-3 to New York to spend a week in the markets each month.)

There was usually a split between the views of those who lived in New York, whether with Elsie Jacobs, later with other Winkelman's resident buyers, or with the Kirby Block buyers. L.W., an instinctive merchandising genius, would spot the new trends and push the planning process in their direction. In the context of the market, he would develop a consensus among the buyers, merchandise managers, and himself about the types of merchandise that would be defined, planned, and controlled in the coming period. They would wind up with a preliminary unit sales projection by price and a percentage allocation for each type within a price.

That plan would be translated into a unit purchasing or buying plan. Advertising plans were established, and merchandise was earmarked for windows. This process became more sophisticated over the years, but L.W. was consistent in expecting delivery of new, exciting merchandise much sooner than reality would suggest. In fact, he was almost always ahead of the market. Merchandise would arrive in Detroit anywhere from one to three weeks later than he thought it would.

And so began my monthly trips to the New York market in the fall of 1947. We would have meetings in the office with our several resident buyers in the early morning on merchandising, advertising, and/or windows. We would also meet with the Kirby Block buyers.

There was always something for me to learn from the Kirby Block buyers, since the individual buyers were quite knowledgeable about fabric and color trends and, to some extent, the particular styles that were reordering in the market. Their style and selling information was always suspect because of potential conflicts of interest on the part of the Kirby Block buyers. We suspected them of taking money from manufacturers and promoting their merchandise accordingly.

The Leon Winkelman approach to the individual markets (dresses, coats, suits, etc.) was quite simple. Shop the market from high price down to low price. Dig out the new ideas, and try to interpret them at volume prices. Then sit down and put together a unit sales plan by price and a percentage for each type within price, and then create an open-to-buy plan.

L.W. had a three-tiered price philosophy: higher price points to introduce new fashions, moderate price points for volume business, and low prices to bring in traffic. His philosophy worked extremely well in those days, and Winkelman's developed a unique reputation as a moderate-priced fashion store.

As I visited manufacturers' showrooms with the group, I was faced with what seemed for a time to be an unsolvable mystery. How could the buyers know which styles from a line were likely to sell the best? They were supposedly buying according to the taste levels and fashion interests of our customers. But that was not true; our merchandising approach was generating business in style types, colors, and fabrics that our customers did not know or understand. (This is why I did not, and do not now, trust customer preference surveys. They reflect the status quo, but that is not good enough in projecting future demand.)

My father did not dispel my puzzlement; he maintained that merchants are born, not made, and that the secret ingredient was "flair," which he certainly possessed.

Over some months, I applied my scientific wiles to this seemingly unscientific process. I monitored the selection of dresses by the buyers, recording my own predictions in advance. When the sales numbers were analyzed, *voila!* I discovered that I could predict success as well as anyone in the dress division.

My confidence was further bolstered when I took a sketch of a high-priced lace-trimmed stole dress and arranged for one of our manufacturers to make it up to retail at $39.95, high for the Winkelman's price structure of that day (probably equivalent to more than $200 today). I also worked out manufacturer support for an ad (not common in those days) that ran in our best media fashion page, the back page of the Sunday *Detroit Free Press* fashion section. Once again I was successful, and my inferiority complex disappeared. The dress reordered, something that was very unusual at our highest price point.

Advertising and Window Display

Ad meetings were free-for-alls, with each merchandise division bringing in samples and L.W. pressing to advertise the latest ideas from the market, which in many cases would not be delivered in time for the ads, causing great strain and many last-minute changes. We would discuss fashion themes for ads and windows, leaving the exact wording and supporting copy to the advertising department, although we would have emotional discussions about that aspect as well.

L.W. and I.W. had hired Manny Hartman away from the *Detroit Shopping News* in the mid-1930s. Manny became the manager of the Highland Park Store and advertising manager for the company. It was Manny who worked out what proved to be excellent positions in the newspapers. Those positions were obtained gradually over about fifteen years, and they included:

1. The back page of the Sunday *Detroit Free Press* fashion section for the newest, higher-priced fashions.
2. The front page of the Friday *Detroit Free Press* section for volume-priced advertising that would run with several sketches and a theme.
3. Five columns on page four of the Thursday *Detroit News* for a volume-priced ad with a theme.
4. A half-page across the bottom of the front page of the fashion section of the Wednesday *Detroit News* for three or four sketches featuring a volume-priced theme.
5. For low-price items and specials, the Sunday *Detroit News*, the *Detroit Times*, and/or the *Detroit Shopping News*.

Under Manny Hartman's direction, and with L.W.'s approval, Winkelman's advertising was modeled on that of Lord & Taylor, using large stylized sketches drawn by our own artists and featuring a specific merchandise theme.

Window planning was even more complicated, since a theme of one or two colors was planned for each of the two alcove show windows in each store. A window was broken down into four units, each with two mannequins, or one mannequin and a draped item, plus two or three small accessory items.

A distant cousin of mine, Frieda Rosenthal Rambar, coordinated the window planning. Frieda had great talent but was a difficult person with whom to work; she was arbitrary and opinionated and unable to build consensus with the merchants.

Each window unit normally had an assigned function, with better merchandise and fashion statements at the front near the street to appeal to the passersby on the sidewalk and cheaper merchandise at the back in units four or eight. The "good window" told a fashion story utilizing higher-priced merchandise in one or two colors without price information or one or two mannequins with a price-tagged item of the same character draped with the price showing on the floor below. The "inexpensive window" had its emphasis on fashion ideas at moderate and low prices, with price tickets on most of the merchandise.

The window process was tedious for those planning it and for those executing it at the store level. The conventional wisdom, as correctly articulated by L.W., was that a presentation would be more effective if the merchandise for the windows was planned centrally rather than determined individually by each store.

Tour of the Store

By 1948, with newly-constructed hanging sportswear alcoves at the front of each new store, sportswear was included in the window in the form of blouses with skirts and sweaters. Until that time, blouses had been kept folded and on shelves behind the "smallwear" counter that occupied the first third of the store on one side. Smallwear included slips and nightgowns along with handbags, gloves, and jewelry.

The millinery department occupied the first third of the store on the opposite side. In the center, at the front of the store, were four tables for presenting the most important promotional merchandise as designated by the main office merchandisers. Each table would have a five-by-seven-inch sign indicating the nature of the goods and the prices.

The ready-to-wear floor, at the back of the floor space, had concealed stocks of dresses, coats, suits, and furs on one side and fitting rooms on the other, with the store office at the rear. In its heyday, continuing until 1960, ready-to-wear was extremely productive with very high turnover. There were three or four costumers and two single racks of merchandise on the floor, featuring the important or advertised merchandise in coats, suits, furs, and dresses with appropriate signs and copy to tell the story.

In the late 1940s, merchandise inventories were corrected by collecting the ticket stubs manually from the merchandise sold and checking the stubs off on the unit control and store distribution records at the main office.

Each Wednesday morning, the dress merchandising people would meet with L.W. in a designated store to review every dress that was more than two weeks old for possible markdown. Turnover was forced with early markdowns; L.W. would often say, "The first markdown is the cheapest."

Looking at each garment to determine its quality, appropriateness, and timeliness was a very important and revealing process that kept the stocks fresh. Later, the process became too cumbersome, and markdown reviews were conducted with samples at the main office. As Winkelman's grew bigger and carried more and more so-called brand merchandise, the manufacturers would insist on holding back markdowns until a certain date.

We fought that policy because we knew that it was much better to keep our stocks clean and fresh in order to maintain a faster flow of new merchandise. While the generic name of the retail game may be distribution, we knew that fast turnover was the key to profitability and that having stocks clogged with slow-selling merchandise could only breed disaster. In the long run, if you don't take markdowns, you don't do any business.

Into Merchandise Management

Toward the end of 1948, I was told that Jerry Morton, the general merchandise manager, would be terminated and that I would be taking on that responsibility. Morton had come to Winkelman's from the Allied Department Store in St. Paul, Minnesota, where Earl Puckett, the cost-cutting chairman, would continually ask, "What are you doing about what you know?" Such clichés may sound absurd today, but they were part of the retail world at that time.

Jerry Morton, it seems, had insisted on an employment contract at what I.W. considered a very high price for Winkelman's. So when I.W. and L.W. perceived that I was making good progress, they decided to dump Jerry. I had learned a great deal from Jerry Morton. I had a high regard for him and considered him a friend.

I declined the title of general merchandise manager, because all of our merchants had considerably more knowledge and experience than I had. I could visualize myself getting caught in the crossfire between L.W. and the other merchants. Instead, I chose the title of general merchandise administrator, which worked very well for me and for the company for the next two years, after which I accepted the general merchandise manager title.

When I met with the divisional merchandise managers for purposes of planning, I was often deeply bothered as they confronted planning problems with the query "What will L.W. think?" My answer was always the same: "I don't give a damn what L.W. will think. It is your responsibility to make the decision." In this way, I was able to help them build confidence in themselves, in one another, and in me. Yes, we did have arguments with L.W., and sometimes that would change their minds. But more often than not, encouraged by me, they stuck with their own decisions and L.W. accepted them.

By this time, I was conducting the advertising and window meetings. I established my position at the middle of the big conference table rather than on the end. Manny Hartman and the top layout artist would attend the advertising meetings, and Frieda Rambar, along with her assistant, would attend the window meetings.

I also conducted the weekly unit meeting with the three store supervisors and the head of store operations, at first Manny Hartman and later Harry Gersell. Each Tuesday morning, we would discuss the trends in the previous week's unit selling, the effectiveness of advertising and windows, and the planning for the next several weeks. The feedback from store operations people was extremely important to the merchandise planning process.

Along with Ben Goldstein, who supervised all nonselling activities in those early days, I conducted a weekly administrative meeting at which we would review our merchandise commitments, as well as factors relating to our gross margin (merchandising profit), our expenses, and our developing systems. Ben and I would think through the organization of the business and discuss ways to move it ahead profitably. We eventually worked out the dollar system for evaluating our stocks and commitments in relation to a dollar sales plan.

Ben was a great intellectual force in my life, both in the business and outside it as well. He, Manny Hartman, and I represented all of the functions at Winkelman's. Ben reported to I.W., while Manny reported to L.W. for advertising and to I.W. for the stores, and I reported to both I.W. and L.W. This arrangement with an expansion of policy responsibility continued until 1956.

Manny Hartman had been the glue that held the business together when I.W. and L.W. would stage one of their not-infrequent arguments. Manny would calm the waters and facilitate compromise, a most valuable contribution at the time.

One of the early conclusions of our administrative meetings was that the manual stub system of unit control was obsolete and should be replaced by a mechanized punch-card system. The manual system involved a two-part ticket stub attached to each garment at the warehouse. One part was removed at the time of the sale. Each night, the stubs for that day's sales were sent to the main office, where they were used to correct manually the unit control records of the store stock. This was a very inefficient and time-consuming process.

To undertake this rather profound system change in 1948, in the late afternoon each Monday we convened weekly meetings of all division managers to do the intricate planning. We decided to tie the unit control system into the accounting system, an expensive but ideal concept.

This design included the on-order information and all of the accounting related to the flow of merchandise from the time it was ordered until it was either sold or marked down and out of stock. All of the accounting and charge account systems were included.

We chose what turned out to be a costly system based on assigning an individual serial number for almost every item in stock. Serial number inventories would be taken periodically in order to correct the unit control records in terms of markdowns, customer returns, and items missing from stock altogether. Sales information, in the form of merchandise stubs, then punch cards, and later punch-card ticket stubs, was sent to the main office each night for processing into reports that would be on our desks the next morning.

A redesign and simplification of the system many years later, with the advent of point-of-sale electronic cash registers, separated the merchandise and accounting systems and used an SKU (stock-keeping unit) number to track identical merchandise of the same style, color, size, and price. By the 1970s, point-of-sale cash registers permitted us to poll the individual store registers each night and transmit the information by telephone directly to our mainframe computer so that reports could be available the next morning with greater accuracy and ease. Technological change had finally come to retailing.

Reports of stock and sales in any merchandise category, price, size, or color could be analyzed from a printed report by individual buyers. A few years later, this could be done by merchandisers using CRT (cathode-ray tube) computers at their desks. If the registers in the stores could be kept on-line to the mainframe computer by means of a dedicated telephone line, merchandise and accounting information could be kept current at all times.

We would be getting ahead of ourselves in our 1980 attempt to use the computer as a means of establishing formulas for distribution patterns and automatic replenishment of stock on relatively staple merchandise, such as hosiery and intimate apparel. Ultimately, the name of the game would be customization of individual store stocks in order to capitalize on each store's customer profile, again utilizing new technology to improve productivity, especially in communities with little or no advertising that had previously generated a chain-wide common demand.

Also, by 1980, we would be using census analysis to determine store locations. I had worked out a test with J. C. Penney, comparing its analysis of customer profiles for individual stores with our own analysis based on census data, recognizing that J. C. Penney would draw from a much greater radius than Winkelman's. The consistency of the data was amazing. For the first time in my experience, I could have confidence in marketing information to help us locate stores and establish a merchandise profile for them within our overall merchandising plan, providing the optimum sales and profit potential for each individual store. Until that time, I had read developer marketing information with a great deal of skepticism.

Back in 1948, at about the same time as we were developing our punch-card systems, I was reconfiguring the New York office. I found it chaotic and poorly organized for the simple reason that no one had ever taken the time to analyze it.

At that time, the New York office consisted of three rooms with four or five unrelated telephone lines plus a telex connection with Detroit. The telex was used on a contract basis twice a day, at nine in the morning and three in the afternoon. The entire setup was inadequate for a rapidly growing young company.

Sample rooms were needed to accommodate the manufacturers' sales-men who would arrive each morning to show the buyers merchandise or to review some aspect of merchandising for styles that had already been purchased.

A switchboard and a telephone operator/receptionist were needed to control traffic and handle incoming calls. Space was needed for the buyers of each of the five merchandise divisions: dresses; coats, suits, and furs; sportswear; intimate apparel; and accessories. Of course, today's compact telephone systems, faxes, and personal computers would have brought miraculous improvements to the operation.

When the modifications and new layout were completed, the functioning of the office improved dramatically. It worked efficiently until about 1960, when Kirby Block moved around the corner on Seventh Avenue to what was then the J. C. Penney Building, and we decided that buyers should be located in Detroit. We then moved to a smaller, independent space at Sixth Avenue and 44th Street, about two doors away from the Algonquin Hotel.

One of the battles I undertook in the late 1940s was to bring order out of the chaos of ad and window planning. L.W. would go to New York, and, working with the merchandise managers, insist on creating ad and window plans that were full of wonderful new fashion ideas but completely unrealistic in terms of merchandise deliveries. Back in Detroit, the plans would be completely revised, realistically, at the next ad and window meetings.

While L.W. was remarkable in his instincts and his quest for effective merchandising unit controls, I found that I was able to simplify them. It should be noted that my father's concept of merchandise control was sound. As a matter of fact, dollar controls were not used in merchandising for many years, until the arrival of the computer. L.W.'s thinking was that if the units were properly planned, the dollars would take care of themselves. Indeed, for many years, this proposition was a practical truth that eliminated the necessity for time-consuming conversions of units to dollars, or vice versa. Obviously, only a great merchant and superior planner could afford the risk.

By 1948, I.W. had become more and more nervous about this approach. As a result, when Ben Goldstein and I developed the new punch-card system, the on-order/open-to-buy analysis was developed as an integral part of that system to provide both dollar and unit figures with respect to our commitments for merchandise. However, that part of the system had to be separated from the rest, and we were unable for several years to have an effective dollar commitment report.

The Remington Rand representatives who had installed what proved to be an unworkable punch-card system and hardware left town and were never seen or heard from again. The system had not been properly designed, and we had compounded the problem by assigning a man with merchandising background to manage the new data processing division, when a competent technician was what was required.

It did not take long from the time the Remington Rand representatives departed for us to realize that there had been a serious mistake. We moved quickly to hire Dick Landers away from Chrysler, and in a few months, Dick had the data processing division humming. Some thirty years later, Dick retired after supervising our shift into computers and creating what was probably the best electronic data processing operation in retailing at that time.

At first, in the early 1960s, there were huge vacuum tube calculators, such as the Univac I and then the Univac II. Finally, during my tenure at Winkelman's, we purchased a Univac III. These were state-of-the-art mainframe computers of their day, all manufactured by Remington Rand (later Sperry Rand).

In 1952, we had placed an order for the "Potter Ticket Reader." Our order was the second for Potter, with Sears having placed the first. We were planning to use the reader to read optical font ticket printing as a replacement for our laborious process of hand-pulling punch cards from a tub file in each store as garments were sold.

But meanwhile we developed a punch-card ticket stub that provided a simpler answer to the problem in the days before point-of-sale registers. The punch-card ticket stubs could be read in the same way as the punch cards themselves. The only continuing problem was that of missing stubs, which averaged about 10 percent. This punch-card ticket system meant that we could cancel the order for the Potter reader. The fact is that we were on the leading edge of systems research, a major feat for a relatively small company.

With point-of-sale cash registers, it is simple to capture 100 percent of the sales information at the register, either manually or with a wand that can read the price ticket. This ensures that each sale is accounted for and eliminates the errors common with successive manual handling of the ticket stubs.

Expansion and Competition

From 1948 through 1951, I.W. was leading the Winkelman's expansion effort and negotiating excellent leases with landlords in the Detroit area. Ed Quint—our general counsel and a partner in the law firm of Butzel, Levin, and Quint—developed a pattern for leases that was comprehensive and meticulous. Ed was probably the most exacting legal draftsman I have ever met.

Overall corporate policies, including expansion, finance, and budget control, were developed by Hartman, Goldstein, and me. They were presented separately to I.W. and L.W. I.W. took the lead on new store locations and landlord relations. Over ten to fifteen years, Manny Hartman was given the responsibility for real estate and store leases. Much later, about 1978, Ron Leonetti succeeded Manny in supervising the real estate division, which included store design, decor, and construction.

In 1952, we began to face up to the question of whether we could compete directly with Hudson's, when the plans for two regional shopping centers— Eastland and Northland—were conceived by architect Victor Gruen, the father of the regional shopping center in the United States.

While Eastland Center was to have been the first such center to be completed, building was delayed because Crowley Milner decided at the last minute not to participate, with the result that Northland Center was built first.

Gruen, a refugee from Austria who had immigrated in 1938, lived in Los Angeles, where he had been designing freestanding stores for Joseph Magnin. Passing through Detroit, he visited with Oscar Webber, then chairman of Hudson's. Gruen wanted to know about Hudson's expansion plans. He was told of a 20,000-square foot corner in Grosse Pointe.

Gruen suggested that such a small piece of property was not appropriate for Hudson's and sold Webber on his concept of a regional shopping center. This became the prototype for the major retail shopping center development over the next thirty years, as cities expanded and people moved to the suburbs. Al Taubman, trained as an architect and businessman, perfected and expanded the concept into a huge moneymaking machine, the Taubman Company.

The enclosed, air-conditioned mall was nonexistent in the early 1950s.

Victor Gruen designed the first one for Dayton's in Minneapolis, which opened shortly after Northland Center.

In order to prime myself for decisions to come, I flew to Seattle in 1952, to see firsthand the largest open-air shopping center of the time. It was a series of connected strips of stores with traffic generators in the form of a department store, large market, or variety store every one hundred fifty to two hundred feet.

In Seattle, I met Peter Best, president of Best Apparel. In those days, Best's was primarily a very large shoe store. The Best family sold out a few years later to the Nordstrom brothers, starting the great retail chain of large specialty stores that is still thriving today. The Nordstrom stores have featured great customer service and depth of stock in their major areas of merchandising. At the same time, Nordstrom's emphasizes sales service that has all but disappeared in the major department stores of today.

We have all had the experience as shoppers in a department store of being told, "That's not my department," or, worse yet, "It's over there." It is the department stores that have, in reality, been responsible for the growth of discount operations. Even worse is the situation in the cosmetics departments of department stores, where anything outside the immediate area is not only "not their department," it is not even their store: the cosmetics manufacturers put their own employees in the department stores.

The department store emphasis on using advertising money to promote labels and brands has established many brand names. The corresponding emphasis on markdown money and return privileges, along with customers' unwillingness to pay the quoted price, has left department stores vulnerable to the discounters that negotiate better prices, take shorter markups, and sell the same merchandise for substantially less.

Specialty stores, on the other hand, with greater merchandising talent, have been able, by emphasizing fashion newness, to maintain customer interest and purchasing. At Winkelman's, we took advantage of this by emphasizing that "Fashion Is Our Specialty," and we did not deviate from that approach. At the same time, good customer service was a hallmark of Winkelman's business.

After my visit to Seattle, I went to Framingham, Massachusetts, where there was a pioneering two-story center on one end of which was the Jordan Marsh store. I returned to Detroit convinced that the regional center concept would be successful and that we could compete directly with Hudson's. Up to that time, we had countered Hudson's efforts at merchandise exclusivity with "Hudson's is downtown, while Winkelman's is in the neighborhoods." I felt strongly that with our record of growth and strong resource relationships, we would be able to buy from the manufacturers we wanted with very few exceptions.

Victor Gruen was hired to design our Northland Center store in order to adapt our store design to the new concept of the shopping center. Up to that time, Charles Agree had designed Winkelman's stores and made up in cost control what he lacked in creativity. Our stores followed a basic pattern of design, and that was quite unique in its day.

Because of my intellectual interest in design, Peggy and I would invite Victor to dinner at our Roselawn home and have lengthy discussions of design, politics, conditions for Jews in Europe back in the 1930s, and so on. Victor's local manager, Karl Van Leuven, also became a good friend.

At Van Leuven's Christmas party in early December 1953, Lee Hills, the publisher of the *Detroit Free Press*, and I almost came to blows because of the tension generated by the first long newspaper strike. The major strike issue, in addition to wages and fringe benefits, was union featherbedding, which would delay cost-saving improvements.

The strike caused me great concern about our ability to generate the planned level of Christmas sales without newspaper advertising. I was openly critical of the failure of the newspapers to communicate with their advertisers so that they could plan appropriately.

Lee Hills, who had come to the party directly from a negotiating session, became very emotional when I challenged the lack of communication, and he took off his coat, ready to fight. Cooler heads prevailed, and Harry Winston, a mutual friend, separated us.

Ultimately, the Christmas business materialized nicely, the strike was settled after Christmas, and we became good friends of Tina and Lee Hills. Lee did a marvelous job later as the chairman of the Founders Society of the Detroit Institute of Arts (DIA) while continuing to do an outstanding job as the publisher of the *Detroit Free Press*.

My relationships with the publishers of the *Detroit News* and the *Detroit Free Press*, Peter Clark and Lee Hills, were very strong, as were my relationships with the editors, Martin Hayden, Frank Angelo, Neal Shine, and David Lawrence. David Lawrence became publisher of the *Detroit Free Press* and later moved to Miami where he took over as publisher of the *Miami Herald*. Of course, the fashion editors were also good friends.

Because of the layout at Northland Center—with Hudson's in the center and specialty stores between Hudson's and the parking areas—Northland was the first regional shopping center where it was anticipated that customer traffic would flow equally from the front and the rear of a store, establishing a need to create two entrances. In strip shopping centers, up to that time, the major traffic came from the sidewalk in front of the store. There was usually a small rear entrance, often with an annex display window, which provided access to the parking lot behind the store.

At Northland Center, the potential traffic pattern meant that window displays should be planned for both entrances and that the store office should be in the middle of the store across from part of the enclosed ready-to-wear stock room.

The design of the whole center—with Hudson's in the middle, surrounded on three sides by strips of specialty retail stores and with the only direct access to Hudson's at the lower level on one of the four sides—was remarkable. Parking space for six thousand cars was provided around the outside of the center, and an elaborate pattern of roads and highways was created.

With the John Lodge Expressway from downtown Detroit being completed at about the same time, it was possible to provide ingress and egress from the expressway to Northland Center parking lots. The underground truck delivery design kept the flow of merchandise separate from the flow of customer traffic.

These innovations helped make Northland Center successful. The J. L. Hudson branch of four hundred thousand square feet was the largest branch

Winkelman's officers, 1958. Seated (left to right) are Manny Hartman, Isadore Winkelman, and Stanley. Standing (left to right) are Stanley White, Harry Matelski, Harry Gersell, Harry Matlin, and Tony Vinci.

store for any department store, and Northland Center itself, with more than a million square feet of floor space, became the largest shopping center in the country for several years.

On the negative side of the ledger was the damage to the downtown shopping district and to the social fabric of the city. This was probably inevitable but was hastened by the sheer magnitude and success of Northland Center and by the carving up of the city with expressways. Designed ostensibly to provide easier access to downtown Detroit from the suburbs, the expressways instead became the arteries for moving out of the city and to the suburbs.

Lack of a rapid transit system, which had been opposed by the Big Three auto companies, was another significant factor in the movement of middle-class white families to the suburbs. The insensitivity to potential human problems in the city, coupled with a narrow-minded opposition to rapid transit that other cities have supported, helped to bring about the very serious negative economic conditions that Detroit has experienced since the mid-1950s.

Credit Pioneers

In about 1952, I.W. went through a divorce and was for most purposes detached from the business for a year or more. While we met with him occasionally to keep the expansion program on course, Hartman, Goldstein, and I managed the business. At this time, we decided that we needed to offer our customers credit in addition to layaway, which had been our only method of deferred customer payment.

We hired Bill Patterson from Neusteter's in Denver and established an advanced system of revolving charge accounts that permitted our customers to pay a percentage of the balance each month rather than have the entire balance due within thirty days, as was the conventional department and specialty store approach at that time.

We were pioneers in a system that has been widely adopted by most retail stores and has become fundamental to the credit card industry. The system was ideally suited to the needs of our customers, who, for the most part, preferred to make small payments and pay a monthly interest charge on the balance. The finance charges went a long way toward paying the cost of the credit operation.

The large charge account balances that resulted from our new revolving accounts necessitated a new approach to financing our accounts receivable. This led to a landmark revolving credit agreement with the Detroit Bank and Trust Company (now Comerica), negotiated by Ben Goldstein and I.W.

In the past, when corporations needed cash, they would work out a

A typical late seventies Winkelman's store front

short-term financing agreement with a bank to borrow the funds to meet their irregular financial requirements. Short-term financing had usually involved a period of at least thirty days each year in which there would be no outstanding loan. This was obviously impossible for Winkelman's, based on the size and continuity of the credit accounts receivable. It should be noted that until the advent of the revolving credit charge account, financing of any kind had been unnecessary for Winkelman's.

In a couple of years, our credit system became so successful that the J. C. Penney Company hired away Bill Patterson to create a comparable system for Penney's. Today the system is practically universal and includes the major credit cards.

The relationship with the Detroit Bank had begun in the late 1920s when Joe Dodge was chairman. The relationship would continue on a very positive basis until 1984. Ray Perring, an elegant man and Joe Dodge's successor, was chairman when the revolving credit agreement was created.

Initially, our accounts receivable were pledged as collateral for the loan, but that provision was dropped after the arrangement matured. We would have periodic meetings with Perring and the senior officers of the bank to discuss business and economic trends in a general way over a glass of sherry and a pleasant lunch in the bank's executive dining room.

Shortly after the development of the revolving credit agreement, Wendell Goddard, a senior vice president of the bank, joined the Winkelman's board of directors. Peggy and I were invited to the wedding of his daughter, Sarah, to Phil Power, the publisher of *The Observer & Eccentric Newspapers* of Michigan. Sarah was on the board of UNESCO (United Nations Educational, Scientific, and Cultural Organization) and became a very constructive member of the University of Michigan's Board of Regents until her untimely death in 1986, at which time Phil succeeded her on the Board of Regents.

When Wendell Goddard retired from the bank in 1966, he was succeeded on the Winkelman's board by Milton Drake, a marvelous man and senior vice president of the bank. Milt died of a heart attack several years later. His successor on the board was Rod Craighead, then chairman of the Detroit Bank and Trust. Rod continued to serve on the board until Milton Petrie took over control of Winkelman's in May 1984.

Rod Craighead was succeeded by Don Mandich. Peggy and I enjoyed being with Georgia and Don Mandich on many occasions. Don's interest in heraldry and his book on the subject are fascinating to us. In addition, I had the pleasure of working with Georgia on the Citizens Advisory Committee to the Wayne County Probate Court, of which I was the chairman.

More recently, I have had a very positive relationship with Eugene Miller, the current chairman. It began when we worked together on the board of the Health Care Institute, located on the site of the then new Detroit Receiving Hospital, connected to Wayne State University. The Health Care Institute was an experimental approach to clinical medicine that both Gene and I thought was worthwhile. Unfortunately, the experiment was not successful; the physical facility became a more typical clinic operation. It was many years later that Gene asked me to serve on the board of Comerica's new family of mutual funds, named Ambassador Funds.

Challenge from the Teamsters

Also in 1952, the Teamsters Union began "informational picketing" in front of the main office and warehouse of Winkelman's. Such picketing was a legal way to put pressure on companies that were not organized. The Teamsters showed up on Parsons Street in seven black Cadillac limousines, which they parked in front of the entrance in an effort to intimidate everyone.

We had just hired three new vice presidents, who arrived on the scene as the Teamsters goons from Jimmy Hoffa's home union, Local 299, were doing the informational picketing.

With the help of Lillian Horenbein and her Business Careers office in New York, we had hired Albert Cohen away from G. Fox in Hartford, Connecticut, to direct our advertising program. Harry Matelski was brought in from a department store in Fort Wayne, Indiana, to manage our human resources division. We also hired Anthony Vinci away from Macy's in New York to manage our nonselling activities, including accounting, credit, and the warehouse. Each of these men did a remarkable job for Winkelman's and spent more than thirty productive years with the company.

Tony Vinci and Al Cohen were initiated into the company by riding shotgun on Winkelman's trucks as we continued to deliver merchandise to the stores. The Teamsters roughed up a couple of our people, and, as a result, we were able to get an injunction against the union that put a stop to its organizing effort at that time. While we had no objection to a union if the employees wanted one, we were not about to be intimidated by the Teamsters without a fight.

In 1964, we would experience a second, much more subtle effort by the Teamsters to organize the warehouse employees and truck drivers. This time, the employees, demonstrating their support for black power, were in favor of the union.

The Teamsters would have been successful on that occasion except for the fact that one of our warehouse employees, who was leading the organizing effort, impregnated one of the women in the warehouse. A National Labor Relations Board election was won by Winkelman's.

About two years later, the Teamsters did win an election and organized our warehouse employees and drivers. The only difficulty in the negotiations was the union health and welfare plan, which would have been very costly to the company and, at the same time, would have provided fewer benefits to the employees. Fortunately, for them and for the company, the warehouse employees elected to keep the Winkelman's benefit plan.

What our warehouse employees did not know was that the Teamsters were probably the least sensitive of the major unions at that time when it came to black people.

Business relationships with the Teamsters were generally straightforward and well managed by the union. Winkelman's was not an exception. We worked well together. As a matter of fact, when reality settled in a year or two later and the warehouse union members wanted to decertify, management took the position that it was strictly up to them. We would not help them in that effort.

More Growth

In 1956, I.W. and I found my successor as general merchandise manager. Edwin G. Roberts had spent about thirteen years with Henry the Hatter, a men's retail hat chain in the New York area owned by Ed's first wife's father.

Ed had a master's degree in business from the Harvard Business School. After Henry the Hatter, he had moved to Interstate Department Stores, then to Rich's Department Store in Atlanta. Two years later, he moved to the Macy's Department Store in the same city.

Roberts's background seemed ideal, with merchandise management experience in chain store, basement department store, and upstairs department store ladies' apparel. What wasn't ideal, of course, was the number of moves that he had made, although each move was upward and broadening for him. Ed was deeply troubled psychologically by the suicide of his father at the time of the 1929 stock market crash. This showed up in our testing of him prior to employment and, more obviously, afterward, when he would sit at meetings drawing pictures over and over again of the same 1929 Buick, with the spare wheel on the side, that had belonged to his father.

Aside from this, he seemed fine. Ed was on the rebound after divorcing his second wife, a Parisian showgirl with whom he had a son, Jean-Marc, who was exactly the same age as our son, Roger, two years old. Ed took great pleasure in Roger and in the fact that we had some mutual friends. This made him feel very much at home in Detroit.

Roberts owned an MG convertible, another deviation from the pattern of Winkelman's executives, who drove more conservative and modest Detroit-made automobiles.

The understanding with Ed Roberts was that he would come in and work directly with me for a year and then take over as general merchandise manager with full authority. Ed was a sharp, hands-on merchant with excellent resource relationships of his own. He also had strong relationships with the fashion magazines, something that I had not developed.

The magazine relationships were very social, and until 1956 I had felt they were not worth the effort. We did run some national ads that were probably good institutional advertising but not productive in terms of sales. I did appreciate the opportunity to sit down with magazine fashion people to discuss trends in fabric, color, and styling.

About this time, L.W. and I developed a close relationship with Paul Honig, the president of Anglo Fabrics. L.W. and Paul got along famously, and twice a year I would take all of our merchandise managers and buyers into the Anglo showroom at 1407 Broadway, in the high-rise apparel building that had just been completed on the site of the old Metropolitan Opera House.

Paul Honig would show us the new 100 percent wool fabric line for the coming season and provide us with color cards. In some instances, we would urge a coat or suit manufacturer to buy a particular fabric and certain colors so that exclusive styles could be made up for us.

Based on our meetings with Anglo, the magazines, DuPont's textile division, and others, we would develop our own color card for the coming season and work with our manufacturers in building their lines. After the higher-priced lines opened at the beginning of each season, we would suggest styling, fabrics, and colors to be made up at moderate prices, something that was unique at that time in apparel retailing.

Stanley White, our coat and suit merchandise manager, was very proficient at working with the designers to accomplish our fashion and merchandising objectives. By this time, we required sufficiently large quantities that we could buy complete cuttings of two or three hundred garments.

We had developed a very strong, very successful higher-priced early-fall coat business in May and June of each year. This preseason coat event was the envy of other retailers and admired by the manufacturers, who were able, based on our early-season sales results, to take important positions on fabrics and colors that would make a substantial profit for the season. On one occasion, we bought a large quantity of cashmere piece goods for an undercapitalized manufacturer in order to protect the price of our cashmere coat promotion for the coming season.

This early-fall coat business was mainly a layaway business until the late 1950s, when we gradually shifted the sales to our revolving credit accounts, thereby reducing returns significantly and transferring the responsibility for layaway supervision from store management to the central credit department.

By the time I retired in 1984, technology had improved to the point that we could send direct mail to zip codes that appeared to have the best potential; to customers who had previously made coat purchases; to our best customers; or to customers whom we felt, for any reason, had particular potential for the annual coat event or for any other of our promotional events.

Of course, advertising and direct-mail costs had risen substantially by the 1980s. Yet technological advances made it possible for us to reach our customers. That is why our own charge account customers were so valuable to us. Their loyalty and support had a very positive effect on our profitability.

In 1956, the Russek's store on Woodward Avenue, one block north of Hudson's in downtown Detroit, became available. After considerable debate about the advisability of a multiple-floor operation, we decided to go ahead. We would inherit an excellent shoe department, which would be on the mezzanine. Ed Roberts and I worked on the layout together.

Ed felt strongly that the dress department should be on the second floor, with coats and millinery on three. I was concerned about the limitation of suggestive selling that would result from the separation of coats and suits from dresses, but I agreed to go along.

We had decided to use the New York architecture firm of Copeland, Novak, and Israel, with Larry Israel as the partner in charge of this store

Mayor Louis Miriani cuts the ribbon for the opening of Winkelman's
downtown store in 1956. Isadore Winkelman is to the mayor's right, Leon
Winkelman on his left, with Stanley next to Leon. Behind Isadore,
from left to right, are Peggy Winkelman and Josephine Winkelman.

design. After Northland Center, we had shifted from Victor Gruen to Louis
Redstone for the design of our Eastland Center store but felt that the
department store and multiple-floor specialty store experience of Copeland,
Novak, and Israel would be worth the additional cost for the design of the
downtown store.

Eventually, the shoe operation was leased to the Wohl Shoe Company
out of St. Louis, and shoes were added to the larger and newer stores. We
designed several labels of our own, including "Pacesetter" for shoes.

In fact, we had been designing our own labels since the late 1940s, when
we came up with the name "Zipster" to be used on our most important
zipper-lined coats.

In the late 1940s, the primary fabric for our Zipster coats was wool
gabardine, just as it was for suits, with the best fabrics from a quality and
price point of view coming from the American Woolen Company. Wine
and hunter green were the dominant fashionable colors at that time.

Our biggest source of Zipster coats was Charlie Klein, a flamboyant Seventh Avenue entrepreneur with a passion for boat racing. One year in the 1950s, Charlie drove his boat in the annual Gold Cup race on the Detroit River. Unfortunately, he did not win, and his powerful boat wound up on the bottom of the river.

In retrospect, we could have done just as well or perhaps better with the downtown store by using Louis Redstone or Victor Gruen as the architect.

The grand opening of the downtown store was a great civic occasion, since very few companies were moving into the city, even at this early date. Mayor Louis C. Miriani was on hand for the ribbon cutting as Winkelman's came to downtown Detroit with appropriate fanfare in the *Detroit News* and the *Detroit Free Press*.

Changes, Career Moves

Ed Roberts helped to generate a major change in our hosiery business. Since 1940, Winkelman's had been using the Sapphire Hosiery Company for our branded hosiery business. Sapphire was run by Ralph and Theodore Schwartz from their offices in the Empire State Building in New York.

The Schwartzes were fascinating personalities. They serviced Winkelman's throughout World War II when there was a great shortage of nylon, which, a few years earlier, had replaced silk as the fiber of choice for the best ladies' hosiery.

Sapphire had the finest retail accounts in the country to sell their full-fashioned nylon stockings with seams at $1.95 per pair, a price that impressed me, even as I was just learning about merchandise, as being much too high for the average Winkelman's customer. Sapphire eventually did give us access to some nonbrand hosiery for our promotions, and of course this helped. But it was still a far cry from the fifty-nine cents per pair for silk stockings that prevailed before the war.

And then, along came seamless stockings, which Sapphire refused to make on the philosophical grounds that only full-fashion stockings were important and that seamless stockings would be a passing fad. How wrong could they be?! Like so many other corporate leaders who refused to move with the times, the Schwartzes made a fatal mistake. The result was the sad end to the Sapphire Hosiery Company.

In 1954, after Roberts had looked over the hosiery market carefully, he arranged a lunch meeting at the Algonquin Hotel in Manhattan with Alex Haimes, who at that time was managing the nonbrand hosiery business of Kayser Roth. We met to discuss proposals for a major restructuring of Winkelman's nonbrand hosiery business. Haimes proposed that Winkelman's develop its own brand of seamless stockings plus additional promotional hosiery. L.W. was also present for the meeting, giving our action plan his full endorsement.

In effect, we would be establishing the same price structure for hosiery that we utilized in our business generally. In this case, it would be Sapphire for the high-priced brand, the Winkelman's Bel Canto hoisery for our moderate-priced brand, and Starmist for our promotional low-priced brand.

Once again, Al Cohen and the advertising staff came up with great, appropriate brand names, labels, and package designs.

Our relationship with Haimes and our seamless hosiery business grew by leaps and bounds as a result of the restructuring and the packaging of the new stockings. Over the years, Mady and Alex Haimes became close family friends. In all of my retailing experience, I have avoided close relationships with manufacturers, with this one exception, because I wanted to make sure there was no conflict of interest.

While Ed Roberts was a good merchant, his presence triggered an upheaval in 1956. The feeling among the top executives was that I would become president and no longer involved in merchandising. Ben Goldstein, the great intellect, adviser, and supervisor of our accounting, personnel, and warehouse divisions, decided to accept the presidency of the Ernst Kern Company, which operated a downtown Detroit department store. Ernst Kern had decided to retire and put Ben in charge as the CEO. But Kern's was an obsolete store with no expansion plans, and Ben Goldstein wound up presiding over its demise. From Kern's, Ben would take on the presidency of Franklin Simon, the specialty chain operated out of New York. But once again, he was unsuccessful and left retailing to work with the Small Business Administration in Washington.

A short time later, in 1958, Roberts himself found that Winkelman's was too restrictive for him and decided to become president of the national ladies' specialty chain Peck and Peck, based in New York. But it, too, was obsolete, and before long, Ed left Peck and Peck to become the president of Franklin Simon, also in New York, the same group of stores that Ben Goldstein had been unsuccessful in managing.

Roberts reshaped Franklin Simon's merchandising around the "young individualist" idea and was very effective in building its profitability. He was so effective that Dayton's invited Ed to go to Minneapolis to head its specialty division, which included jewelry stores.

In his next move, Roberts came back to Detroit as the president of Hudson's, which had been bought by Dayton's to form the Dayton-Hudson Company. Ed reinvigorated Hudson's with his creativity and keen merchandising sense. He and I had continued our friendship even as Ed married for the third time, this time to a childhood sweetheart. That marriage lasted

Stanley with Tony Vinci at Stanley's fiftieth birthday reception,
1972. Tony became president of Winkelman's shortly after.

for only thirty days. But then Roberts married a young designer from a New York lingerie firm. Ed and Joan stayed married for close to twenty years, until Joan's death from cancer in Los Angeles. They had two children together and spent happy years in Detroit until he was hired as president of the May Company Department Stores in Los Angeles, a position he never should have accepted. The rigid management of the May Company would not tolerate Ed's entrepreneurial approach.

Hudson's was never again as sharp as it was with Ed Roberts as president, and the May Company experience proved disastrous to Ed. He was fired after a couple of years and was never the same again. After Joan's death Ed began drinking, and the problem became so serious that I strongly urged him to get help. He appreciated my candor and did get help. The last time we saw Ed, he was building a house with a woman down on the Baja Peninsula. He would later suffer a fatal heart attack. It was a sad ending for one of the best merchants this country has seen.

After Ed Roberts left Winkelman's, I decided to promote Stanley White to the position of ready-to-wear merchandise manager and Harry Matlin, an excellent sportswear specialist and our New York office manager, to smallwear merchandise manager.

These moves led to the resignation of our excellent dress merchandise manager, Sidney Alpert, who was a good personal friend. Sid decided to go into business for himself in California, a major mistake that led to a near-fatal heart attack.

The shakeout resulting from the hiring of Ed Roberts was continuing. Our new senior officer roster now included, besides I.W., Manny Hartman and me, Harry Matlin and Stanley White who split the merchandising responsibilities, Tony Vinci handling the nonselling functions, Harry Gersell in Store Operations, and Harry Matelski managing Human Resources.

Before long, Stanley White told me that either he or Harry Matlin should be the general merchandise manager because he felt the two-division arrangement would not work. My response was quick and decisive, since I have never permitted myself to be intimidated: "Then it will have to be Harry Matlin." This change led to a stable merchandising organization for the next several years.

Immediately, I was in touch with Business Careers and Lillian Horenbein to find a replacement for Stanley White. Luckily, I found a very good one in Jerry Chazen, who came to Winkelman's in about 1960 as our ready-to-wear merchandise manager and vice president. Jerry had been a buyer for Lit's, a department store in Philadelphia. He appeared bright and capable of making the transition into chain store merchandise management.

Within two years, we brought all of our buyers to Detroit to live and reduced the size of our New York office in the process. Murray Robbins, one of our New York resident buyers, remained in New York to manage a small staff of resident buyers.

At about this time, I became very concerned that our junior sportswear and junior dress businesses were not experiencing the same explosive growth from the post-World War II baby-boomers as were the junior apparel market and many retail stores.

"Junior" in ladies' apparel has always related to size patterns and not to age. The junior figure has a shorter waist and relatively larger bust and hips than its "misses" counterpart. At the same time, there has always been some confusion about age appeal of junior merchandise if only because of the name.

I hired Milton Goldberg, a consultant and former department store merchandise manager living at the time in Florida, to come to Detroit and work with me on correcting the situation. Milton was a sound merchant with a warm, personable management style.

Goldberg worked with me and with the merchandise managers in designing a survey to evaluate the customers' views on junior/young merchandise and store environment. Analysis of the survey results led us to conclude that the closed ready-to-wear stocks in Winkelman's stores were obsolete and that in order to make an appropriate merchandise statement to attract younger customers, it would be necessary to present our merchandise in open stocks and separate the younger merchandise from that for our more mature customers. We would also need to provide a more appropriate environment for the younger merchandise.

We knew from our experience in opening a small part of our sportswear stocks beginning in 1948 that doing the same with our junior merchandise would be productive. But we also knew that we would have to carry a substantially larger inventory, which would require a much larger investment and, at the same time, slow our merchandise turnover significantly.

Making the decision was somewhat easy due to the fact that our profitability was at an historically high level. Yet despite this fact, we would be making a very substantial investment in store remodeling and in improving the decor to coincide with our revised merchandise objectives.

The Death of L.W.

Unfortunately, and at the same time fortunately, L.W. was not around to fight for the survival of the selling system that he and I.W. had created back in 1928. My father died suddenly, and prematurely at age sixty-three, of a heart attack on November 6, 1958.

I was in a New York coat showroom on that Thursday afternoon when I received the call with the very sad news. Somehow, Peggy and I managed to get back to Detroit that evening to be with my mother and to proceed with arrangements for the funeral. More than eight hundred people attended the funeral held in the Brown Memorial Chapel of Temple Beth El. It was a fitting tribute to a great merchant and a great human being by his many friends, by Winkelman's employees, and even by Winkelman's customers.

By coincidence, the board of directors of the National Association of Women's and Children's Apparel Salesmen (NAWCAS) met in Detroit about ten days later. It had already named Leon Winkelman its "Man of the Year." This posed a difficult emotional dilemma for me. Should I appear at the convention to accept the award on behalf of my father?

After considerable thought and a great deal of anguish because it was so close to the time of L.W.'s death, I did decide to attend the NAWCAS banquet, where I accepted the award posthumously for my father. It is a beautiful bronze plaque that to this day hangs on the wall of my office beneath his photograph.

After L.W.'s death, I.W. proved to be very uncomfortable with the idea of being chairman and CEO with me as president and COO, although it was obvious to the officers and directors that it would have been appropriate. While we continued to work together for the next fourteen years until his retirement in 1973 because of ill health, the relationship was negatively affected by his inaction.

In retrospect, I attribute I.W.'s failure to put us on an equal footing to his ego. He felt that "I. Winkelman" meant "I am Winkelman's." He was nevertheless supportive of my leadership and management of the operation.

While I.W. continued to be responsible for leasing, store construction, finance, and corporate policy, he had little to do with operation of the business. The hiring of Ed Roberts had brought about greater involvement on my part in all aspects of the business. I.W. urged me to develop as broadly as possible, while, at the same time, his ego was protecting his own position as president and CEO.

By the time of L.W.'s death, Tony Vinci had been promoted to senior vice president and given the responsibility for all of the nonselling divisions except personnel. Tony worked with I.W. on finance and bank relationships in which I participated in terms of policy. Tony reported to me for the operation of accounting, data processing/systems, credit, and warehouse. He was a strong leader and an extremely competent manager who would become the president of Winkelman's when I became chairman and CEO upon I.W.'s retirement in 1973.

Outside the business, Tony had strong commitments to the community. He became the president of the Episcopal church in Grosse Pointe and an officer of the Red Cross, with which he continues to work in Washington, D.C., where he and Evelyn have lived since Tony's retirement in 1984.

Merchandise Presentation

After the death of L.W., the Management Committee—consisting of me, I.W., and Ben Goldstein—was established. As chairman, I was in a position to develop new policies and to coordinate the management of all aspects of the business. My experiences with Peggy in the world of art and design gave me the understanding I needed in order to supervise the planning of store design and decor.

I was able to apply my knowledge of store productivity by department area within each store to new store layouts as well as remodeling old stores. By the 1970s, it was clear to me that store layouts and decor became obsolete within a few years. Therefore, a continuing approach to remodeling was essential in order to generate a fresh environment and adapt to the latest productivity information.

In Winkelman's stores as well as many others, merchandise presentation became uninteresting to customers who were not impressed with looking at sleeves on a rack filled with merchandise where only the garment on the end could be seen in full. We were always looking for new ideas, for fixtures and signs that would enhance the appearance of the merchandise and generate improved consumer interest. Merchandise presentation became more and more important.

To consumers, department stores have become increasingly boring, with the same merchandise on similar fixtures and with infrequent injections of new merchandise and especially different colors. Customer boredom would be a subject of the dean's seminar I conducted on "The Crisis in Retailing" at the University of Michigan Business School in 1988. My concerns were presented in an editor's feature in the January 1989 issue of *Fortune* magazine. Dean Gilbert Whitaker had recommended that I write up the seminar for publication.

I had previously developed the Isadore and Leon Winkelman Chair in Retail Marketing beginning with Allen Smith, Acting President, and consummated with Harold Shapiro, President, in 1980. At that time Claude Martin was named the Winkelman Professor. Claude has been reappointed several times and has held the position for nineteen years.

In the dean's seminar, I concentrated on two problems. The first involved the damage being done to retail businesses and their employees by leveraged buyouts and hostile takeovers. The editors avoided the subject in the *Fortune* article, as they were not ready to deal with it. The second problem, which

Claude Martin, far left, named that day as the Isadore and Leon Winkelman Professor of Retail Marketing, 1980. To his left are Stanley; Harold Shapiro, President of the University of Michigan; and Gil Whitaker, Dean of the Business School.

became the basis for the *Fortune* article, was the lack of merchants in the retail world to replace the original entrepreneurs. The result of this void was new CEOs coming from accounting or real estate orientations, or, if they came up through merchandising, they were oriented to figures and not to the merchandise itself.

Area productivity within stores and increasing merchandising productivity received all of the emphasis, with little or no thought about uniqueness in concept, merchandising, and presentation. The stores run under this sort of emphasis reflected, and still do reflect, a lack of point of view, which simply stated means that they are boring and too much like other stores.

Why would successful merchants, especially in department stores, not see the need for unique presentation? Their training, from assistant buyer to buyer to merchandise manager to store president, was based on figures rather than on the merchandise. There was also a flawed relationship with vendors, which stressed advertising money, markdown money, and return privileges instead of negotiation for the lowest price and selection of merchandise based on a store's unique approach.

The fundamental problem lay with the training of assistant buyers who were not left in a department long enough to learn about the merchandise, its construction, and the manufacturing process. They were moved to another department after a few months, so that all they really had an opportunity to learn were the figure aspects of the particular segment of the business.

As buyers, they were told which resources to buy from, so they had little opportunity to be creative. Instead, they would walk into a showroom and ask the manufacturer what was important for the coming season. The answer, of course, would be the same for all of those asking the question, because the manufacturer made more money by making fewer styles. The result: all buyers were buying essentially the same merchandise, setting the stage for the boredom of store presentations in almost every case.

What's more, the pressure for advertising money and markdown money meant that the buyers were not getting the lowest price and that by advertising the product at the recommended retail price, they gave the growing discount store segment a marvelous opportunity to sell the same label merchandise at a significantly lower retail price.

With service in conventional department stores cut to the bone in the name of expense control and the merchandise priced unrealistically, is it any wonder that discounters have grown so rapidly? Without a long-term change in approach, the department store, as we know it, will become obsolete.

While Winkelman's continued to make progress in improving gross margin, our profitability was weak when compared to the stars of the industry, especially The Limited and Petrie Stores. Our stock price at about twelve times annual earnings told us that the financial world was not willing to rate us with the best, although Winkelman's was regarded as a well-managed business.

We continued to remodel stores effectively and to improve productivity. But in our expansion outside Detroit, where we were the dominant factor with our large advertising program and very favorable leases, the stores were slow to become profitable.

In Cleveland, where we were able to build a similar chain of stores, it took many years to generate a profit. Advertising costs were high and sales volumes slow to build. This was similar to the problems of building profitable stores in upper Michigan, although we were aided in Michigan by our very strong reputation in Detroit, where our profit was excellent in the thirty-four stores within the metropolitan area.

Chicago, which we entered in 1976, proved even more difficult with its extremely high rents and impossible advertising costs. We opened stores in the major new centers and the Water Tower center on North Michigan Avenue but had missed the opportunity to get into Old Orchard and Evergreen Park in the late 1950s.

In 1954, we had turned down Evergreen Park and made the decision to go into Cleveland instead because the rent at Evergreen Park was very high, and the shape and location of the available space were very unusual.

In general, our process of management by objectives worked well, and for the most part we achieved our objectives over the years. But I became concerned with our long-term profitability and our inability to generate planned sales levels in Chicago.

As a part of our effort to improve productivity, we had been working to reduce advertising costs in the 1970s and had shifted to circulars and newspaper inserts successfully in the Detroit area but to a negligible degree in upper Michigan, Ohio, and Chicago.

The concern for our future direction and our developing weakness in merchandising caused me in 1978 to bring in Stanley Goodman, the recently retired chairman and CEO of the May Company. Stanley was a brilliant man, a renaissance man, who brought the May Company through the transition from a family-run department store chain to one committed to and practicing professional management. Stanley was the chairman of the National Retail Merchants Association (NRMA) when I met him.

I myself had been a member of the board of directors and a vice president of NRMA for about twenty years. I received a silver medal in 1982 for my work as chairman of the Consumers Affairs Committee. (It was also in 1982 that I received a large "diamond" from Carol Channing at a recognition luncheon given at the Plaza Hotel by one of the textile mills.) Tracey Mullin, now the president of the NRMA successor organization, the National Retail Federation, was the staff person assigned to the committee. As a committee, we managed to force attention on consumer relations and problems that until that time had been ignored by the board.

At the meeting following the 1967 Detroit riots, I managed to force a discussion of the legal implications of civil unrest on cities and on retail stores. During most of my tenure, I was at odds with the Legal and Governmental Affairs Committee, because the committee in my opinion was either ignoring many issues or in opposition to proposals for governmental action. I still can't understand why big retailers favored state-by-state legislation of credit sales with different internal controls for each state, rather than one national law that would be much simpler and cheaper to administer.

One of my most interesting involvements with the NRMA was as a member of the International Committee. We met each January at the time of the annual convention. The members of the committee, the CEOs of major stores around the world, were fascinating. Georges Meyer, president of the Galeries Lafayette in Paris, became a good friend. We would meet twice each year in the store and then, on another day, Peggy and I would have lunch or dinner with Noelle and Georges Meyer.

Stanley Goodman would come to Detroit two days a month to work alongside me, evaluating my approach and participating in policy discussions. We would visit stores to evaluate content of stocks and merchandise presentation. Stanley would challenge our thinking on both broad and narrow subjects. I had lost confidence in our merchants in the mid-1970s and was looking for an independent evaluation as well as additional options for making improvements.

As a consultant to Winkelman's, Stanley Goodman would stay in our home. Each morning, he would run two miles despite severe cold in the winter, come back to shower, and have breakfast. Then, as we drove to the office downtown, he would meditate in the car. His interests were wide-

Stanley with actress Carol Channing, who presented him with a large "diamond" at the Plaza Hotel recognition luncheon given by a large textile manufacturer. 1982.

ranging, especially in music and the arts. Stanley, chairman of the St. Louis Symphony and an excellent violinist in his own right, would play chamber music with visiting soloists.

Our discussions were very stimulating, his questions penetrating. We would talk about the various aspects and problems of the business, which helped to sharpen my own decision making.

At one point, I hired a motor home, in effect a motorized conference room. With our officers and Stanley Goodman, we drove from store to store in the Chicago area in search of better answers. Our board of directors was pleased that Stanley was working with us, although some of our officers were not happy with this intrusion into the status quo.

The aftermath of Stanley Goodman's consultation included several personnel changes and some buyer reeducation, but the more fundamental problem of profitability of the Chicago stores was not solved. There was no question that the future growth of the company would depend on generating good profit in Chicago and other stores outside Detroit. The concerns of our board members caused me to hold a board meeting in Chicago and to take the entire board on a tour of the Chicago stores, as I had done with Stanley Goodman and our merchants.

It appeared that the answer would lie in our ability to customize the stocks of each store directly by relating the composition of each store's

The Winkelman's board of directors during a tour of Chicago stores, 1980.

stock to the consumer demand in the particular store. This approach was now technically feasible without exorbitant cost by virtue of computer programming. It would have been impossible a few years earlier.

Such customization of individual store stocks was unnecessary in areas such as Detroit and Cleveland, where our dominant advertising program generated a similar demand in all stores. Certainly, they too could benefit from customization, but it was not a top priority for those highly profitable stores.

The Board and the Takeover

While my merchandising and promotional activities would always be very demanding in terms of time and travel, I had important and at times urgent activities in my role as Winkelman's COO and later, from 1973 to May 1984, as chairman of the board and CEO.

The Winkelman's board of directors until 1951 had included L.W. and I.W. along with their personal advisers, Ed Quint and Samuel Rosenthal. Sam was a distant cousin who grew up in Manistique in the Upper Peninsula of Michigan. He was a brilliant young man who went to the University of Michigan and then on to Harvard Law School. Later, Sam was a partner in what became one of the largest and most prestigious law firms in Chicago. Sam was a mentor of mine and provided me with important insight as I grew in stature within the business.

Manny Hartman, Ben Goldstein, and I became senior vice presidents and members of the board in 1951. Board meetings were scheduled quarterly. Frank Siedman of the Siedman & Siedman accounting firm in Grand Rapids attended the board meetings and conducted the annual audit.

The Siedman firm did the accounting for the major Grand Rapids furniture companies. As Winkelman's grew, I.W. decided that we needed the benefits of associating with a large accounting firm that could provide other services besides the audit. The relationship with Siedman & Siedman continued until after the company went public in 1959, when Arthur Andersen became our accountants following the death of L.W. Its specialists were able to supply significant tax advice and consulting on retail operations that were beyond the scope of the Siedman firm.

The board continued with the same composition for a number of years, until I.W. decided that it should be enlarged with Lou Berry and Dave Pollock. I believe that I.W. was looking for personal support from the new board members. Lou Berry was a real estate investor and close associate of another investor, Max Fisher. Dave Pollock, a lawyer involved in politics and real estate, was a close friend of I.W. My relationships with both of them were good, and I was confident that I could deal with them on any issues likely to come to the board.

At the time of L.W.'s death, I was executive vice president and somewhat distressed that I.W. did not become chairman so that I could become president. Even though I was only thirty-six at the time, I had proved that I could do the job and had the organization behind me.

I.W. had the ultimate problem of not completely trusting other people and of being reluctant to change the status quo. Yet I.W. was sufficiently open-minded and committed to the growth of Winkelman's that he attended a four-week management course at the American Management Association in New York in the mid-1950s. I.W. had developed the unusual management style of thinking through expansion questions and coming to a tentative decision. After he had convinced everyone, he would then back off and become the devil's advocate. In a sense, this was good because it did prevent some mistakes. But it kept everyone off balance.

With I.W.'s death in 1973, I was faced with a critical choice. With great regret, I concluded that those directors over the age of seventy-five should retire from the board. This included Lou Berry, Dave Pollock, and Sam Rosenthal. At this time, I also developed a position guide and job specifications for future directors.

I decided against bringing onto the board I.W.'s son Eric, who was working in real estate and was hell-bent on becoming I.W. the Second. I also decided against Beryl Winkelman, I.W.'s widow, who, although a pleasant and constructive individual, in my view could add nothing of substance to our deliberations.

I chose instead to create the strongest possible board for the good of the business and to take my chances with the members of I.W.'s family in not hiring them. In retrospect, I have no regret for this decision, because the effect on the business was a very positive one. (On the other hand, in the long run, I.W.'s family would sell out to Milton Petrie, giving him the opportunity to gain control of the company.)

Our new directors would be Harold Shapiro, about to become the president of the University of Michigan; Alan Schwartz, a close friend and prominent attorney who served on the boards of many large public companies; Brod Doner, the head of the Doner Advertising Agency; and Jack Robinson, the chairman of Perry Drug Stores. The one other inside director was Tony Vinci, our president, who had replaced Ben Goldstein when Ben left in 1958.

The dynamism of the new board was refreshing and very stimulating to me and to the other executives of Winkelman's. We would work well together until Petrie gained control in early 1984.

Eric Winkelman's sale of stock to Milton Petrie in 1982 established the pattern for others to do likewise. These included Beryl Winkelman, whose sale of her substantial holdings was the immediate cause of Petrie's gaining control of the company. While the price at which these family members sold their shares was slightly above the American Stock Exchange price at the time, it did not reflect the true value of the business.

Milton Petrie began his retail career in Detroit working for Norman Hayden, who had a small chain of fairly successful lower-priced ladies' specialty stores, Robelle Shops.

Petrie then went to Hudson's, where he became the advertising manager of the basement store. About 1930, he opened his first Red Robin Hosiery Store next to the third Winkelman's store at Grand River and Grand Boulevard in Detroit. Petrie went bankrupt during the Great Depression, but he started growing his business again, vowing to maintain a strong cash position in order to prevent another failure.

During his time in Detroit, Petrie met my father and uncle as well as other members of the family. In fact, he was always an admirer of Winkelman's and eventually wanted to acquire our operation as a stepping

Stanley with Walter McCarthy, chairman of Detroit
Edison, and Don Mandich, CEO of Comerica, 1982.

stone to a moderate-priced fashion business, as opposed to his low-end
Marianne stores.

In later years, Petrie and I would meet periodically to compare notes
on business and retailing. During the 1950s, he had acquired Lerner Stores
stock that developed a value of $132 million in about ten years. This liquidity
funded the rapid expansion of Petrie Stores in the 1960s and 1970s. Petrie
would needle me periodically regarding our 3 percent after-tax profit on
sales versus Petrie's 10 percent profit after taxes. At the same time, we at
Winkelman's continued to update our stores. In addition, we paid dividends
without interruption from 1959 on, and Winkelman's never lost money in
any year.

Petrie then accumulated 20 percent of Toys R Us stock after learning
that Toys R Us had successfully taken over a defunct Interstate Department
Stores space in an eastern shopping center. But Petrie was forced into a
standoff agreement under which he could buy no more Toys R Us stock.
Petrie also bought The Limited stock and Harris Stores stock before
turning his attention to Winkelman's.

The performance of the Toys R Us stock masked the weakening of Petrie
Stores even as Petrie brought in a series of presidents in an effort to develop
a successor. Each new president would leave, if only because Petrie would
not let him alone to do the job. His two superannuated merchants were
wedded to the status quo.

Petrie spent money on remodeling but did not change the merchandising
of the stores, which operated mainly under the names of Marianne and
Stuart's. As indicated earlier, Milton would needle me regarding our 3 percent after-tax profit and high expense rate compared to his 10 percent after-
tax profit, which was truly remarkable at that time. Our leases were more
favorable than Petrie's, but our advertising costs, selling costs, systems costs,
and investment in organization were high. We had strengths that, from our
point of view, made it worthwhile, even as we worked strenuously to reduce
expenses and improve profitability.

The stage was set for Petrie to accumulate Winkelman's stock, which
he did from those individuals who wanted liquidity—just over the market
price. Ultimately, everyone would have been better off if we had agreed
to stick together and work out a sale to someone else. Yet this option was
never seriously explored. At the same time, it was not my objective to sell
the company.

The ultimate liquidation of Winkelman's was approved in January 1998
by the bankruptcy court handling the Petrie Chapter 11 proceedings. The
liquidation of Winkelman's was approved despite the fact that Winkelman's
remained a viable business. The sale of Winkelman's shares to Milton Petrie

by Eric and Beryl Winkelman had set the stage for the final curtain for Winkelman Stores, Inc.

Crowley's had agreed to buy Winkelman's in late 1997, but the board of directors of Crowley's turned down the deal in early January 1998, sealing the fate of Winkelman's. The Petrie people had made the decision to sell or liquidate Winkelman's by the end of 1997.

The closing of all Winkelman's stores was sad to contemplate. The final act in this drama put a sudden end to the prospects of the company continuing in business and perpetuating the family name. It was also the denouement for the many loyal employees.

My retirement as chairman of Winkelman's was precipitated by a telephone call from Milton Petrie in February 1984 in which he told me, "Don't go," just prior to my scheduled departure for the spring pret-a-porter (ready-to-wear) showings in Paris. In addition to working with our merchants and buyers to develop styling for 1985, I was to moderate a session of the International Congress of Retailers in Paris.

I replied to Milton's directive by saying, "OK, Milton, I won't go," and then canceled my trip. Since that was a good indicator of things to come when Milton would take over control of the Winkelman's board of directors in May at the annual meeting, I went to the Petrie office in Secaucus, New Jersey, the following Monday to tell Petrie that I planned to retire under the terms of my contract. Our board had predicted that I would endure about thirty days of Milton's idiosyncrasies.

Petrie had gradually gained control of Winkelman's as he provided a ready market for the stock of those family members and former executives who wanted to liquefy their holdings. The stock of the company, which had traded on the American Stock Exchange since 1959, was lightly traded with a very small float, so that offering a few thousand shares for sale would result in a depressed stock market price. Thus gradually, over a ten-year period, Petrie gained control of the company.

I had tried unsuccessfully to work out an agreement that would maintain the position of management. With all of the legal talent we had working with us, no one could provide a practical answer. I view this as the greatest management failure of my career.

4

Flair for Travel

In Touch with Fashion around the World

During his tenure with Winkelman's, Ed Roberts had urged me to explore Europe as a source for merchandise and ideas. He contacted Milton Bluestein, president of the Plymouth Shops in New York. Milton was kind enough to ask me to accompany him and his buyers to Europe in the spring of 1957. Thus began my visits to overseas markets, which continued two to three times a year until my retirement in May 1984.

The European Scene

Peggy accompanied me on every overseas trip but one. Her companionship, her fluent French, and her own fashion perspective provided continuous inspiration, as did her growing interest in illustrated books from as far back as the development of movable type by Gutenberg in 1454. We had opportunities to meet interesting people and to enjoy the culture of each country and city that we visited. Because Peggy was with me, we made many friends in Europe, in the Middle East, and in the Orient.

L.W. had visited Europe in 1956 and had helped to lay the groundwork for my trip. He met with commission agents in London, Paris, and Florence with whom I had already made contact. With my encouragement and guidance, he purchased the merchandise for an outstanding window from Emilio Pucci. L.W. had agreed with Ed Roberts and me that the timing was right.

In February 1957, Peggy and I went first to London, where we worked with Jim Warburg of Baker, Warburg—a fine and reputable buying office. This was the same firm from which L.W. had purchased piece goods in 1937, when he and my mother took me along, at the age of fourteen, on their first trip to Europe. Jim and Betty Warburg became good friends over the years. We would get together for dinner and theater or visits to their home at Leisurlea on the Thames in Weybridge, Surrey.

It was several years later that I met retired Major General David Belchem, when Jim Warburg merged with Great Universal Stores (GUS). Belchem, who had been chief of staff to General Montgomery in North Africa, was in charge of a number of GUS acquisitions and was used as a consultant by Sir Isaac Wolfson regarding Wolfson's investments, especially in oil, in Israel and the Middle East. In Italy, we worked with Enzo Tayar, who ran an office with his brother, Frank. We developed a close friendship with Enzo and his first wife, Vicki. The Tayar Brothers office was by far the best in Florence. Because Italian knitwear, leather handbags, and gloves became so important, the dollar value of Winkelman's imports from the Italian market rose to a level of $1 million at first cost or about $3 million at retail, a very profitable business for all concerned.

Throughout most of the 1960s, we employed a young Italian woman, Luciana Corsini, as our own buyer within the Tayar office to ensure that sufficient attention was paid to the placement of our orders, to the follow-up and pressure to meet the manufacturers' delivery commitments, and to the inspection of merchandise before it was shipped.

Luciana came to Detroit for our Italian promotions and traveled all over Italy with our people. In the summer of 1961, with our children—Andra, Margi, and Roger—accompanying us, we made an exploratory trip to Venice, where we found interesting glass and expensive handbags. A few years later, nearby Vicenza would become the center of 18-karat gold jewelry manufacturing.

On that first trip in 1957, Peggy and I met Milton Bluestein, his wife Gaby, and the Plymouth Shops buyers in Florence, where, working alongside their buyers, I was able to place merchandise testing orders for about one hundred thousand dollars at retail. I bought sweaters, handbags, and, in Naples, leather gloves. In Florence, I bought another inspirational window of printed summer sportswear designed by Emilio Pucci.

Gaby and Milton Bluestein were a pleasure to be with, as were Milton's buyers with whom we spent a great deal of time. We all spent Easter weekend together at the Villa d'Este, an incredible small hotel (later a large meeting center) on Lake Como. The city of Como was, and is, the Italian center for luxurious silk fabrics, and we purchased marvelous printed silk scarves there.

In foreign travel with merchandise managers and buyers, deluxe hotels and fine restaurants were the rule—a bonus for the long hours and irregular schedules that this kind of travel required.

Winkelman's needs were different from those of the Plymouth Shops in

Stanley's first buying trip to Europe. Left to right: Stanley, Milton Bluestein, Enzo
Tayar, Gaby Bluestein, Vicki Tayar, a buyer for Tayar Bros., and Peggy, 1957.

terms of the character of merchandise and the prices that would be right
for us.

Before that first European buying trip, Roberts and I had called the
Winkelman's buyers and merchandisers together to communicate our
thinking. I would be representing them in a new market and wanted their
recommendations for what to purchase. I advised the merchants and buyers
that as the business grew, many or all of them would be buying overseas.
As a result of the meeting, I was given an open-to-buy from the head of
each department where we knew that appropriate merchandise would be
available. Of course, like all good buyers, I overbought between the March
trip and a return visit in July of that year, as the merchandise was very
attractive and well-priced for our stores.

It was on that first trip that our friendship with Bernard and Marie-
Therese Aubremont blossomed. We had met Bernard, who was traveling
with his good friend Sam Rosenthal, during the time that Peggy and I were
doing a little fishing at Islamorado, Florida, in November of 1954. Bernard
was a Parisian banker who owned a six-floor apartment building facing the
Bois de Bologne. At one time he gave Peggy two books beautifully bound in
blonde leather with the gold crest of Marie Louise, printed in English when
Marie Louise was the Duchess of Parma. The subject of the two-volume set
was the defeat of Napoleon's fleet by Lord Nelson at Trafalgar. The books
were published in 1814.

Through the Aubremonts we became close friends of their daughter and
her husband, Drs. Lise and Lucien Bouccara. Lise is an ophthalmologist
and Lucien was a gynecologist strongly committed to Israel. His great-

grandfather was the Grand Rabbi of Tunis and had attended the Balfour Conference in Basel in 1917.

We had lunch or dinner with the Aubremonts and the Boucarras on each trip to Paris until the untimely deaths of Bernard and Lucien a number of years ago. We would talk by telephone between trips and compare notes on many subjects. Bernard seemed like part of our family. He and Marie-Therese came to Detroit for Roger's wedding. At an earlier time they came to Detroit with Lise and Lucien as well as their grandchildren. During their stay, I hired a bus to take us all, including our children and grandchildren, to Greenfield Village.

In July, when Peggy and I returned to Italy on our own, and in the heat of summer, I made the most important purchase. We went to visit Tayar on a Mediterranean beach at La Spezia just north of Pisa. There I met Umberto Severi, who would later become the "King of Capri," where he developed a major knitwear production facility. At the beach, Severi showed me samples of wool knit dresses at an unbelievable first cost of four dollars each. The value was incredible, so I bought several hundred as a test.

Severi had harnessed the process of cottage work. He measured out yarn centrally, helped people who lived nearby to acquire knitting machines, and then inspected the finished product before shipping it to the purchaser. At first, our buyers were aghast when they discovered that the sizing of the dresses was very erratic. To bring order out of chaos, we sized the goods ourselves.

I invited the foreign consuls in Detroit to a managers' meeting, where I showed the spectacular photographs I had taken along with the merchandise. (This was the beginning of my work as a professional photographer.) The results were excellent. The merchandise sold very well, and we realized about a half million dollars at retail that first year. We were on our way to developing a very exciting and profitable new aspect of our business that would hit a peak of more than $3 million a year at retail from Italy alone.

I also attended the Italian couture showings in Florence, in the grand ballroom of the Pitti Palace. The showings took place in a fairyland setting, with buyers from all of the best specialty and department stores around the world occupying seats with the names of stores in large letters emblazoned on the backs. In the summer of 1961, Margi and Andra sat in the Lord & Taylor seats as they accompanied Luciana, Peggy, and me to the presentation of the collections. One of the highlights was the "Ballo in the Boboli," a marvelous ball held outdoors in the magnificent Boboli Gardens on the Pitti Palace grounds.

On that same trip, Peggy and I took Andra and Margi to the Lido night club in Paris for the spectacular show. The next morning Roger, age six,

Peggy and Stanley stand at the entrance to Pitti Palace
in Florence for the Couture Press Showings, July 1961.

looked at the program and came into our room crying, "You didn't take me to see the naked ladies!"

In Paris, the couture collections were presented in the individual ateliers of the designers. It was particularly exciting to be there along with their famous customers as each collection was presented.

A New Fashion Approach

In 1958, Stanley Marcus put together the "French Fortnight" promotion for Neiman Marcus. We had run into Stanley in Italy as he was assembling the Neiman Marcus import program in February of that year. (In those days, orders for fall merchandise were placed in February in order to ensure delivery by July.)

In October 1958, I flew to Dallas to be on hand for the Neiman Marcus event. From a promotional point of view, it was very well done, both in the press and in the store. However, the impact of the French merchandise itself was thin and much less than I expected. I attended some of the special events—including the art exhibits Stanley Marcus had arranged to complement the merchandise—and was welcomed to the store by a number of Neiman Marcus executives.

These were marvelous lessons for me as I contemplated the problems of making a presentation in more than thirty stores in Michigan, Ohio, and Illinois. The downtown Detroit store presented an exciting opportunity to create special events, including art exhibitions.

The cost of entry to the couture collections was usually one garment, which we would buy and then bring into the United States in bond so that we did not have to pay the duty. After we had used it for promotional purposes with the press and sent it to New York to be copied, we would then ship it back out of the country.

In the 1960s, I made an arrangement with Alexander's in New York to obtain, without cost to Winkelman's, the original couture garments Alexander's had purchased in France and Italy so that we could use them with the press. Alexander's appreciated our willingness to buy into the special cuttings of the copies that they would promote in New York. Our purchase reduced Alexander's exposure to markdowns and enabled Winkelman's to promote the merchandise without buying an entire cutting. Our ready-to-wear merchandise manager and the coat and dress buyers had great respect for their counterparts at Alexander's.

In those days, there was a race among Macy's, Ohrbach's, and Alexander's to be the first to advertise copies of the newest couture designs in New York in March and September, with each store featuring an evening charity event for a very select guest list. Since we were the only ones in Michigan featuring

Peggy and Stanley at the *Ballo* in the Boboli Gardens of the Pitti Palace, July 1961.

the couture copies at that time, we could well afford to wait until the end of September to feature them.

The Impact of Imports

With Christian Dior's "New Look," which had been introduced in the summer of 1948, we determined to make Winkelman's the store that would feature the copies as soon as they could be available and, in the process, to become the center of new fashion controversy. Fortunately, we had Sidney Blauner and his Suzy Perrette company to provide us with the copies at remarkably low prices. In those days, Christian Dior had to be featured as Monsieur X, but that did not deter us.

With skirt lengths lowered to mid-calf after seven years of wartime

Stanley with French consul Jean Le Diréac at the opening exhibition from the Mourlot Press of Paris at Winkelman's downtown store, 1966.

Peggy and Stanley with Metropolitan Opera diva Regine
Resnick and artist Arbit Blatas at their Venice apartment, 1982.

restrictions on the use of fabrics, the Dior move was both dramatic and timely. We ran a full-page ad declaring that Winkelman's was the store for new fashion ideas. We did not expect the copies to sell especially well, but more often than not, we were able to discern trends that we could translate into substantial business. In addition to mid-calf skirt lengths, the new silhouette had a rounded waistline and was tightly belted.

With the radical, overnight change in skirt lengths, Winkelman's developed a very profitable aspect of our alterations business by inserting a midriff into our customers' suits, thereby making them appear more fashionable. Even those customers who could afford to buy the new look did not want to buy an entire new wardrobe all at once.

While high-fashion trends were important to our future merchandising direction, the Italian knit business became the key to a profitable import business. In London, working with Jim Warburg's people, I found handbags, a limited sweater business, and some coats. There were also interesting coats in Amsterdam.

In Paris, Odette Guigue's Continental Purchasing Company buyers helped us find excellent promotional handbags. There were also blouses and silk scarves. (In October 1998, we took Odette to a special dinner honoring her eighty-fifth birthday.)

In Brussels, we bought beaded handbags at amazingly low prices. In Copenhagen, through Peer Herschend, we found a source for hand-knit ski sweaters that were very well priced.

In Switzerland, where Fritz Reiman was the commissionaire (buying agent), there were wool gloves and scarves and some gift items, but the prices were very high. I found little for Winkelman's in Austria, where the merchandise was too basic on the one hand and too high-priced on the other.

Most of our commissionaires were members of the same international group of buying offices. They would meet once a year, each time in a different city, where they would compare notes and work together to solve mutual problems.

Plymouth Shops did an excellent business in needlepoint-trimmed black leather accessories. This brought us to Frankfurt, Germany, where Offenbach and the annual Leather Goods Fair were just across the Main River.

Just twelve years after the end of World War II, with the Holocaust still very fresh in our minds, we found Germany difficult to visit. On our first visit, when we took the overnight train from Paris, customs officers at the border came into our compartment in the middle of the night to inspect our baggage. That was not an auspicious beginning, although Peggy and I continued to attend the Offenbach fair. We found the Germans very evasive about their wartime experiences, although we knew that most of them had been involved in the military.

After about 1962, we would not visit Germany again until after I had retired, when Peggy and I decided to go to the Salzburg Music Festival in 1985. We also visited Munich and Berlin on that trip. Peggy's intellectual interest in books and our curiosity about the great artists and writers of Germany brought us back. This time, we found a new generation of Germans and a strong commitment to democracy. The great writers, artists, and musicians continued to fascinate us, as did the question of how a country with such a marvelous cultural heritage could have committed the heinous crime of exterminating six million Jews.

Holocaust memories became a part of our family when Roger married Linda Schwartz. Linda's mother, Irene Schwartz, was a victim of Auschwitz. Her husband was killed there, and her baby was ripped from her arms and killed in front of her. It was only by her sheer determination and resourcefulness that she survived. More recently, through the research of Steven Spielberg, Linda learned that forty-seven members of her family died in concentration camps. Irene still bears her Auschwitz numbers on her arm as a constant reminder of that horrible experience.

New Dimensions of Travel

Because of our interest in art, books, and music, travel would be continuously challenging and satisfying to Peggy and me for many years to come.

Rapid technological developments in transportation and communication had provided a profound and lasting impact on Winkelman's and on the lives of Peggy and me and our family. The development of a substantial and profitable import business resulted in two hundred transatlantic crossings, twenty crossings of the Pacific, and three trips that involved circumnavigating the globe.

Aircraft improved—from the four-propeller-driven Lockheed Constellation we'd flown in on our first trip in 1957, to the first transatlantic jet-engine Boeing 707 and later the Boeing 747, to the supersonic Concorde. Travel time had been cut from ten or twelve hours down to three and a half hours for the supersonic. While the improvement in transportation has been remarkable, hijacking and terrorism have created security problems that offset some of the great gains.

Not incidental to all of the exposure to fashion and culture in the many countries we visited was the development of friendships in each place, many of which are still flourishing forty years later. In London, besides Jim Warburg, we are in communication with Betty and Sidney Corob, whom we met through Detroiters Wanda and Mac Fader after they had met the Corobs at a resort in Portugal in 1956.

Sidney has been involved in real estate in central London since we have known him. The first time we met Betty and Sidney, he was wearing his bowler and driving a Jaguar. That was on our first London visit when we were staying at the Savoy Hotel. Sidney took us for a ride along the Thames and promptly ran out of petrol in both tanks. In more than forty years since, he has not gotten over his embarrassment—in part because I remind him periodically.

Sidney has also been active in the British Roundtable of Christians and Jews. In 1995, in recognition of his strong community commitment and action, he was made a Commander of the British Commonwealth by the queen. Sidney has also been very active in Israel, where the Corob Walk has been created just outside the Yaffe gate to the ancient city of Jerusalem. Betty Corob is on the board of the Center for Jewish Studies at Oxford University, where the Corobs have established a chair in Yiddish literature. We have spent many wonderful hours with them and their children at Squires Mount, their fabulous home in Hampstead that was built in 1714. Our children have visited them, and on one occasion they have come to see us in Detroit. We have also been their guests for the Glyndebourne Opera, where we dined before the opera in formal dress, on the meadow grass, with beautiful china, crystal, and edibles brought by Betty and Sidney.

Nigel and Eunice Lion are friends we met through Betty and Sidney Corob. We have had many marvelous times together and through correspondence. On one occasion they took us to meet the librarian at Westminster Abbey where we had the privilege of examining the Abbey's collection of manuscripts and early printed books. Nigel and I have spent time jousting over the origins of biblical tales and the question of visits to the earth by extraterrestrial beings.

On two occasions, Peggy and I entertained our British friends at elegant dinners at the Connaught Hotel, where we stayed many times over the years.

In Paris, we continued working with Odette Guigue and her Continental Purchasing Company on the rue Royale. While our purchases were never huge, we became good friends and continue to see her many years after her office closed and we both retired. Odette was instrumental in getting me invited to couture showings and, beginning in the mid-1960s, to the pret-a-porter showings.

We met Christian Bricard, the president of the Belle Jardiniere Department Store on the banks of the Seine, on our first trip to Paris. We have become good friends over the years, meeting for dinner twice each year. We spent one weekend at the Moulin, their estate, outside Paris, with Christian, his wife Anne-Marie, their two lovely daughters, and their four magnificent golden retrievers.

Christian retired from Belle Jardiniere and became involved for a short time with the work of Ted Lapidus, a pret-a-porter designer who had a number of boutiques. The Lapidus venture did not succeed, and Christian involved himself more and more with hunting.

The Bricards, whose Paris residence is on the Avenue Montaigne a block from the Rond-Point on the Champs-Elysees, was purchased many years ago. Villeoiseau, a fairy-tale sixteenth-century chateau with nine-foot-thick exterior walls on four hundred acres, is about fifty miles south of Paris. There they raise ducks, partridge, and rabbits for the hunt. We spent one spring weekend at the chateau with Anne-Marie and Christian when wild daffodils were blooming in profusion in the woods. We also spent a fall weekend at Villeoiseau during the hunting season, when friends of the Bricards would come for *la chasse* on Saturday and Sunday.

La chasse is a misnomer, since the "hunters" stood along a line with their guns at the ready, while beaters and dogs flushed the game toward them. While Peggy and I were dressed appropriately for *la chasse*, neither of us did any shooting, except with my camera. The results of the day's shooting— that is, of the gun variety—were laid out very formally in front of the

chateau, and a careful count was recorded. The formal dinner afterward
was a delightful experience.

Fashion Developments Then and Now

The next very important fashion development, after Dior introduced his
"New Look" in 1948, was the demi-fitted suit of Balenciaga in the mid-
1950s. As with most new ideas, the Balenciaga styling innovation took
several years to gain acceptance in the United States, whereas in Europe it
was accepted immediately. By contrast, Dior's "New Look," introduced a

Peggy and Stanley with an unidentified hunter participating in La Chasse at
Villeoiseau, the estate of Christian and Anne-Marie Bricard, 1975.

few years earlier, had met with instant success in the United States. In the interim, we had witnessed other Christian Dior and Yves St. Laurent styling innovations, including pyramid coats and flyaway boleros, that generated important sales volume for Winkelman's.

One of the most interesting style changes during my career was the miniskirt, which got its start in London in the early 1960s and was designed by Mary Quant. The miniskirt, however, would not have been possible if it were not for the invention of sheer panty hose, eliminating the need for garters to hold up ladies' stockings.

With one stroke of design genius, girdles became obsolete and slips and petticoats much less important. All eyes were on young legs. Miniskirts became a craze overnight in Europe but could not be given away in the United States for several years. This American slowness to accept new fashion ideas was nothing new, but the miniskirt took an unusually long time to win acceptance in the United States.

As a part of the continuing education of our buyers, merchandisers, and store managers, I would photograph the latest developments in retail stores in Paris, London, Milan, Rome, and Florence. I would also sit at the outdoor corner table on the Boulevard Saint-Germain at the Deux Magots Cafe, taking pictures of people on the streets wearing the latest fashions. This was a ritual for many years.

In the latter 1960s, Andre Courreges created a structured look that did not fit tight to the body. It was a very modern version of the tunic with tights that men wore in the eighteenth century. Even today, jackets and tights are part of contemporary fashion. Karl Lagerfeld, the great design leader of the 1980s and 1990s, has been designing jackets worn with tights for a number of years.

Fashion design today is fragmented, with many niche designers such as Armani, Versace, Missoni, Sonia Rykiel, Kenzo, and Thierry Mugler. The niche designers actually have little influence on fashion direction. Likewise, the work of highly creative designers such as Vivienne Westwood, Jean-Charles Castlebejac, and Jean Paul Gaultier is so extreme that they exert little influence on fashion direction.

A number of designers—such as Christian Dior, Yves St. Laurent, Givenchy, and Valentino—have been strong fashion leaders and very influential in establishing fashion direction since World War II, but today are pretty well dated.

Dior may be an exception if John Galliano lives up to the promise of the creativity in the first couture collection he designed for Dior for spring 1997. Galliano had designed for Givenchy for several seasons but was unable to capture the Givenchy spirit.

The dominance of individual Parisian designers has diminished as they

Peggy (left) in Paris with Winkelman's merchandise managers Arthur Epstein, Sportswear Merchandise Manager; John D'Ascenzo, General Merchandise Manager; and Loretta Howison, New York Office Manager, 1978.

have gotten older and the great ateliers have taken to importing design talent. Examples are British designers John Galliano at Dior, Stella Mc-Cartney (daughter of ex-Beatle Sir Paul McCartney) at Chloe, and Alexander McQueen at Givenchy. Besides these three English designers, two Americans—Oscar de la Renta at Balenciaga and Marc Jacobs at Louis Vuitton—also have joined the Paris scene.

Gian-franco Ferre was an outstanding Milanese designer who created the Christian Dior collection for a number of seasons, until his untimely death. While his Dior designs were mediocre, Ferre's signature collection in Milan was outstanding.

A few years ago, Christian Lacroix arrived on the scene from the atelier of Madame Gres. Lacroix created an immediate sensation with his lampshade skirt and unusually flamboyant mixtures of fabric textures and colors inspired by his background in Provence. For a few years, Lacroix was an important leader who influenced fashion direction at many price levels; more recently, he has produced a more subdued collection and a lower-priced sport collection that are selling better. As a consequence, that inspirational spark of fashion leadership that generates followers is all but missing.

The German-born Karl Lagerfeld is an outstanding creative design talent who has had a tremendous influence on fashion all over the world. King Karl, as he is affectionately known, created the first pret-a-porter line in the early 1960s for the House of Chloe. Lagerfeld designed for Chloe for more than thirty years.

Lagerfeld was contracted to revive the House of Chanel by designing a couture collection and a pret-a-porter collection each season. This most creative of creative spirits has generated a new feeling of youth and creativity that has sparked a great revival of that legendary name. Tweed jackets and skirts are still the earmark of Chanel, but in ways never dreamed of by Coco Chanel. In addition, King Karl created his own signature Karl Lagerfeld line that featured very advanced design ideas. And, if that weren't enough, Lagerfeld has designed for the Fendi sisters in Milan for many years.

A real problem in fashion today, of course, is the aging of the designers whose names are on the atelier door and the extreme difficulty of finding creative replacements for them within the spirit of a given atelier.

Most of the major fashion firms were very small in the 1940s and 1950s. They have grown very large since, with multiple lines—including men's, children's, shoes, jewelry, and, above all, perfume, which is the most profitable part of their business.

The couture and pret-a-porter fashion houses have opened boutiques in various European countries, the United States, Japan, Hong Kong, and Singapore. This tends to create a negative influence on fashion creativity, as salability rather than design creativity has become the most important criterion.

There had traditionally been couture showings in January and July for the immediate spring or fall season. Now, the March and October pret-a-porter showings are geared to delivery in-store for September and February selling, and are attracting larger and larger audiences and press coverage. No longer are designers creating one-of-a-kind styling. Rather, they are going after the high-priced fashion business around the world.

Generating Excitement

Generating customer interest and excitement was always a challenge for Winkelman's, made more difficult in areas outside Detroit where we could not afford the same sort of extensive advertising program. At the same time, it was in Detroit that our primary institutional reputation and profitability were at stake.

We worked hard to establish our own identity and customer loyalty. Each spring and fall, beginning in the early 1950s and continuing for many years, we created a storewide color promotion that was featured in almost all departments.

First, we shopped the piece goods (fabric) market to determine the specific color to be featured. We then arranged for particular manufacturers to buy the piece goods and make up garments exclusively for Winkelman's.

Windows, color ads, and floor plans were put in place to emphasize the specific color. With one exception—peach blossom (there may still be some of it left forty years later)—these color promotion events were very successful. They enhanced our reputation and gave us a competitive advantage. White with brown in the early summer of one year was the most successful of all.

I could never understand the failure of manufacturers and other retailers to exploit this unfulfilled consumer demand for a strong visual presentation. As a matter of fact, I believe that a white-with-brown promotion could be successful today if any retailer is willing to risk the investment. But without real merchants managing retail businesses, it is not surprising that it does not happen.

Until 1958, there were few Winkelman's stores outside Detroit. In Detroit, we relied heavily on our fashion presentation in store windows and Sunday *Detroit Free Press* ads stressing particular fashion ideas. In addition, we utilized large volume-priced ads on current fashion themes for weekend business, which is when 70 percent of the week's sales were realized.

The concept was developed by Manny Hartman and further enlarged upon by Al Cohen as we increased our dominance in Detroit newspaper fashion advertising. We were able to negotiate excellent positions in the fashion section, the first news section, or the front page of another section.

We would sometimes take a full-page ad to introduce a new trend—such as the Dior "New Look" in 1948, the demi-fitted suit from Balenciaga and the chemise dress by Yves St. Laurent in the 1950s, the structured look created by Andre Courreges, and the Mary Quant miniskirt of the early 1960s. Our objective was to make Winkelman's the store for new ideas in fashion, adapted from the most creative designers of the day.

Our approach had changed dramatically with the first buying trip to Europe in 1957. Based on my evaluation of the potential of European merchandise, we developed an approach emphasizing the fashion aspects of European merchandise.

Department and specialty stores for the most part did not attempt to develop a fashion approach to their imported merchandise programs. Rather, they worked through their buying offices in order to have enough buying power to purchase basic merchandise in quantity at very favorable prices. This was a much less risky but also less interesting approach to importing. Since Winkelman's operated as a chain, we already had sufficient buying power to negotiate prices that were very competitive.

The couture, both French and Italian, was supplying the overall inspiration until the late 1960s. We exploited the new trends with the original garments we were receiving by agreement from Alexander's plus the copies that we had purchased from Alexander's cuttings in New York.

Al Cohen would arrange a meeting with the fashion editors from as many cities as possible where we had stores, with press releases for those editors who could not attend. At the press conference, usually at the Detroit Press Club, I would explain the fashion trends and models would show the individual garments.

These meetings were followed by newspaper ads and in-store promotions utilizing our display windows and internal visual presentations with signs. It was a great way to build our fashion reputation and at the same get a jump on the competition.

Our relationship with the Bluesteins and the Plymouth Shops merchants flourished. We continued to meet them in Europe for a number of years after that auspicious beginning in 1957. Gradually, through our participation in the Tayar office in Florence, we came to know and work with the Joseph Magnin people who were headquartered in San Francisco. Jerry Magnin, who currently owns the Ralph Lauren boutique in Beverly Hills, and Donald Magnin were our initial contacts. Our merchandise managers and buyers developed close working relationships.

At the same time, Peggy and I developed friendships with Elaine and Donald Magnin and with Ellen (Magnin) and Walter Newman. Ellen was a very good merchant. Walter managed the real estate function of the Joseph Magnin stores. And, of course, Cyril Magnin, Mr. San Francisco himself, was their leader.

These relationships became especially important for joint purchasing, where minimum quantities were very high and there was a mutual interest in the merchandise.

The relationships with Plymouth Shops and Joseph Magnin stores were in their infancy when I worked with Al Cohen to develop our first import promotion. While Italian knitwear was potentially the most profitable, we also imported Italian cowhide handbags and French calf handbags, Italian leather gloves, German needlepoint gift items, English knitwear and handbags, Belgian beaded handbags, and coats from Holland.

In 1957, when Peggy and I first visited in Florence with Emilio Pucci in his palazzo on the via Pucci, a stone's throw from the Duomo, the grand cathedral of Florence, we asked him about the paintings on the walls of the showroom. The best ones had been painted by Alvaro Monnini, who had been designing print patterns for Pucci. Our interest delighted Pucci, and he put us in touch with Monnini. We worked out a potential Florentine painting exhibition in Detroit, timed to coincide with our first import promotion in the fall of 1959. Back in Detroit, I worked with Al Pepzinski and George Mancour at the Gallery Four on Livernois to arrange the exhibition.

The painting exhibition gave Winkelman's an institutional handle, a special community event that was very positive. Joy Hakanson (now Colby), the art critic of the *Detroit News*, reluctantly covered the opening. She was surprised by what she saw and wrote a favorable review. At that time, it was practically unheard of for corporations to support art exhibitions.

The Italian art exhibition was the first of many special events, mostly related to our import program. From 1960 to 1982, there were events every fall. Between 1960 and 1970, our import promotions were built around original couture garments and their copies, which were at the leading edge of fashion at the time. The moderately priced imported merchandise was presented through creative ads, windows, and interior displays with signs to emphasize fashion newness.

Starting in 1970 and until 1982, we developed a more spectacular format. Working with Al Cohen, we created and sponsored a Cultural Center Open House in mid-September each year that involved the entire Detroit community. Woodward Avenue was closed off. Winkelman's paid the operating costs of keeping the Detroit Institute of Arts, the Detroit Public Library, and the Detroit Historical Museum open for the evening.

On one occasion, in 1970, Peggy and I along with Harry Matlin had

Peggy and Stanley with the Duke of Bedford at Woburn Abbey, 1970.

lunch with the Duke of Bedford in his Palace, Woburn Abbey, while I was negotiating to bring his Rembrandt paintings to Detroit as an adjunct to one of our European promotions. The duke had converted the grounds into a zoo in order to raise money to maintain the building. We ate in a large dining room with many Canaletto paintings on the walls and a parade of two-foot-high sterling silver minutemen on the table. It was a heady, but unsuccessful, day.

We arranged for special exhibitions at each of the cultural institutions and for a group called the McKinney Cotton Pickers to present a jazz concert in the middle of Woodward Avenue. In addition to newspaper advertising, announcements were included in a charge account statement enclosure to Winkelman's four hundred thousand charge account customers in the metropolitan area and in mailings by the cultural institutions themselves. Press coverage was excellent, which, of course, gave Winkelman's a substantial institutional plus in recognition of our commitment to the city of Detroit.

Outside Detroit, our press coverage was also excellent, although our ability to duplicate major institutional events was obviously severely limited.

However, the development of a television advertising program in the 1970s, with merchandise filmed on location in Italy, France, England, and other countries, provided a new and powerful method of communicating the excitement of the import events in Michigan and in Ohio. For Chicago, the costs were just too high.

Also prohibitive were the costs associated with the major advertising agencies in cities like Detroit and New York. However, Al Cohen was able to find a young man in Milwaukee—Duke Marx of the Marx Advertising Agency—who could produce the TV spots that we wanted for a favorable price. Al and Duke would go off on location in the spring of each year to shoot the commercials for the fall event.

The Discount Effect

In 1961, we became concerned about the inroads of discounters and their potential effect on our business. We decided to open leased departments in the new discount stores through our newly created Contemporary Merchandise Corporation (CMC).

The first Kmart store opened in 1961 on Ford Road in Garden City. While we were not ready for the first Kmart, we did go into two others later in that year, one in Bloomington, Indiana, and the other outside Minneapolis. In addition, we took on a leased department in one of the first Meijer Thrifty Acres stores in Grand Rapids and a leased department in a GEM membership store outside St. Louis.

We hired a merchandise manager from the Boston Store (Milwaukee) basement and thought we were off to the races. But after one year, we decided to cut our losses and get out of the discount business. We had selected the wrong man to run it and felt that the risk was too great to reorganize and try again. There were, however, two very positive aspects of our costly (about four hundred thousand dollars) experience. We had wisely kept the discount business separated from our specialty business. In addition, we learned that there was a key to selling merchandise in specialty stores at prices that could allow for Winkelman's service, which was greatly admired. That key was, and is today, the fashion approach to merchandising, something we had traditionally stressed.

We had relearned the proposition that desirable newness could be sold at traditional specialty store margins, and that emphasizing newness to the customer through ads, windows, and interior merchandise presentation was the life blood of specialty store retailing. What has baffled me over the years has been the failure of department stores to understand this simple principle.

Zsa-Zsa, Twiggy, and Yoko

Funny things tended to happen on the way to fashion promotions. Once, Manny Hartman was driving Zsa-Zsa Gabor from store to store in connection with a promotion of Oscar de la Renta wigs developed by Ruth Rothschild, the operator of Drake Millinery, our lessee. Manny was driving north on I-75 when he developed car trouble. Not wanting to be late at the next store, Manny and Zsa-Zsa got out of the car, prepared to hitchhike the rest of the way. It was agreed, of course, that Zsa-Zsa was more likely to attract a ride, so she stood out on the expressway. Soon a car stopped and picked them up. When the driver heard the identity of his celebrity passenger, he kept muttering, "My wife will never believe this!"

Another time, toward the end of February, we were running a dress promotion featuring long, lean model-actress Twiggy. We were presented with a ten-inch snowstorm the night before, which all but immobilized the city. I was mobile, though, driving Twiggy from empty store to empty store.

In July 1967, I went to London for three days (the only overseas trip that I have ever made without Peggy) to negotiate the purchase of a knitwear firm, which ended up not working out.

After arriving in London, I called Kasmin, an art dealer, to arrange dinner with him on the Friday night before my return to Detroit. Kas called back a day or two later to tell me that he had an invitation for the two of us to attend a cocktail party being given by the editor of one of the British art magazines.

I arranged to meet him and took a taxi to the address of the flat where the party was being held. Since the door was open, I went inside to the kitchen, where I was greeted by men with flowers in their hair; I ended up with flowers in my hair, too.

The only artist there whose name I recognized was R. B. Kitaj. And then I met Yoko Ono. In a brief conversation, I told her that I had seen the photograph of a dress she had designed in a recent issue of *Life* magazine.

The party was a lively affair with plenty of alcohol but no hard drugs in sight. After a while, Kas asked me to join the group that was headed for the French embassy to watch the Bastille Day fireworks. I declined, deciding just to eat dinner and head back to the hotel. I left the party and started walking across the square looking for a taxi. I heard a female voice calling, "Hey, Stan, wait for me." It was Yoko Ono running after me with a young man in tow. She, too, had decided to forgo the fireworks and get something to eat. I asked her and her friend to join me, so we headed for Fu Tong, a Chinese restaurant on Kensington High Street.

At dinner, we went through the usual "What do you do?" routine. Ono was making a movie in London. She said the project was going fine except

Peggy and Stanley with Yoko Ono at the opening of an exhibition of her work at Cranbrook, 1992.

for one problem: no theater was willing to show the movie. When I asked what the film was about and she replied that its title was *Bottoms*, somehow I knew why no one would show it.

About twenty-five years later, Peggy and I would meet Yoko Ono at an exhibition of her work at the Cranbrook Museum in Bloomfield Hills, Michigan. She was pleased to see us and even more pleased by my description of that evening in London and my mention of the *Life* magazine dress. She said she was trying to piece together recollections of her life before John Lennon and very much appreciated the limited insight that I provided. Ono invited Peggy and me to visit her in New York, something we have not done. (It so happened that enlarged film clips from *Bottoms* were hanging in the Cranbrook exhibition hall. They were not at all erotic, just nude bottoms.)

On to the Orient

After mining the markets of Europe for more than five years and developing a profitable business during that time, I noted that prices were gradually moving higher and business was beginning to shift to the Orient. So in 1963, Peggy and I made our first exploratory trip to the Far East.

We knew that quality merchandise was being produced in Japan and Hong Kong. Taiwan and Korea were just beginning to develop as major sources. Singapore had not yet produced any significant ladies' apparel exports. Most of our time on that first trip was spent in Japan and Hong Kong, with a visit also to Bangkok.

We began working with Bill Conner's office in Japan after learning that many of the top U.S. retailers were doing likewise. Bill had stayed on in Tokyo at the end of World War II to establish himself as a commissionaire working with American companies. Conner employed a former sweater buyer for the Broadway Department Stores in California—Jane Hinckley—who worked especially on sweaters and blouses. Jane's husband was the vice president of the Ford Motor Company in the Far East. Jane was a dedicated buyer who worked on the development of styling for synthetic-fiber sweaters and blouses.

Fujimura became our major volume resource for "fur blend" (rabbit hair and wool) sweaters. Peggy and I were invited to dinner more than once at one of the finest Tokyo restaurants—where we left our shoes at the door and sat on the floor while we ate. After dinner on each occasion, Mr. Fujimura, who was also the head of the Tokyo Stock Exchange, would take out his paints and create traditional Japanese paintings of bamboo for his guests.

On that first trip, we stayed at the new wing of the Imperial Hotel, which was next to the original hotel designed by Frank Lloyd Wright.

The dimensions of the Wright building's design made the original hotel unsuitable for taller Americans, but it was a thrilling experience just to walk through it.

The Imperial Hotel was just off the Ginza, the main shopping district in central Tokyo. The Takashimaya department store was close by, giving us the opportunity to look over the assortment of merchandise presented to Japanese customers. The shopping experience was fascinating, especially in the second basement, where there was a mind-blowing presentation of Japanese antiques from which we made some purchases. Since Takashimaya was a member of the Kirby Block buying office in New York, I had met some of their executives, who now became our hosts.

We were taken to lunch at the Tokyo Press Club by John Rich, the Tokyo correspondent for NBC. John and D. Lee Rich became close friends of ours over the years. We even ran into John by chance in Beijing in 1980, in the lobby of the Beijing Hotel, when John, as vice president of RCA for the Far East, was selling a satellite to the Chinese.

After finishing my work with the Conner office in Tokyo, we left with a car and driver. We stopped to see the Great Buddha of Kamakura on our way to Myanoshita at the foot of Mount Fuji. In Myanoshita, we purchased a series of seventeenth-century Tosa school paintings. After an overnight stay, we drove on to Kyoto.

Rather than staying in Osaka, which was highly industrialized, I decided that we should stay at the Miyako Hotel in Kyoto and that I would take the new bullet train to Osaka, where I would be working with Bob Kothchi, the manager of the Conner Office in that city. Very large quantities were the order of the day in Osaka, resulting in minimal purchases by Winkelman's.

Meanwhile, Peggy was getting acquainted with Japanese culture in the great temples of Kyoto, a few of which I was also able to see. The Ryoanji Temple, with its peaceful fifteen-stone garden, was a highlight for me. Peggy also visited the Red Lantern Gallery, which would become involved the following year in our plans for an exhibition of Japanese art.

While she was in the Kyoto Museum, Peggy met Jim and Dorothy Cahill. Jim, an art history professor from the University of California at Berkeley, was developing the inventory of all art that the Chiang Kai-shek regime had taken with it to Taiwan from China. These treasures were installed in the mountain behind what is now the Palace Museum. We came to have great regard for the Cahills, especially as we became more and more fascinated with Chinese and Japanese art.

We managed to spend a day in Nara, which had been the capital of Japan in the eighth and ninth centuries. The temples and pagodas, the sculptures in bronze and wood, and the artifacts of that very early capital of Japan were astounding to our unaccustomed eyes.

We went next to Kobe, a badly bombed-out city that was still recovering from the war. Pearls and beaded handbags were on my mind as we arrived at this important port on the Sea of Japan. Sorting pearls was a great experience for me, and I selected twenty or thirty strands to buy as a test. I planned to have them strung in New York in order to save substantially on the duty. They appeared to have good sales potential and were extremely well priced. While looking at the pearls I was introduced to a man who had served as the chauffeur for Harry Bennett, the infamous security manager for the Ford Motor Company, at the time of The Battle of the Overpass with Walter Reuther and the leaders of the United Auto Workers (UAW) outside of the Ford River Rouge Plant. He had returned to his native country after World War II.

Stanley sorting pearls in Kobe, Japan, 1963.

Buying handbags was a much different experience. I had observed that Winkelman's best-selling straw summer bags were made in Japan, and I had located the particular resource in Kobe. Cautioned by the buyer that the three-dollar cost (to sell for six dollars) we were paying was very low, I did not expect to find an edge in buying from the source directly. But I was wrong. I was able to buy the identical straw handbags that I had seen in the New York showroom for ninety cents each so that we could sell them profitably for three, four, or five dollars and still be below the competition. Since there was no gamble, except perhaps with delivery and packing, I bought them heavily.

Our first visit to Hong Kong was another remarkable experience, despite the water shortage when the Chinese on the mainland cut off the pipeline to Hong Kong. Water could be used only at certain times of the day, and bath water was saved for washing floors, even at the Peninsula Hotel.

The amenities of the Peninsula—in our experience, the best hotel in the world—were outstanding. These included the lobby lounge, the remarkable service, the boutiques, and, above all, its location with a view of the extremely busy and very beautiful harbor. Its restaurants, Gaddi's and the Marco Polo Room, were both outstanding, as was the mezzanine restaurant with its exciting harbor view. The entire experience in the hotel was both romantic and pleasurable.

I stayed up late at night, transfixed, watching the ships move in and out as the Star Ferry made its way back and forth from the Kowloon Peninsula to the island of Victoria and the city of Hong Kong. During the Vietnam War, there were always many U.S. Navy ships anchored in the harbor. The ships were there to be resupplied and to provide their crews with liberty.

On that first Hong Kong visit, I worked with Bosco Corea, the Chinese office manager for Bill Conner. Bosco was six feet five inches tall and weighed more than three hundred pounds. We would start at the office in the early morning and then move around Kowloon and the New Territories as we visited factory after factory in his Mercedes.

Beaded sweaters were extremely important at that time, as were unusual patterned (jacquard) sweaters, all manufactured from wool yarn and copied from European styles. Selection was easy on that first trip, since the manufacturers had samples they had made up from garments submitted by retailers with the understanding that the styles would not be sold to competitive stores in their geographic area.

The manufacturing plants occupied old buildings. They were makeshift and sloppy, with almost no modern facilities, a far cry from the newly built factories we visited later in Taipei and Seoul. Besides knitwear, I gave major attention to woven fabric blouses, shirts, and dresses as I evaluated the Hong Kong market.

Peggy and Stanley with Bosco Corea, manager of the Hong Kong Conner Office, and Mrs. Corea at Gaddi's restaurant in the Peninsula Hotel, Hong Kong, 1963.

Silk fabrics were available in blouses, dresses, and quilted robes at very good prices. I tested silk shirtdresses that I purchased at four dollars first cost, to retail for twelve dollars. If my projected retail prices seem low compared with what was available at retail in the United States, that was because I was determined to get successful sales results on a profitable basis but without inflating the retail price.

Unfortunately, the silk dresses did not do well, nor did the very good copies of the cotton pique-stitch knit dresses that were identical to those with the Lacoste alligator label that sold at retail for forty dollars. Ours were priced at only sixteen dollars and still did not sell.

These were the days of the Dynasty silk robe business. Dynasty was operated by Franklin Roosevelt (no relation to President Franklin D. Roosevelt). On several trips, we were picked up at the dock in front of the hotel by the Dynasty yacht. After cruising the harbor at twilight, we would be taken to one of the floating restaurants at Tai Pak for a delightful dinner. Dynasty's quilted robes were magnificent, although high-priced for Winkelman's, even when purchased directly in Hong Kong. They provided us with the better robes we needed to balance our moderate-priced branded business and our low-priced promotional business.

The Kowloon Peninsula offered wonderful retail shopping opportunities for items made either on the Chinese mainland or in Hong Kong. Charlotte Horstmann was the outstanding retail source for decorator furniture and furnishings of her own design. Lane Crawford, of British origin, was the prestigious department store. At lower prices, there were all kinds of possibilities. And, of course, the jewelry in those days was exceptional in assortment and value. The electronics business was booming, based mainly on well-priced Japanese cameras, TV sets, radios, and audio components.

Pat Searle, a vice president of the Hong Kong Shanghai Bank, advised me with respect to resources, letters of credit, and other financial arrangements. We would take lunch or dinner together on each visit to Hong Kong. Her assistance was invaluable. On more recent visits, the new and architecturally daring skyscraper designed by noted British architect Norman Foster has provided a most exciting environment for our meetings. We would also meet with the president of the bank to discuss the political situation in China.

Jim Robinson, an NBC colleague of John Rich, was stationed in Hong Kong and became a good friend. Jim had a Chinese wife, the daughter of a general. They lived on the south side of Victoria Island on Repulse Bay with a great view of the South China Sea. We would have dinner together at the Overseas Press Club or at their home whenever we came to Hong Kong.

My father, when he visited Hong Kong in 1957, had met a Chinese maker of embroidered linen whose products were manufactured in the southern part of China. His company became a source of gifts for us to bring back and also for beautiful handkerchiefs with a replica of an individual's signature embroidered onto the linen fabric. I was most impressed by the one that L.W. had made up with his signature and wasted no time in having some made up for myself.

On our first trip to Hong Kong, Peggy and I were taken to dinner by this linen manufacturer at a restaurant in a nearby hotel. We were served barbecued rice birds, a rare delicacy from the rice fields of the southern part of China. Peggy enjoyed the rice birds despite the fact that they were served with their heads still attached. She had not been able to manage such an enjoyment when we were served a similarly whole bird at the Trattoria Sostanza in Florence, Italy, six years earlier.

One of our best lunches anywhere was the buffet on the veranda of the Repulse Bay Hotel overlooking the South China Sea. We liked the hotel so much—even though its water shortage was much more acute than at the Peninsula—that we decided to stay for a few days after our planned return from Thailand.

Bangkok was another fascinating place, with its remarkable temples, its unique religious art, and the mystery of Jimmy Thompson. Thompson may or may not have been a wartime spy. He did, however, create a silk industry in Thailand and then disappeared in about 1960, never to be heard from again.

In the market along the Klongs on a rainy day, I was able to take a great photograph that became the cover of the *Detroit Free Press* rotogravure section in March 1964. Inside was a series of my color photographs taken in Japan, Hong Kong, and Bangkok. Included in the series was a photo of the Sony Building on the Ginza. It was designed by Yoshinobu Ashihara, who also managed to bring Maxim's, the restaurant from Paris, into the second basement. We became good friends of Ashihara and his wife, Hatsuko, when we met in Greece at the Delos IX Conference on Urban Settlements in July 1971.

Yosh had studied architecture at Yale under Marcel Breuer. He returned to Tokyo after receiving his degree to begin a very creative career as an architect and professor at Tokyo University. We have spent time with the Ashiharas on each trip to Tokyo since 1971, either at their home, at a restaurant, or, on one occasion without Hatsuko, at a geisha house. In the mid-1980s, Yosh completed one of his most important commissions, the beautiful Museum of the Japanese People, not far from Narita Airport.

The immediate sales results of my first trip to the Far East were excellent,

Stanley and Peggy, with geishas, as guests of Tokyo architect Yoshinobu Ashihara, 1974.

which caused us to substantially expand our buying plan and develop a promotion on merchandise from Japan and Hong Kong for the fall of 1964.

It was fortunate for me that both Jane Hinckley and D. Lee Rich in Tokyo were members of the American Club and friendly with the staff in the U.S. embassy. D. Lee was particularly interested in Japanese art, having organized exhibitions at the American Club. I therefore had sources available to work out tentative arrangements for a 1965 exhibition of both Ukiyo-e (seventeenth- and eighteenth-century) woodblock prints and contemporary woodblock prints from well-known artists such as Saito. The Yoseido Gallery on the Ginza in Tokyo would supply the contemporary prints, while the Red Lantern Gallery in Kyoto would provide the traditional Ukiyo-e prints. The exhibition would be shown in our downtown Detroit store. I had the counsel of Bill Woods, the director of the Detroit Institute of Arts, who was very knowledgeable about Japanese woodblock prints. Bill provided guidance that I needed in evaluating the artists and the quality of the specific proposals.

Our 1964 visit to Japan, Hong Kong, and Singapore was planned so that we would arrive in Tokyo from Hawaii at the end of the 1964 Olympic Games. I had found a special British Airways flight to Tokyo that would be picking up British visitors and returning them home after the Olympic Games. There were six of us plus a large crew on that flight, which was one of the most memorable that we have taken.

We arrived in Tokyo in time to watch the closing ceremony of the Olympics—on television. In connection with the Olympics, there was an outstanding art exhibition that assembled in Tokyo—for the first time in history—national treasures from all over the country. We saw the exhibition twice because of its extraordinary scope and quality. We also went to the Mingei Museum for the first time and saw works by the great modern print artist Munakata. We stopped on the island of Hawaii on the way home to rest at the very beautiful Mauna Kea Resort.

The 1965 promotion of merchandise from the Orient, almost entirely from Japan and Hong Kong, was geared to sales volume with little fashion excitement, except for that generated by our art exhibition. The Japanese prints, both Ukiyo-e and modern, sold well, and the merchandise itself was outstanding. I received a congratulatory letter from Margaret De Grace, an executive of the Detroit Institute of Arts, saying, "I think you have an aesthetic—and commercial—coup on your hands. Cheers for Winkelman's (and Stanley and Peggy) in producing a show with charm and good taste."

It was in 1970 that we took Roger with us to Japan and Hong Kong. We would have gone to Taiwan as well except for the fact that Roger refused to have his hair cut so that he could be admitted, as there was a law disallowing long-haired males at the time.

Peggy and Stanley at the Mauna Kea Resort on the Island of Hawaii, 1964.

The Middle East

Following our work in Hong Kong and Japan in 1964, we planned to stop in Israel in preparation for our next Mediterranean promotion. Since there were no direct flights to Tel Aviv from Hong Kong at that time, we decided to fly to Teheran, where we could board a connecting flight.

Our stop in Iran turned out to be fascinating and exciting, although when we arrived, worn out, in Teheran at four in the morning and sat down to eat Persian melon before retiring, we knew that things were picking up. Since we had had no time to prepare for visiting Iran, I called the U.S. embassy and asked for the ambassador. He was having his Farsi lesson and could not be disturbed.

Instead, I was connected to the U.S. Information Agency officer, John Reinhardt. I invited him to join us for dinner that evening. He was charming and knowledgeable. We talked about the political situation with the Shah, about the economy of the country and its dependence on oil for export. We also talked about Persian art going back to the Luristan horse culture from 1,000 to 700 b.c. and to the civilizations that preceded it. We talked about the time of Alexander the Great and the ruins in Persepolis.

The next time we would see John Reinhardt would be in Lagos, Nigeria, in March 1971, when he was the U.S. ambassador to Nigeria. I was chairman of New Detroit (the urban coalition begun in 1967 following the riots of that summer), and we were touring West Africa to study the relationship between black people in the United States and those in the African villages. Hearing the Morehouse College Choir sing "We Shall Overcome" at the embassy was a moving experience. The college is located in Atlanta, Georgia.

We were greatly stimulated by the museums in Teheran and their historic treasures. We saw the ancient Jewish ghetto, a walled city within Teheran. Here were poor Jewish people who, in most cases, did not even know they were Jews, although they did practice some aspects of Jewish ritual.

We contacted a family whose daughter had attended the University of Michigan and were invited to their home for dinner. The father was a prominent builder of roads and, of course, a supporter of the Shah. They lived in a beautiful home and were very hospitable. The evening provided great insight into the lives of the upper class at that time.

One morning, we took a seven a.m. flight to Isfahan, where we could see the dome of the Blue Mosque from the airport. We then flew on to

Peggy, Stanley, and Roger in Japan, 1970. Mt. Fuji is in the background.

Peggy with workers in a village near Korogo in the Ivory Coast, 1971.

Persepolis and, during the flight, ate caviar that we had purchased at the airport. We had a tour of the ruins of the great city of Persepolis. It had been created by the Meades and the Persians and laid waste by Alexander the Great in 322 B.C. Late in the same afternoon, we flew back to Teheran after an exhilarating but exhausting adventure.

In Israel, we would receive a telephone call about our itinerary each morning from Chaim Venitzky in the United Jewish Appeal office. We were asked to discuss our feelings about the events of the previous day and our plans for that day. We were also asked if there were any special interests that we would like to pursue. When we indicated an interest in archaeology, I was immediately put in touch with Avram Biran, the director of antiquities for the State of Israel, who invited us to meet with him. Avram, who had received his doctorate from Johns Hopkins University, was an enthusiastic practitioner of his profession. One day, we paraded around his office carrying large ceramic vessels that were more than two thousand years old.

Thirty-four years later, in 1998, our granddaughter Pamela Barr was in Jerusalem studying for the rabbinate at the Hebrew Union College. She

Stanley and Peggy in front of the Sphinx and
the Pyramid of Cyclops outside Cairo, 1986.

was taken on a dig to Tel Dan near the Golan Heights and while there met Avram Biran, who is now in charge of the archaeology department at the college.

During our son Roger's visit to Israel in 1971, he was the guest of Avram and Ruth Biran at their home for Sabbath dinner and the weekend.

During our short first visit to Israel, we spent time in the Israel Museum with the antiquity collection and had a Sabbath dinner with Ruth and Avram Biran in their Jerusalem home. Our time in Tel Aviv was spent primarily

Stanley with Israeli archeologist Avram Biran at Tel Gezer near Beersheba, 1970.

on merchandise—knits, leather coats, and swimsuits. Ironically, the leather coats were made from pigskin imported from Rumania.

Subsequent visits to Israel would take us all over the country and to a number of archaeological sites. We had also spent time viewing the Dead Sea Scrolls.

On one occasion, I chartered a single-engine airplane in Tel Aviv after another Sabbath dinner with Avram and Ruth Biran in Jerusalem.

Our flight plan took us first to Beersheba, where we took a taxi to the site of Biran's latest excavations at Tel Gezer. We spent about an hour inspecting the site and then took off for Masada. Again we went by taxi to the site, in this case the high plateau overlooking the Dead Sea where a small group of Jews had held out in A.D. 71 against the Romans and then committed suicide rather than be captured.

We had to hurry our visit to Masada, having been warned that military aircraft would be exercising in the area and that we would be shot down if we were in the wrong place at the wrong time. We did fly out on schedule and circled the site of the atomic research facility in Desmona before heading on to Jerusalem. We circled that magnificent city at a low altitude, from which we could identify important landmarks and I could take photographs. From Jerusalem, we flew north to Lake Tiberius, where we landed and rented a car for the drive to Haifa, a beautiful city in which Technion is located.

On the drive south from Haifa along the Mediterranean the next day, we stopped at Caesarea, the site of Roman ruins and a castle from the days of the First Crusade.

Market Changes and More Travels

By 1964, while we were developing new resources in the Orient, our trips to western Europe had become routine in terms of the cities we covered. But major changes were beginning to take place as the markets in the Far East became more important. Our emphasis on buying merchandise was changing to the purchase of samples in Europe, especially in France and Italy, to copy in Japan and Hong Kong, and later in Taiwan and Korea.

The buyers, merchants, and I spent most of our time shopping the boutiques and department stores of each European city, especially Paris, in search of appropriate samples that appeared to have merit for the next selling season, which would be about a year away. We would also develop our color card for that season so that all departments would be using exactly the same colors as they placed their orders. Before leaving each city, we would assemble all the samples we had purchased and decide, tentatively, where they would be sent to develop copies.

Back in the United States, at 25 Parsons Street, we would confirm our decisions regarding which sources we would ask to make up counter samples to be ready for the buyers' next trips to the Orient.

In the mid-1960s, another major change was taking place in Europe that reduced the role of the couture in establishing fashion trends. Karl Lagerfeld, as the designer for Chloe in Paris, was the first to make up a collection of pret-a-porter. His idea was to build new styling into a collection that would sell in stores without the confining implication that the styles were one-of-a-kind and handmade, as was the case with the couture.

While the individual styles cost much less than those of the couture, they were still high-priced and, in most cases, machine-made. Showings began to take place in March for fall merchandise and in October for spring of the following year. Couture showings, on the other hand, continued to take place in January for spring and in July for fall.

Initially, the pret-a-porter collections were presented in various locations around Paris, Milan, and London. In time, Paris provided three tents, each holding up to four thousand press members, buyers, favored customers, and celebrities. The tents were put up by the French government in the Cour du Louvre. This was a courtyard at the eastern end of the museum where the main entrance was located. At that time, the tents were set up for the presentation of the collections over a ten-day period twice each year. The arrangement was a little crude, but it worked effectively until the new pyramid entrance to the Louvre was opened in 1991.

Adjacent to the new underground entrance to the Louvre, the French government created an area, the Carousel du Louvre, with four auditorium spaces of different sizes for the presentation of the pret-a-porter collections. This area offered all of the amenities that had been lacking with the tents and included a group of boutiques as well as a mezzanine with many excellent small restaurants and, of course, modern toilet facilities.

With the advent of pret-a-porter design in the mid-1960s, I personally led the effort to buy the Chloe collection, which was also being bought by Claire Perrone and Hattie Belkin, operators of better fashion stores in Birmingham and Troy, Michigan. The minimum purchase was high for Winkelman's, as was the price for the merchandise, but buy it we did for three stores.

We also bought Kenzo and two or three other collections. I regarded our pret-a-porter presentations as the successors to the couture events we had been featuring, eliminating the purchase of the couture copies and still giving us the opportunity to copy or adapt the styles that we felt had merit.

Our promotional approach shifted to the new direction in our meetings with the press and in a limited advertising program that emphasized the actual pret-a-porter dresses, suits, and coats rather than copies of couture garments as we had done in the past.

While we did not expect to make money on Chloe and the others, we received more than our money's worth in publicity, in the strength of our fashion reputation, and even in the resulting markdowns. Many Grosse Pointe matrons drove across town to Lincoln Center at Greenfield and 10½ Mile Road, long before the completion of the I-696 expressway, to take advantage of the styling and the prices.

In 1967, our European merchandise promotion was highlighted in the downtown Detroit store by an exhibition of prints from the Mourlot Press in Paris. The particular exhibition was put together by the Redfern Gallery in London and circulated in the United States by the State Department. There was an excellent catalogue prepared by Redfern. The French consul Jean Le Diréac and I opened the exhibition.

On our next trip to Paris, Peggy went to meet Fernand Mourlot, who was the print maker for Picasso, Matisse, Chagall, Braque, Miro, and Calder. She was so impressed by Mourlot and his remarkable press that she asked me to go with her again so that I could meet him and take photographs. As a souvenir, we were given a copy of the very colorful Chagall poster that was being printed at that moment for the opening of the new Metropolitan Opera House at Lincoln Center in New York in September 1966. We also received a poster by Tezechkovitch depicting the waterfront at Menton on the Cote D'Azur in the south of France.

Our meeting with the press that year highlighted the relatively new strength of the European pret-a-porter collections plus the fashion aspects of our import program along with the Mourlot Press exhibition. The media coverage was excellent, as with each passing year the fashion editors looked forward to our import event with an increasing sense of anticipation.

In 1968, our emphasis was on Paris once again. By this time, we had decided that the romance of western Europe along with the fashion excitement of pret-a-porter was more important institutionally than frequent promotions of merchandise from the Far East that had greater immediate sales potential. This time, we chose to feature contemporary art from the well-known Galerie Denise Rene in Paris. Peggy and I had met Denise in Paris and had discussed the possibility of an exhibition of works from her gallery on the Rive Gauche, where she featured graphics and multiples. I was convinced that we were in a position to handle paintings and sculpture on the third floor of our downtown store, where our exhibitions were being held.

The opening for "Galerie Denise Rene in Paris" took place on the evening of December 2, 1968, on the third floor of the downtown store. The exhibition drew excellent traffic, and many items sold. Denise Rene, who had come to Detroit for the opening, was happy with the result, and so were we. Peggy and I have seen her many times since, usually at the annual FIAC (Foire Internationale D'Art Contemporain) show of art from galleries around the world at the Grand Palais in Paris.

By this time, we had long since abandoned Ed Roberts's idea for the downtown store that dresses should be on the second floor and coats on the third floor with millinery. Instead, we had combined coats, suits, dresses, and furs on the second floor to take advantage of suggestive selling opportunities and to reduce selling costs.

Our Italian commissionaire, Enzo Tayar, was present in Detroit for our 1968 event and for discussions of our plans for the "Salute to Italy," which was a year away. I met with Emilio Pucci to determine his willingness to participate in our television production by talking about the merits of Italian merchandise. Emilio agreed and provided us with an excellent TV presentation in his rich baritone voice and Italian accent, at no cost to Winkelman's. This would be our most powerful European promotion to date.

The Milanese department store La Rinascente was another important contact as we developed our plans. I had worked with their manufacturing people, attempting to develop ready-to-wear at a price that would work for Winkelman's. The results were not encouraging because of problems with size patterns and price.

Our friend Count Aldo Borletti, the president of La Rinascente, was killed in 1969 in a fall from his horse while riding along the shores of Lake Como. He had been a friend for many years after we'd met in the New York office of Kirby Block.

It was Borletti who came to our rescue when Peggy and I were arriving by train in Italy from Zurich with our children in 1961, only to be stopped at the border town of Chiasso by a strike of Italian railroad workers. When I telephoned the count from Chiasso, he offered to send a limousine for us. I was embarrassed to tell him that one limousine would not be sufficient, and so he sent two, one for the five of us and one for our baggage. The limos took us to Milan to meet him and then, afterward, all the way to Florence, some two hundred miles to the south.

For the Winkelman's "Salute to Italy" event in 1969, the Italian ambassador to the United States, Egedio Ortona, came to Detroit to preside over the opening. I arranged with Walker Cisler, the president, for a special meeting of the Economic Club of Detroit to provide the ambassador with a platform for his comments on Italian-American relations, and more particularly on the subject of the opportunities for Italian merchandise in the United States.

In our downtown Detroit store, we had uniformed Swiss guards from the Vatican, a number of gondoliers from Venice, and several artisans. One was a leather goods maker, and another was a jeweler who, during his stay in Detroit, created a magnificent 22-karat gold medallion for Peggy, who was in the hospital with a back problem at the time.

We had arranged for the Detroit premiere of the new Michael Caine movie, *The Italian Job*, at what is now the Music Hall Theater. The movie played to a full house with a great audience.

There were special restaurant menu items from Florence and Rome being prepared by the downtown hotels and restaurants, including the London Chop House.

The consul of Italy, our good friend Luigi Lauriola, held a reception honoring Ambassador Ortona at the Whittier Hotel. He invited the leaders of the Italian community and other notable Detroiters. The headline in the John Detroit column in the *Detroit Free Press* read: "Luigi's Party Wall-to-Wall Celebrities."

Henry Ford II was there, as was Tony De Lorenzo, the vice president for public relations at General Motors (GM). Also mentioned in the article were our daughter Margi and our son, Roger, who accompanied me while their mother was in traction at Harper Hospital.

"Italy Staging Detroit Capture—Peacefully" was the headline in the *Detroit News*. The accompanying photograph showed Peggy looking over a piece of Venetian glass with Luigi Lauriola. The article also mentioned the red, white, and green flag of Italy flying over Woodward Avenue. Washington Boulevard was renamed "Via Veneto" following the declaration of Mayor Jerome P. Cavanaugh making September 7–13 "Salute to Italy Week." The *Detroit News* column also discussed the wide range of furniture, art objects, food, and travel information, all of which was the result of two years of planning by our people working with the Italian government.

The year 1970 saw a shift in emphasis as we planned ahead for our "Focus Mediterranean" promotion in 1971. Al Cohen worked out a domestic tie-in with Plymouth dealers on the occasion of the fortieth anniversary of the Plymouth Division of Chrysler-Plymouth. A contest was created with a new Plymouth Fury III hardtop, a new wardrobe, and Winkelman's gift certificates as prizes.

Our focus that year was on American-made merchandise as a change of pace, and to provide another highlight, we challenged five of the top young American designers, including Calvin Klein and Jane Justin, to create garments for the year 2000, which at that time was thirty years away.

Also in 1970, Winkelman's began annual sponsorship of its Cultural Center Open House, as we paid the cost of keeping the DIA, the Detroit Public Library, and the Detroit Historical Museum open for an evening in September to start off the new season. With Woodward Avenue closed to traffic by a city council resolution, a jazz band playing in the middle of Woodward, and special events in each of the institutions, a new community event was put in place that would grow in importance with each succeeding year. The year 2000 styles were exhibited at the Detroit Institute of Arts. A seminar at the DIA had the designers interpreting the individual thinking behind their work. All of this was a part of our "Uniquely USA" effort.

The *Detroit Free Press* ran a photograph of Peggy and me with Calvin Klein and Frank Rachman, the president of Beverly Paige. The article described the opening of "Uniquely USA" and the special openings at the cultural institutions, which twelve hundred people attended.

We had given a dinner at the Pontchartrain Hotel before the opening for the many manufacturers who were important to Winkelman's and to whom Winkelman's was important. They had come to Detroit to meet our people, to visit stores, and to participate in the festivities.

Today, the creations for the year 2000 lie in the storage area of the Detroit Historical Museum. It would be most interesting to resurrect them at this time of the new millennium, to assess the vision of these designers thirty years later.

The year 1971 and the April pret-a-porter presentations in Paris found me invited to an exotic dinner at the famous Tour D'Argent restaurant looking down on Notre Dame cathedral. The sponsors of the pret-a-porter showings were our hosts for the dinner. It was a fabulous evening with store owners and leading merchants from around the world on hand for a tantalizing feast. Of course, the food and wines were superb, with the specialite de la maison, *caneton roti Marco Polo aux quatre poivres* (roasted duck with four peppers), served as the main course.

By this time, preparations for our fall event were well under way. In Paris, I arranged with noted designer Jean Barthet to present his collection in Detroit as part of our "Focus Mediterranean" event. I then flew to Barcelona for a day to arrange for the important Spanish designer Andres Andreu to present his collection as well.

Earlier in the year, we had gone to the Marbella area of Spain and to Andalusia to look for Spanish crafts and leather goods. On the Iberian Airlines flight, we met a couple we would see again the next night in the bar of the Marbella Club. In the bar, we exchanged the usual pleasantries with Bud and Peggy Yorkin and learned that they were staying in a villa owned by actor Jose Ferrar. Peg Yorkin became frustrated because we did not recognize her husband as the co-producer of the three most popular shows on network television. "But his photograph was on the cover of *Time* magazine last week," she declared. And indeed it was, along with the photograph of his senior partner, Norman Lear.

For a number of years, Peggy and I had been spending a week in July at Beaulieu on the Cote D'Azur in the south of France, and then a second week at the picturesque alpine town of Crans-sur-Sierre where the temperatures were much cooler. But July 1971 would be different, starting with a visit to Greece in search of merchandise and special events for "Focus Mediterranean" in the month of April. Walker Cisler suggested that I contact Constantinos Doxiades, urban planner and head of the Center for Ekistics in Athens. Cisler had worked with Doxiades in implementing the Marshall Plan for rehabilitating Europe following World War II. Doxiades invited us for lunch at his home.

During lunch, Doxiades asked if I could attend the Delos IX Conference on Urban Settlements aboard ship in the Aegean Sea during the first week of July. It turned out to be a fantastic experience. We picked up the ship in Piraeus, the port for Athens, on July 12 and set sail for Olympia. For seven days and seven nights, about two hundred of us—participants, companions, staff, and student observers—held meetings every morning on the problems of human settlements and went ashore each afternoon to visit important sites with the best archaeologists of Greece as our guides.

Some of the participants included Harvey Cox, dean of Harvard's Divinity School; Buckminster Fuller, architect and inventor of the geodesic dome; anthropologist Margaret Mead; Jonas Salk, creator of the polio vaccine; Francoise Gilot-Salk, artist and painter, and mistress of Pablo Picasso; Larry Halperin, architect and designer of Girardelli Square in San Francisco and, much more recently, the Franklin Roosevelt monument in Washington; Barbara Ward; and Erik Erikson.

It was exciting to be involved with some of the world's best minds. Doxiades began the conference by saying that architects are criminals for the manner in which they design human settlements, especially apartment buildings. This touched off a lively debate that became the centerpiece of the conference. The final session was held at twilight in the amphitheater on the island of Delos, with torches burning on the periphery as the final reports were read from the ancient stage. The setting was unforgettable.

The final banquet took place in the town square of a small village on the island of Rhodes. It was a very festive occasion; Peggy and I were at a table with Bucky Fuller and others. At one point, a group member came over to the table and said, "Winkelman, someone is looking for you." It turned out to be a former Chrysler worker who had been born in that village, had lived and worked in America, and had moved back after his retirement. He wanted to tell me that his wife had been a good customer of Winkelman's.

The following summer, Roger was invited to be a student observer at the Delos X conference, the last in the series. Roger's roommate was Marshall McLuhan's son. He also had the assignment of taking Arnold Toynbee back to the ship at night. For Roger, too, it was a mind-blowing experience.

The collections of Jean Barthet and Andres Andreu were presented on models in our downtown store. Peggy and I also gave a black-tie dinner at

Stanley and Peggy at the Parthenon, 1971.

Peggy (far right) at a banquet of Delos IX in a village town square on
the Island of Rhodes with (from far left) Herb Strawbridge, CEO of
the Higbe department stores in Cleveland; Mrs. Strawbridge; and
Buckminster Fuller, architect and designer of the Geodesic Dome, 1971.

the Pontchartrain Hotel to kick off "Focus Mediterranean" and to introduce
the designers to Detroit.

Among the invited guests were Flo and Bunky Knudsen. As Peggy and
I arrived at the hotel, we noticed Flo and Bunky going into the bar. We
asked them to join us upstairs as we put out the place cards and checked
to be sure that everything was in order for the dinner. The evening was
very exciting for us and our sixty guests, and when it was over, I stopped by
the *Detroit Free Press* building as I usually did to pick up a copy of the next
day's paper. To our shock and amazement, the headline told us that Bunky,
who had been the president of Ford Motor Company, had been fired that
very afternoon by Henry Ford. We marveled at the graciousness of Flo and
Bunky in attending our dinner and enjoying themselves as very good guests
at such a difficult time.

In the same year of 1971, in addition to our Mediterranean event,
Winkelman's sponsored the second annual Cultural Center Open House.
The Detroit Public Library presented "Mediterranean Montage," a graphic
exhibition of old and new maps, books, and artifacts tracing the influence
of Mediterranean culture on American life. The DIA presented "Shalom
of Safed," an exhibition of painting and biblical prints by Shalom, one of
Israel's most gifted artists. There was even a special concert by the Detroit

Symphony Orchestra, "A Hellenic Evening," with Andreas Paridis, director of the Athens Symphony, conducting to raise money to establish a Greek Room at Wayne State University.

We had arranged an Italian wine- and cheese-tasting reception and special Mediterranean menus in various restaurants in Cleveland and Detroit. There were also Portuguese basket weavers, Greek icon painters, and Italian leather craftsmen at work in our neighborhood stores.

The *Detroit Free Press* ran a half-page on the front of a section with a banner headline reading "A Sizzling Beginning for Focus Mediterranean" and photographs of Andres Andreu and Jean Barthet plus five of the pret-a-porter styles from France, Italy, and Spain. Also quoted was a model who said backstage that "Senor Andreu may not be able to speak English, but he can sure say 'no bra.'" Prices were quoted as ranging from seven dollars for a Portuguese shirt to three hundred dollars for a coat, designed and manufactured in Rome by Onebene Zendman.

Winkelman's continued to be the exclusive sponsor of the Cultural Center Open House for twelve consecutive years, through the fall of 1982. The concept was revived as a special community event in the 1990s with no reference whatsoever to its origin or to Winkelman's role in building its acceptance. *C'est la vie!* We do have great memories of these events and of the special exhibitions we helped to create. We still enjoy meeting people who recall with pleasure the annual open house.

After 1971, our yearly merchandise presentations continued to be timed to coincide with the open house. The theme would change each year as we attempted to emphasize the fashion message of the day. We would also interpret the latest fashion developments and trends from pret-a-porter and our imports from Europe and the Orient. We recognized that the emotional appeal of our "Salute to Italy" and "Focus Mediterranean" could not be duplicated.

In 1974, Yvonne Petrie, fashion editor of the *Detroit News*, wrote a beautiful article—really a fashion editorial on Winkelman's—accompanied by photographs under the headline "Change: Will Detroit Accept European Ready-to-Wear?" Two of the four costumes in the photographs were designed by Karl Lagerfeld for Chloe. Meanwhile, the *Cleveland Plain Dealer* trumpeted "Europe's Best Is Adapted for U.S." The garments in the photographs were all supplied by Winkelman's.

At the 1976 Cultural Center Open House, Mayor Coleman Young, who had avoided visiting the DIA, appeared in a *Detroit News* photograph taken on the steps of the DIA with Fred Cummings, the director of the DIA; Fred's wife, Judy Cummings; Clara Jones, the director of the Detroit Public Library, and Mr. Jones; and Peggy and me. It was for this open house that we had invited our friend Stella Blum, the director of the Costume Institute of the Metropolitan Museum in New York, to give a lecture on the history of fashion at the DIA. Her lecture was in connection with an exhibition of nineteen historic costumes dating from 1776 to 1900, which we had also underwritten.

Fred Cummings, in a letter of thanks following the open house, made a number of points that bear repeating:

> What an outstanding idea it was to invite the Mayor to endorse this event. The tour of the cultural institutions was also most opportune since it allowed us to present ourselves from a point of view that we could select without the constraints of committees or commissions with strict agendas and guidelines.
>
> I know that the Mayor felt quite comfortable in this atmosphere just as we did.
>
> Once again, cultural concerns benefited from the leadership of a local corporation, but, of course, of a local corporation guided by one family and not an anonymous corporate entity. Winkelman's, in this respect, is distinctive and has my great support and appreciation.

Exploring China

October 1976 marked my first exploratory trip to China and to the Canton Trade Fair. Since it was not possible to obtain visas in the United States, I applied in London. We had planned to go with someone who was knowledgeable about Chinese merchandise, but, at the last minute, this person was unable to leave New York.

We therefore arrived in Hong Kong uncertain about what we could accomplish at the Canton Trade Fair. To attend, one had to have received an invitation in advance from Chinatex, one of the seven large government trading companies. I did manage to obtain an invitation at a time when few American businesses were sending their buyers to China.

While we had the necessary credentials and a general hotel reservation, we did not know the name of the hotel or its location in relation to the fair. We left Hong Kong for Canton by train on a Saturday morning knowing that the sixty-mile trip would take four hours.

On the train, we were lucky to meet the Boston owner of Prestige Sportswear, with whom we did a substantial business. He was traveling to Canton with his daughter and son-in-law. Since Winkelman's did considerable business with Prestige, we talked at length about the business potential with Chinatex. I learned that Prestige Sportswear was developing velveteen jackets for the next fall season and would be working at the Canton Trade Fair with a Chinese agent called the "Dragon Lady." I told them of my plight. In response, they suggested that I work with the Dragon Lady after they had completed their work with her, in about two days.

Travel through the New Territories of Hong Kong to the border of China was fascinating all by itself. In those days, it was necessary to get out of the train at the border and walk across a bridge to the town of Sum Chum. There, everyone had lunch in the railroad station, exchanged money, and passed through Chinese immigration.

Looking out from the station, one could tell that a major change had taken place by the colors of the clothing people wore. Whereas in Hong Kong women on the street wore bright and varied colors, in Sum Chum, and later in Canton, the women wore somber shades of black, white, gray, and navy.

Mao Tse-tung had died only ten days earlier, and China was on the verge of significant change.

The trip to Canton that Saturday was comfortable and particularly interesting as we rode through the lush farmland being tilled by numerous workers with water buffalo attached to simple plows. At the station in Canton, we were channeled onto buses.

We were then driven through the city on wide streets with little traffic except for bicycles. We were taken to the hotel we had hoped for, directly across a wide boulevard from the trade fair buildings. As we were registering, I was asked if I would like to have an interpreter, and I was immediately assigned a young lady to work with me.

Having been warned that Monday morning was a difficult time to schedule appointments, I suggested that we meet in the lobby at three on Saturday afternoon and go to the fair building where Chinatex was located in order to set up an appointment for Monday morning. On the way in to the fair buildings, we passed displays of some of the most modern and powerful-looking farm equipment that I had ever seen.

"Where is it being used?" I asked, mindful of the primitive farming that we had witnessed from the train. "It's used up north," was the reply. In fact, most of it was being used politically to enhance Chinese influence in Africa.

After making an appointment with Chinatex, we walked back to the hotel to rest before dinner and the acrobatic show we planned to see afterward. Just as we arrived in our room, the telephone rang and we were told by our friends from Boston that the Dragon Lady had invited us to dinner along with them. The meal was excellent, and the Northern Garden Restaurant became our favorite on that trip. The conversation was even more interesting.

It was agreed that I would working with Veronica (the so-called Dragon Lady, who was born in China but kept an apartment on Park Avenue in Manhattan) beginning on Wednesday for the last two days of my stay.

On Monday morning, Peggy and I, along with our interpreter, departed at the appointed hour and went to the very large building devoted to Chinatex, the Chinese National Textile Corporation; all the signs were in Chinese. Somehow we found the same room we had visited to make the appointment. We sat down at a card table in the middle of the room. We were joined there soon after by the young lady who had made the appointment the previous Saturday and also by the janitor (everybody was involved in the negotiations in those days). The room was sterile-looking with white tile floors and floor-to-ceiling glass cases around half the room containing crude displays of various kinds of merchandise.

I had decided that I would be looking for velveteen jackets, knowing that they were selling for about forty dollars in the United States. The discussion was all in English, with my interpreter rarely involved. I asked if there were any samples of velveteen jackets in the cases. There were none. Then I asked her to look in the back room. Sure enough, she came back with two ratty-looking samples from which I decided that I could work. My next query was about color, as I remembered the lack of color I'd seen in the clothes worn by those on the streets in Sum Chum and Canton. I was shown a color card with about a hundred colors. Obviously, this would not be a problem. My next question was about minimum quantities; we compromised at one thousand of a style.

We turned our attention to styling. Fortunately, Peggy was there to serve as a perfect model. Gradually, I suggested the changes that I thought were needed, including buttons and linings that would have to be shipped in from Hong Kong. Peggy was fascinated by the proceedings and was a tremendous help in the restyling process.

We worked out three colors for each garment and set up appropriate quantities by size, based on information that I had brought with me from Detroit. The price, I was told, including cost and freight, would be less than ten dollars per jacket, enabling us to sell them very profitably for thirty dollars or less. Shipping was to be by air to Seattle and then by truck to Detroit.

Size specifications? Of course, I had them with me and would be happy to let her copy them. I could pick them up the next day. Imagine my surprise when I was told by this very young woman from Dalien that my size specifications were wrong. She correctly pointed out the errors in grading from size to size.

"Do you have J. C. Penney size specs?" I asked. She did, and she agreed to use them and to send me samples of each jacket in each size in the colors we had agreed upon. "But the contract cannot be contingent on the samples," she advised. At the same time, she agreed to make whatever changes we wanted from the samples when the order was put into production.

I was to return the following day to sign the contract. When I read the document, everything was exactly as we had agreed, but a new element had been added. There was to be a letter of credit through a third country other than the United States or China. "How about Hong Kong?" I asked.

"Hong Kong is a part of China," she replied.

"You're right," I answered, "but how about the Hong Kong Shanghai Bank?"

"Oh," she said, "that's fine. The Hong Kong Shanghai Bank is British."

There was quite a contrast between this meeting and my work with the Dragon Lady the next day. The conversation turned immediately from English to Chinese as I prepared to sample sweaters, blouses, jewelry, and gift items.

Since we were ready to leave Canton after working with her for two days, I gave her the same kind of detailed instructions that I had used for the velveteen jackets regarding sizes, colors, fabric, and shipping instructions. I asked her to sign the contracts on my behalf.

Meantime, Peggy and I toured Canton, the location of the academy once attended by Chiang Kai-shek, Mao Tse-tung, and Chou En-lai. We drove along the Yellow River and even visited the Canton Zoo to see the pandas and the Chinese tigers.

Speaking of the Yellow River, we drank "Yellow River Orange"—or Tsingtao beer—with our meals plus the 110-proof Mao Tai on occasion. No one drank the water. For restaurant meals, it was important to tell the young man in the baggy pants at the hotel desk before making the reservation, which established only the price of the dinner, "No dog! No snake!"

I noticed that the headline in the Hong Kong newspaper as we crossed the border leaving China read, "Peanut Farmer Elected President." Jimmy Carter had won the presidential election back in the States.

About four weeks later, I received the contracts that Veronica had concluded. Very little of the content was what I had specified. "Assorted" colors or sizes in an order was *verboten* at Winkelman's. In a telephone conversation with her, I was told that this was the way the company did business.

While no one we worked with in Canton would give us their name on that first trip (anonymity was the order of the day; there was no fraternizing with foreign visitors), I had taken careful notes. I sent an immediate letter to Chinatex indicating that my instructions had not been followed and requesting that the contracts be changed if they were interested in any further business.

Sure enough, three weeks later, I received amended contracts written exactly as I had specified. Now for the confrontation with the Dragon Lady. I decided to wait and confront her personally at her apartment in New York in January.

When we finally did meet and I advised her that Chinatex had rewritten the contracts for me, her comment was, "That is the first time that has ever happened."

The purchases were made about ten months before we intended to promote the merchandise. The samples did arrive in March 1977. The quality was excellent, and we cabled our approval with some minor changes.

The velveteen jackets were selling very successfully in the fall of 1977 as Peggy and I went back to the Canton fair once again. We were still holding the jewelry and gift items as potential Christmas gift possibilities.

The *Detroit News* did a half-page story headlined "Ah, So Old New Look—It's Jewelry from China." The photographs showed jewelry coming out of a wooden crate and me holding a group of necklaces.

In preparation for that first trip, I had put together information about Detroit, its people, its institutions, and its buildings that was well received by the Chinese people we had met. We had been briefed for that trip by Professor Michael Oksenberg, an economist we knew at the University of Michigan's Center for Chinese Studies.

For the second trip, we had the advantage of a copy of a letter written by Leonard Woodcock, then head of the U.S. Liaison Office in Peking. Leonard had written a detailed account of his first few months in that position after his appointment by our new president, Jimmy Carter.

China had seen significant changes in the twelve months since our first visit. We arrived in Canton this time to see the Gang of Four being hung in effigy as the last vestiges of the Cultural Revolution were being eradicated. The rigid discipline had been eased slightly in the interim, with people now willing to tell us their names. This time, we did know in advance that we would be staying in the same hotel. Yet the large white-on-red propaganda signs were still very much in evidence, both at the Hong Kong border and within the fair itself.

During this trip, I was negotiating our way out of the contracts with the Conner offices in Japan and Hong Kong as we prepared to tie up with the May Company's overseas buying offices.

To complete these transactions, it was necessary for me to make several overseas telephone calls to Japan, Hong Kong, and the United States. My objectives were achieved, but with great difficulty, since the Chinese telephone system was still very primitive compared to that in Hong Kong or Japan.

It must be remembered that none of what I was doing would have been feasible without the benefits of jet aircraft and efficient telephone and telex systems. Even with jet aircraft, we were sometimes in the air for fourteen hours at a time. Telex was adequate for long-distance rapid communication of the written word, but it required typing the message on the machine and then sending it to its destination automatically, once a connection was completed, to the machine at the other end. Fax machines had not yet arrived on the scene to provide instantaneous transmission of multi-page typed or handwritten documents.

At the end of this 1977 trip to China, we planned to fly to Paris by way of Bombay and Moscow after returning to Hong Kong. Our train from Canton arrived in Hong Kong in the afternoon, but our flight to Paris would not leave until midnight. Our friends at the Peninsula Hotel came to our rescue by providing a room without charge for a luxurious bath and nap before we headed for the airport.

Our plane was delayed, so I changed airlines only to discover hours later, after our arrival in Paris, that our baggage had not made the transfer and had wound up in London. The airline provided us with toothbrushes and paper night shirts. This happened to be the only time I had ever traveled without wearing a tie. I walked across the street from the Ritz Hotel the next morning to Charvet and purchased what proved to be a very expensive tie. We were happy that our baggage was found, but it was a nuisance to have to go to the airport the next day to bring it through customs for a cursory inspection.

After 1977, our Chinese business hit a hiatus until 1980, because no one from Winkelman's was able take the time for the extra travel to China.

Our switch to the May Company overseas buying offices was being completed just prior to the time that Stanley Goodman, the retired chairman of the May Company, came to Winkelman's to consult with me. I had previously met Martin Moss, the man who was running May Company's overseas buying offices, at May headquarters in London and had worked out our arrangement with him, subject to corporate approval.

It was necessary for Stanley to reassure the general manager of May Company in Cleveland that he should accept us as a fee-paying account rather than have the fee go to another buying office.

We knew that their buyers were much too busy to be concerned about what we might be doing as competitors in Cleveland, just as they should have known that our buyers would be too involved with what we were doing to be concerned about the plans of the May Company.

This move was, in reality, the beginning of the process of consolidation of retail businesses and their buying offices that resulted from mergers, acquisitions, and leveraged buyouts, through which many competitive firms wound up within the same corporate structure.

With the May Company, we had the advantage of a worldwide organization with representatives in every major market providing us with assessments of trends in their particular area.

We had also hedged our bet a few years earlier when we hired Nigel

Peggy with Georges Meyer, the president of Galeries Lafayette
department store, on the roof of Galeries Lafayette, Paris, 1988.

French in London and his specialists in fashion developments in styling,
fabrics, and colors to provide guidance in these areas. I had met Nigel
French years earlier through Milton Bluestein and the Plymouth Shops.
We would meet twice each year with Nigel and his people to compare
notes on current trends and future direction.

Leonard Woodcock had negotiated successfully with the Chinese. As a
result, the U.S. Liaison Office was upgraded to an embassy, and a Chinese
embassy was established in Washington.

Deng Xiao-ping had come to Washington, where he spoke at the National Gallery. Peggy and I were on hand for his speech with a group from
the faculty of the University of Michigan and a Professor Schwartz from
Harvard.

The echoes were so bad that the chairman's remarks and those of his
interpreter were unintelligible. Afterward, I used my press pass to obtain
copies of his remarks, which we discussed over a late dinner.

The next day, as we were returning to Detroit, Leonard, Doug Fraser,
and Millie Jeffrey were waiting along with us to board the aircraft when
Peggy asked Leonard if he was ever lonesome in Beijing. The group
broke into semihysterical laughter at her question, and Peggy was very
embarrassed. Peggy apologized for asking her question, but the next day
she laughed, too, when she read that Leonard would be marrying Sharon
Tuohy, the embassy nurse.

Our third trip to China took place in 1980. Peggy and I were accompanied by Carol Marchetti, the manager of Winkelman's New York office, and two young market representatives from the May Company office in Hong Kong.

Before our departure, I had called Michael Oksenberg in Washington. At that time, Mike was the head of the China desk at the National Security Council (NSC), where he worked for President Carter's NSC chief, Zbigniew Brzezinski, his former mentor at Columbia University. I asked Mike if he could use the NSC's communication system to invite Sharon and Leonard Woodcock to be our guests for dinner in what was now called Beijing.

Great changes had taken place in China. The train from Hong Kong now went straight through to Canton in less than half the time it took in 1977. Gone were the huge red signs, and in their place were posters advertising various products, including cosmetics. And the people were wearing colorful clothes.

Even more striking were the human changes. The people we worked with now carried calling cards, and it was possible to talk with them about their lives and their families. We could even entertain them at lunch or dinner. Until that time, we had been able to have conversations with some Chinatex people only at the dinners to which Peggy and I were invited. At those dinners, I would exchange toasts with our hosts as we drank mao-tai and attempted to stay sober.

Manny Eagle, the president of R&K, the dress division of Jonathan Logan, was coming to the Far East for the first time with a couple who owned a New York blouse manufacturing business. We had arranged to meet for dinner on their first night in Canton in a restaurant at the top of a downtown building.

My visit to the desk in the lobby to make dinner reservations followed the usual procedure. I selected the price of the dinner and gave my usual admonishment: no dogs, no snakes.

Peggy and I arrived at the appointed hour and were ushered into a large room with a circular table set up at one end. We waited and waited for our guests to appear, but no one did. Finally, I decided to walk through the restaurant and, in the process, found the four of them looking for us. It seems that the Chinese custom was to record reservations by hotel room number. Of course, Manny Eagle and his traveling companions had no idea what our room number was.

They were all very hungry, having not eaten a decent meal since they left the United States. We sat down at the table. We talked. We drank mao-tai and Tsingtao beer along with some appetizers that not everyone appeared to be eating. After about thirty minutes, a waitress appeared with a beautifully garnished platter holding a suckling pig. At this point, our dinner companions started to laugh. Then they laughed until they cried. They all lived by kosher dietary laws that forbade eating pork.

Peggy and I were not aware of this, and it had not occurred to me to declare "No pig" when I had ordered the dinner at the hotel, since no restaurant had served us a suckling pig before. Peggy waved to the waitress to take the pig away, thinking that she would bring back something else. About fifteen minutes later, she came back with the pig cut up and its skin scored on a platter. More laughter and crying were heard. At this point, I declared, "I don't know about you, but I am going to eat the pig." With that, I picked up my chopsticks and ate some of the pig with plum sauce and scallions. It was excellent! Soon, all but one of our guests had joined Peggy and me for what proved to be a delicious dinner.

We relived that incident when we read Theodore White's autobiography a few weeks later. In it, he recounted a dinner in Chungking when he was covering Chiang Kai-shek and Chou En-lai for *Time* magazine. White had been invited to dinner by Chou along with some of Chou's staff. The scenario was exactly the same as our dinner with Manny Eagle. When the suckling pig arrived at the table, White said that he could not eat it, to which Chou replied, "We have offended our guest. But Teddy, things in China are not always what they seem." He picked up his chopsticks and pointed to the pig and said, "That is not a pig. That is a duck." And with that, they all picked up their chopsticks and ate the duck. White added that he had been eating it ever since.

We traveled to Beijing by train, a comfortable overnight experience. We went by taxi to the Beijing Hotel, the best known hotel in Beijing, where many people found it difficult to get reservations. This was the Peninsula Hotel of Beijing, so to speak, where one could run into friends from around the world. Indeed, we did run into John Rich in the lobby. John had become vice president of RCA for the Far East and was in Beijing attempting to sell a satellite to the Chinese.

We also ran into an associate of Jan Berris from the U.S.-China trade office in New York. Jan was a Detroiter who became the executive director of the National Committee on United States—China Relations, Inc. I had been in touch with Jan prior to our first trip to China in 1976 and had become a member of the organization, along with many of the faculty of the University of Michigan. Jan provided a great deal of useful information and contacts, and I provided minor financial support for her efforts.

Charles Yost, the former head of the U.S. Liaison Office in Beijing, was the chairman of the committee at that time. Among the directors were George Bush, eventually President Bush; Father Hesburgh, president of

Stanley with Chinatex visitors at the McGregor building
on the campus of Wayne State University, 1983.

Notre Dame University; and Ralph Lazarus, CEO of Federated Department Stores.

Peggy and I attended a number of the committee's meetings in New York and are very much committed to improving relations with China.

On two occasions, Jan asked Peggy and me to entertain visitors from China. The first time, we were the hosts for nine representatives of Chinatex, six of whom we had met previously in China. We invited them to our home for dinner, where we were reminded that we had met the others as well when we were in China. None of them had been in an American home before.

It was a remarkable event, during which we attempted to answer their many questions. In the course of the evening, I was able to photograph the group on the deck outside our living room. The next day, we took them to the McGregor Conference Center at Wayne State University to meet some of the faculty.

The second occasion occurred after our third trip to China, when Jan Berris called to ask Peggy and me to entertain a group of Chinatex representatives from Henan Province who were stopping in Detroit to visit the UAW leadership on their way to meet with farmers in Kansas City. This time, we arranged a dinner at the Hyatt Regency Hotel in Dearborn. We invited Leonard Woodcock, by then the former ambassador to China, to join us. Among our guests was the former head of the Bank of China. Peggy and I were presented with a beautiful scroll painting of shrimp that now hangs on our living room wall. The head of the delegation invited us to visit the new excavations in Henan Province.

Unfortunately, we have not been back to China since 1980. However, in 1996, we were privileged to see a spectacular exhibition of material from the excavations of the past ten years at the British Museum, "Mysteries of Ancient China." As it turned out, much of that material came from the new Henan Province excavations.

In 1980, we shopped the primitive department stores in Beijing, looking for art and craft objects that we might import. During our stay in Beijing, we were taken to the Great Wall by a woman from Chinatex. We rode to the wall in a new sixteen-passenger Toyota microbus. There were five of us, including Carol Marchetti, our New York office manager; the two representatives from the May Company Hong Kong office; and our Chinatex interpreter. It was a bitter cold February day, but the trip was nevertheless very exciting.

We climbed to the top of the wall and stayed there just long enough to take in the view and snap a few pictures. On our way back, we stopped to see the magnificent Ming tombs and the sculptures along the boulevard leading up to them.

We ate more than our share of Peking duck during our stay, washed down with Tsingtao beer.

The climax of Beijing for us was the dinner with Sharon and Leonard Woodcock. Leonard had called us just after our arrival to ask if we would mind having dinner, just the four of us, in the embassy; they had been attending too many banquets and would like a quiet evening at home with us. We were delighted to accept their invitation. The embassy building was impressive, and we were extremely pleased to have the opportunity to be there. The dinner was excellent, and we waited afterward for a signal from Leonard that the servants had departed and we were left with only the "bugs" before beginning serious conversation. At that time, the Chinese were notorious for installing secret listening devices for eavesdropping on foreigners working in sensitive areas.

Leonard and Sharon were very active and maintained contact with dissidents, especially dissident artists, some of whose work adorned the embassy walls. After a long evening of intense conversation, Leonard drove us back to our hotel in his Volkswagen.

We see the Woodcocks in Ann Arbor or Detroit periodically, and we have dinner together once or twice a year. Leonard continues to visit China and to do consulting work in connection with his trips there.

Leonard and Sharon also joined us for dinner along with Maestro and Mrs. Gunther Herbig and Max Uhlman, an artist from East Germany, for a small dinner party at the time of the opening of the exhibition of paintings from East Germany at the University of Michigan Museum of Art in February of 1990. Peggy and I were the catalysts for the development of that exhibition, which opened at Harvard's Busch-Reisinger Museum in

Peggy and Stanley on the Great Wall of China, on a very cold day, February 1985.

Peggy with actor Peter Ustinov at the opening of the Russian
Art Deco exhibition in the Tate Gallery, London, 1995.

September of 1989 and at UCLA's Wight Gallery in December of that year,
just at the time that the Berlin Wall was coming down.

The exhibition idea was developing as we attended the Salzburg Music
Festival in August 1985. We decided to drive north to Prague and Dresden
on our way to East Berlin and West Berlin.

Prague had always fascinated us as a city, and we looked forward to our
first travel behind the Iron Curtain. In addition, Peggy and I planned to
meet with five Dresden painters and to serve as a catalyst for an exhibition
of paintings from the Deutsche Democratic Republic.

We had viewed an exhibition of Thirteen East German Painters at the
Barbican Museum in London earlier in the year that was organized by David
Elliott, the director of the Oxford Museum of Modern Art. Peggy and I
were to see David Elliott again at the opening of the Russian Art Deco
Exhibition at London's Tate Gallery for which Peter Ustinov was the host.

When we met David at the Oxford Museum, we learned that the British
had a relationship with East Germany and the United States did not. Despite
the anticipated political difficulties, Peggy and I were nevertheless inspired
to stimulate such an exhibition in the United States. We had been in touch
with Sam Sachs, the director of the Detroit Institute of Arts and with Evan

Maurer, the director of the University of Michigan Museum of Art, both of whom had shown some interest. We felt it was especially valid at university museums. We had also written blind to the five Dresden artists, advising them of our interest and asking them to meet with us and then join us for dinner at our hotel.

We drove north from Linz on the Austrian border to Prague where we spent three days in that troubled city. The music was marvelous and the Jewish synagogues and cemeteries most impressive, but the city itself was a mess both physically and spiritually. This was a sharp contrast from the vital city we visited with the Association Internationale des Bibliophilies (AIB) after Russian domination had ended.

In Dresden four of the five artists and their wives were waiting for us at the Academy of Art in the studio of Hubertus Giebe, one of the artists, when we arrived late. We were driven from our very modern hotel by another of the artists, with whom I had talked in my pidgin German, and his brother, a chemical engineer, who told us that he would be our interpreter since he spoke very good English.

The scene in the studio of Hubertus Giebe was a joyful one as Peggy looked over many of the artists' paintings and drawings and I photographed the scene. Their work was an outgrowth of German Expressionism and showed none of the social realism that one would expect in a communist country. They were anti-war and anti-Nazi to be sure, but the sources of their inspiration were good communists like Picasso.

The eleven of us then dined in a private room, with flowers on the table and French champagne, at our hotel where the sign outside read, "HOTEL RESIDENTS ONLY." There were many toasts and an avoidance of politics. Our commitment to the artists was to pursue the possible exhibition as catalysts in every way we could. Because of the circumstances surrounding this gathering, strong friendships developed in just a few hours with each of them that have lasted for many years.

From Dresden we drove north toward West Berlin only to find Checkpoint Charlie in East Berlin closed on that Sunday evening. At the Sunday checkpoint, I made the mistake of admitting to a few East German marks—we did not know that it was illegal to take East German marks out of the country—and was to exchange them at the railroad station. I drove instead to the Metropole Hotel where Peggy went in to buy something. She came back with two large jars of pickles, which she had insisted on buying from a display in the restaurant, to get rid of the money.

Those jars of pickles stayed with us in the car as we spent several days in West Berlin. We visited many libraries and museums, studying the visual arts from the fifteenth century to German Expressionism in this century. We also went back to East Berlin by subway to spend time in the Pergamon

Stanley and David Elliott, director of the Oxford Museum of Modern Art, at
the opening of the Russian Art Deco exhibition at the Tate Gallery in
London, 1995. A painting by Wassily Kandinsky hangs in the background.

Museum, with the huge altar from Pergamon on the Turkish coast and the
very colorful Gates of Babylon that we had never seen before. The scene
in West Berlin was very hectic, while that in East Berlin was quiet almost
beyond belief.

From West Berlin we drove to Frankfurt, stopping on the way that
Sunday afternoon at Mainz to visit the Gutenberg Museum just as it was
about to close. Again Peggy arranged for us to come back on Monday,
despite the fact that the museum was closed that day, to see the collection
and meet with Hans Halby, the director. After the museum closed that
Sunday, we sat down on a park bench just outside. As we were sitting there,
a group of four of the town bums were gathered at another bench about a
hundred feet away. Peggy, at long last, took the pickles out of the car and
made a formal presentation to the chief bum, who was wearing a crushed top
hat. The response to her presentation was a low bow from the chief followed
by bows from the others and clapping as the presentation was made.

Our second visit to the Gutenberg was most exciting. We reviewed the
history of printing, which began with publishing of the Gutenberg Bible in
1454 after Gutenberg had developed moveable type.

In Frankfurt, once again, we visited museums and libraries, including the
new museum designed by Richard Meier. In the libraries, we were looking
with the curators of the collections at manuscripts and early printed books
published in the fifteenth through seventeenth centuries.

And then, it was on to Heidelberg for three days, on each of which we spent major time at the Heiliggeistkirke and the exhibition marking the six hundredth anniversary of the University of Heidelberg Library. It is the only time we have seen a waiting line all the way around a block to see a book exhibition. The exhibition itself was remarkable for its scope and historic importance. It seems that in 1623, at the time of the Thirty Years' War, the Pope ordered the library's collection sent to the Vatican in order to avoid capture by the enemies of the Emperor. In fact, the books were not returned until the time of this exhibition—in 1986—and they were sent back in their entirety to be shown in Heidelberg.

While in Heidelberg, we met with Elmar Mittler, the director of the library, who told us of the very difficult negotiations with Father Leonard Boyle, the director of the Vatican Library. We invited Elmar Mittler to speak to the Friends of the University of Michigan Library and provide an illustrated lecture about the exhibition. This he did the following year.

For many years, going back into the 1960s, I had been using a tape recorder to document both the business and the personal aspects of our travels. In the early days, I used a reel-to-reel tape recorder that was bulky and difficult to handle. Gradually, I moved to a much smaller cassette recorder that, by comparison, was a pleasure to use. More recently, it has been the micro cassette recorder that fits easily into my pocket. My use of a tape recorder has created a few incidents along the way, the most notable of which took place at the Kenzo Boutique on the Place de Victoires in Paris when Kenzo himself was ready to fight with me, even though he should have been aware of the fact that Winkelman's was a customer of his. Kenzo became very angry with me for recording my observations as I walked through the boutique.

On another occasion, I ran into Marvin Traub, the CEO of Bloomingdale's, as I was analyzing the merchandise presentation in the New York store, something I did every month. Marvin and I were friends, and there was no problem with my tape recording about the merchandise I was seeing in his store, yet I felt a little uncomfortable.

From Beijing, in 1980, the five of us traveled by train to Dalien (in my school days, it was known as Darien, Manchuria), a port on the Yellow Sea where the velveteen jackets were made.

We had been unable to make reservations at a hotel in downtown Dalien and settled for a resort on the Yellow Sea. This resort had lain fallow since the Cultural Revolution, when it had been a favorite escape for Chou En-lai and other Chinese leaders. For us, it was a special treat despite the need to take sponge baths in the shower because of the condition of the bathtub, a rusted and cracked specimen with some strange insects running around in it. Unfortunately, it was too cold at that time to swim in the Yellow Sea.

Our lady friend from Chinatex, whom we had met on our first visit to the Canton Trade Fair in 1976 and who worked with me again in 1977 in Canton, was on hand to greet us in her home city of Dalien in 1980. She took us to the factories where the velveteen jackets were made. We were in for a number of surprises in the process. The factories themselves were in improvised buildings of various kinds. They were well organized and very clean. Before long, we began seeing many labels from retailers around the world. I remember the Pierre Cardin label on jackets of the same quality that we had purchased and sold for thirty-nine dollars that would be sold in Cardin boutiques for several times that amount.

Since France had no labeling law comparable to the one in the United States, purchasers would assume that the jackets were made in France because that was the location of the retail business.

From Dalien, we returned to Beijing where Peggy and I departed for Paris, directly this time by way of Calcutta on Air France. We were on a flight that did not exist in 1977 when we were required to return to Hong Kong in order to fly to Paris. By this time, it was also possible to fly into Beijing directly from the United States.

Golden Anniversary

Winkelman's fiftieth anniversary, "Celebrating 50 Fashionable Years," was the highlight of 1978, with a history of Winkelman's, a design contest cosponsored by DuPont with a scholarship as the prize for the winner, and a promotional effort geared to the working woman.

Once again, the heads of our major sources were on hand for all of the anniversary events and a luncheon in their honor at the Standard Club. There were several father-and-son teams and one represented by three generations attending the luncheon.

Both Governor William Milliken and city council president Carl Levin (running for the U.S. Senate at that time) were present, as was Dick Simmons, representing Mayor Coleman Young. Al Taubman was also on hand to be introduced as the developer of the Fairlane Center and a major force in the creation of the Renaissance Center. Each center, including the two Winkelman's stores, would be visited that afternoon.

My brief summary of Winkelman's history emphasized the following:

- On our fiftieth anniversary, Winkelman's had eighty-six stores in three states.
- In addition to the Detroit market, which we had saturated, there were twelve stores in Michigan outside Detroit. Saginaw opened first in 1937.
- The Westgate store in Cleveland opened in 1954. It was the first of twelve stores in Cleveland, followed by five other Ohio stores.

- The first of six Chicago stores opened in 1976 in the Water Tower.
- In 1973, the first of eight Today Stores, geared to the young contemporary customer, opened in suburban Detroit.

I introduced Governor Milliken as a fellow retailer of Milliken's in Traverse City who had made it big as governor of Michigan. I then announced that, as a Democrat, I would be supporting him in his reelection bid that was six weeks away.

Bill and I kidded each other. Milliken's would stay out of the Detroit market if Winkelman's would stay out of Traverse City. Governor Milliken called me at two one morning when we were in Paris to ask if I would accept an appointment to the SEMTA (Southeast Michigan Transportation Authority) board. I was sufficiently awake to decline on the grounds that my commitment as president of the Metropolitan Fund, the nonprofit urban research organization devoted to solving regional problems, required major time, and a portion of its agenda was focused on transportation.

The main event at the 1978 Cultural Center Open House was "Morals and Modes: 50 Years," featuring columnist Ann Landers and Stella Blum, curator of the Costume Institute at the Metropolitan Museum of Art, who compared notes on changes in dress and in lifestyles over the past fifty years. There were dancers and models to support their discourse. The production was supervised by Audley Grossman.

Bob McCabe had come to Detroit from New York about ten years earlier to lead the professional staff of Detroit Renaissance, Inc., in its effort to rebuild Detroit. In fact, Bob did an outstanding job for many years beyond the opening of the Renaissance Center, introducing two major new annual community events, the Grand Prix Auto Race and the Detroit-Montreau Jazz Festival, during his long tenure as president.

The opening of Winkelman's Renaissance Center (RenCen) store had taken place in April 1978, and Winkelman's was off to a very successful start with the career woman—our principal customer—in our new RenCen store. More than ever, there was a need for customization of store stocks to enhance the profitability of each store.

Women's Wear Daily devoted a page of photographs and copy to the Renaissance Center opening in 1977 and the black-tie dinner. Betty Williams, chairing that event, was quoted as saying, "Darling, I've been working on this party for two years. We only have vice presidents, presidents, and chairmen here." There was an important exception to her comment: the communist mayor of Florence and his entourage were also in attendance.

In connection with the opening of Renaissance Center *Women's Wear Daily* ran a photograph of the chairmen of Detroit's largest corporations and their wives or companions: Henry Ford II, Edsel Ford II, Lee Iacocca

Peggy (center) with Beatrice and Bob McCabe, 1969.
McCabe was president of Detroit Renaissance, Inc.

(then president of Ford), Pete Estes (president of GM), Gene Cafiero (of Chrysler), Joe Hudson, and Max Fisher. There was also a photograph of me talking to Mayor Elio Gabbuggiani of Florence.

Gabbuggiani and Mayor Coleman Young both had careers as labor organizers before entering politics. They complemented each other beautifully. Gabbuggiani had brought with him the famous bronze "Putto with Dolphin" by Verrochio that was usually displayed in Florence in the courtyard of the Palazzo della Signoria.

The presence of the sculpture generated a great deal of excitement all by itself. That excitement became almost too great for Peggy when Signora Incerpi, Mayor Gabbuggiani's assistant, asked her to step out of a meeting in the boardroom of the DIA to discuss a very urgent problem.

"What is the problem?" Peggy asked, bracing herself.

"The 'Putto with Dolphin' sitting over there waiting to be taken to Renaissance Center, there is no insurance."

"Why not?" was Peggy's query.

"No money," was the blunt answer.

Peggy, in a state of near panic, rushed to a telephone to call me. After listening to the story, I suggested that the solution could probably be as simple as calling the Metropolitan Museum of Art in New York and

Stanley with Florentine Mayor Gabbuggiani (left) and the Detroit Italian
Trade Consul (center) at the opening dinner for the Renaissance Center, 1977.

offering that museum the opportunity to display the "Putto" for a couple of
weeks with the understanding that the Met would pay the cost of insurance
beginning immediately.

My own handwritten notes on the subject dated March 23, 1977, about
three weeks earlier, reflected my concern: "Insurance while in Detroit—
cable State Department, Italian Desk."

Luckily, the Met quickly agreed, and the crisis was averted, although I
still do not understand to this day how a priceless, unique art treasure can
be adequately insured.

It was earlier that year that Peggy and I invited members of the Florentine
nobility to join us for dinner at the Excelsior Hotel in Florence, where we
had taken over the main dining room for the evening. We were indebted to
the nobility for their lavish entertainment of our group from the DIA when
we had come to Florence for the opening of the Twilight of the Medici
Exhibition at the Pitti Palace. The only venue in the United States for that
exhibition had been the Detroit Institute of Arts.

We also invited Mayor Gabbuggiani, whom the nobility had never before
met. While in Milan I had run into Eunice Johnson, the wife of John
Johnson, publisher of *Ebony* magazine and a charity fashion show organizer
in her own right, to join us along with her buyer who at one time was a

buyer for my cousin, Manny Winkelman, the general merchandise manager of Lane Bryant.

Everything appeared in order for our Sunday night dinner party as we arrived in Florence on Saturday afternoon. But then, the telephone rang. It was Emilio Pucci calling to say that he must see me urgently prior to the dinner. Could we have lunch with him at the palace on Sunday? Of course we accepted his invitation, and for the first time we arrived at the living quarters in the Palazzo Pucci.

Lunch was served to Emilio, his daughter Laudomia, Peggy, and me in a small dining room with lovely murals on the wall. Prior to lunch, Emilio took us on a tour during which he showed us many beautiful paintings, including one by Botticelli showing a wedding dinner of Puccis and Medicis in which he proudly proclaimed that it was the Puccis who were using the knives and forks.

As we ate, Emilio proceeded to tell us a horror story about the threat of terrorists. He felt compelled to wear a bullet-proof vest. No one could go out of the palace without a bodyguard. And, above all, we were making a terrible mistake in inviting Mayor Gabbuggianni to come to Detroit for the opening of the Renaissance Center. Pucci felt that it would only harden his political positions in Florence. We listened with great sympathy but indicated that the invitation had already been issued by our mayor, Coleman Young.

The dinner was a successful affair with warm conversation and toasts. I had brought with me a bicentennial medal, which I presented to Gabbuggiani with appropriate comments about our democracy. His response emphasized his view of democracy. Everyone seemed pleased.

The next evening, the Contessa Federica Piccolomini, sister of Nando Cinelli, gave a cocktail reception in her palace. During the evening I was introduced to Roberto Gucci, whom I had not met before. We discussed the plans for the opening of the Renaissance Center and the question of the appropriateness of inviting Mayor Gabbuggiani to Detroit. Gucci's comments were reassuring. He felt that the experience of visiting Detroit would be a broadening one and would be helpful to the people of Florence.

In September 1979, the *Detroit Free Press* estimated the attendance at the annual Winkelman's open house at four thousand people as it showed a picture of the crowd crossing Woodward Avenue.

In 1980, we even made the *New Zealand Press* in an article stating that "Winkelman's sells more than 200,000 pure new wool sweaters and 50,000 wool and wool blend coats a year." We had just become the proud owners of a pair of sheep as a result of our wool promotions. The article reported on comments that Al Cohen had made to the marketing staff of the International Wool Secretariat in New York.

Stanley, Andra, and Margi in front of the sail fish they caught off Acapulco, 1963.

Peggy and Stanley in Pasadena at the 1995 Rose Bowl.

In April 1980, after Peggy and I had returned from China, Fred Cummings received a letter from our ambassador to China, Leonard Woodcock, recommending an approach to obtaining a major Chinese art exhibition for Detroit. Leonard indicated in his letter that initial contacts should be made with the Chinese embassy in Washington and that after the project was initiated, there should be a delegation of prominent Detroiters going to Beijing, where the final decision would be made. Leonard further suggested that "such persons should be Stanley Winkelman, Henry Ford, Thomas A. Murphy, Governor William Milliken, WSU [Wayne State University] President Thomas Bonner, UAW President Douglas Fraser, etc."

The 12th Annual Cultural Center Open House in 1982 was the last one sponsored by Winkelman's. Just before it, the *Detroit Free Press* ran an editorial entitled, "Artful: In a Time of Cutbacks, We Need All We Can Get to Raise Our Spirits."

Thus, some thirty years of annual fall promotional events and twelve years of Winkelman's-sponsored annual Cultural Center open houses came to an end—the victims of increasing costs and complexity of arrangements.

Over the years, Peggy and I have been very fortunate to tie in personal travel along with business travel. For many years we would spend the first week of July in Beaulieu, from which point we were able to explore the whole Cote d'Azur. For many years we played tennis with Marilyn and Bernie Pincus either on the clay courts of Beaulieu or those of Monte Carlo. Playing tennis on the center court was particularly exciting. The second week of July we would spend in the mountains of Switzerland at Crans-sur-Sierre. There, we would play tennis and walk in the mountains.

Early on, for at least twenty years, we would spend two weeks at Christmastime with our whole family at Islamorada, Florida, half-way down the Keys toward Key West, where we swam, played tennis, and spent as much time as possible fishing for snapper, yellowtail, and mackerel on the ocean side, while on the gulf side we would catch snook and sea trout. To go fishing, we would rent a boat at Bud 'n' Mary's and keep it in front of The Islander. Most of the time I would go—almost always with Roger, some other family member, or friend—without a guide to fish the weed patches within a quarter-mile of the hotel, or the nearby gulf side. To go after snook, redfish, and sea trout near Flamingo at the entrance to the Everglades usually required a guide, although I did it myself on one or two occasions.

Prior to our annual trips to Islamorada, we traveled to Mexico on several occasions. We would stop in Mexico City and then drive on to Acapulco. On one vacation, in 1963, Andra and Margi each caught a 110-pound sail fish in one morning.

More recently, we have spent some winter time in Palm Desert, California, with a few days in L.A. at the end, and on three occasions we attended the Rose Bowl game in Pasadena. We have stayed in Detroit during recent summers. In addition, we have been spending a week in March and a week in late October first at Vence and more recently at St. Paul de Vence, on the Riviera, as I was covering the pret-a-porter showings as a photojournalist for the *Birmingham Eccentric*, of the Observer & Eccentric Newspapers chain.

One year, the Nice Matin greeted us with the announcement of a nineteenth-century French sculpture exhibition in Monte Carlo of works

Stanley with the artist Arman at his Venice studio, 1995.

that had been acquired by a croupier at the Grand Casino from older casinos that had been torn down or casinos that had replaced the older sculptures with more contemporary works. It was announced that Princess Caroline would be the royal hostess. I called and arranged for press credentials.

The opening was an extraordinary experience. It was well attended, and I was able to take several excellent photographs of Her Royal Highness.

5

Commitment to Community

Social, Religious, and Political Action

Whello was a young man, World War II had caused me to do some deep thinking about my life. Rolling across the Pacific far away from Peggy and Andra made me wonder what I could do to prevent future wars. While this may seem a bit naive, merely an example of youthful idealism, I was profoundly concerned, consumed by my sense of the uselessness and waste of war, to say nothing of the jeopardy, isolation, and vulnerability I felt during the very long cruise aboard the LST-384. It all made me wonder: Why was I there, and what could be done to keep my children and grandchildren from having the same experience?

To explain what brought me to such a state of awareness and concern, I can look back to quite a young age and recall the growth of my social views.

Back when I was in high school in Detroit, the anti-Semitic oratory of Father Coughlin—a Catholic priest from Royal Oak—who made a broadcast every Sunday afternoon on WJR radio, caused me considerable anxiety, as did, to a lesser degree, the anti-Semitic diatribes of Henry Ford and Charles Lindbergh.

Very few of my parents' friends were Republicans, and almost everyone we knew supported Franklin Roosevelt. After all, it was Roosevelt who brought the country back to life after the disastrous 1929 stock market crash and the ensuing Great Depression that, in fact, jeopardized American life itself.

With eleven million unemployed out of a population of sixty million, with bread lines and with apples being sold on the streets for a nickel each, and with the discouragement and despair of people everywhere, there was a growing group of intellectuals ready to give up on our democratic system and embrace socialism or communism.

Had I been five or six years older during the 1930s, I might well have become a socialist, a communist, or a fellow-traveler. At the very least, I would have joined the Americans for Democratic Action.

FDR moved quickly in March 1933 to declare the Bank Holiday that closed all banks for a few days and many banks permanently. This was followed by a proposal to establish the Federal Reserve System. The laissez-faire doctrine of Herbert Hoover and the Republican Party had led to a political and economic catastrophe of unpredicted and gigantic dimensions. More than sixty years later, conservative Republicans appear to be pushing us back toward those failed policies of the 1920s.

The National Recovery Act (NRA) sailed through Congress, as did the Works Progress Administration (WPA) and the Civilian Conservation Corps (CCC). All were designed to put the unemployed back to work and to rejuvenate the economy. The art component of the WPA put starving artists to work on public projects and generated a community of some fine American artists, including Jack Levine, Raphael Soyer, and Stuart Davis.

There were many jokes at the time about WPA workers standing idly, leaning on their shovels, as they were supposedly working to complete badly needed public projects. The CCC created a sense of discipline among formerly unemployed youths. It conducted significant forestation and re-forestation projects and was successful in reducing damage caused by forest fires.

Near the beginning of FDR's first administration, a distant cousin of mine, Wilbur Cohen, who much later became the dean of the education school at the University of Michigan, was one of three authors of the Social Security proposal that was enacted by Congress. That law continues to provide needed benefits to retirees, although it will require some changes to make it viable beyond the next thirty years.

Could all of this constructive activity have been possible without running a significant budget deficit? Could it have happened in the environment created by the Balanced Budget Amendment of 1997? I doubt it. It is my belief that a sense of history should alert all Americans to the dangers of returning to the laissez-faire doctrine of Herbert Hoover and the doctrine now being preached by ultra-conservatives in the Republican Party.

Economic inequities have been growing steadily for the last two decades. The wealthy have been getting substantially wealthier. The number of families below the poverty line has been growing larger, and the real income of the middle class, until very recently, has been shrinking. Society cannot expect this growing polarization to continue without ruining what has been the most productive economic system in the history of the world.

Businesses and corporate executives have become extremely greedy, with little or no commitment to the broader society. That broader society is complacent despite the erosion of living standards of almost half the population, leading me to believe, despite current stock market trends, that we are currently in a period of decline of the American civilization.

Arresting and reversing this decline will certainly depend on a much stronger and more effective political leadership that generates a new level of trust and civility. It also will depend on the willingness of citizens to respond to that leadership and commit themselves to the common good, a consideration that has all but disappeared since the end of World War II.

Selective Service, the draft of World War II, called for a significant commitment and sacrifice for our country. It also provided a leveling, disciplined experience and exposure to all kinds of people. Our society today would be much better if it required a year or two of public service for young people around the ages of eighteen to twenty-two. Designing such a service program would not be easy, and certainly in our present anti-government environment, approval of such a program would be difficult to obtain.

After World War II ended, I met in San Francisco with Herman Camp, the chairman of Camp Millinery, a company that operated leased millinery departments in stores all over the United States. Herman and I discussed concerns I'd felt while cruising the Pacific on the way to the Battle of Japan along with my desire to do what I could to prevent future wars.

His wise response was simple: "Go home and get involved in the community." If I did that, in time I would be able to exert some influence on the political process and could probably be involved at the state or even at the national level.

Study and Involvement

I took Harry's advice. As I was learning about store management and selling and at the same time settling into a most wonderful family life, I was thinking through my personal philosophy along with Peggy, who was also concerned with her own direction.

We were helped considerably by a study group that we were invited to join. It included Ben and Edna Goldstein, Betty and Sol Kurtzman, Hannah and Irving Pokempner, Lillian and Jules Pierce, Edith and Sidney Shevitz, and Mac and Wanda Fader. All of these individuals exerted a positive influence on us, especially in the setting of those years between 1947 and 1956, as did Adlai Stevenson, our intellectual idol, and his runs for president in 1952 and 1956.

The study group met once a month at a different home each month. We would listen to a paper presented by one of the members and then discuss the content and the presentation. Two particular subjects I presented would have long-term influences on my life.

My first paper was on "Group Dynamics," for which I did a great deal of reading of books by Kurt Lewin, the father of group dynamics, who had been an Austrian refugee to the United States in the late 1930s. Lewin established at MIT the Research Center for Group Dynamics, which was later moved to the University of Michigan.

Lewin, Dorwin Cartright, and Alvin Zander all wrote books on the dynamics of small groups that helped me tremendously in various kinds of meetings I would be involved in over the years to come. The discussion of my paper by the group was very positive, if only because no one presumed to have a greater knowledge of the subject than I and because they, too, were stimulated by it.

Even more profound for me was Lewin's *Resolving Social Conflicts.* This book caused me to come to grips with being a Jew in an anti-Semitic world. It stimulated me to develop a very positive attitude toward being a Jew, and it awakened in me strong religious feelings that I have carried with me ever since.

My second paper, on "The Evolution of Modern Architecture," was more challenging, because a number of the study group members felt they were authorities on the subject and did not take particularly well to my intrusion into their domain.

In fact, the discussion was a dynamic one, with basic acceptance of what I had learned and what many of them had long known, namely that there were two primary directions for architecture at that juncture: the organic architecture as practiced by Frank Lloyd Wright and the simple geometric designs seen in the work of Mies Van der Rohe. I find "postmodern" architecture of the 1990s poor by comparison.

We are fortunate to have one of the great architects of the twentieth century—William Kessler—living in Detroit. Kessler was educated at Illinois Tech, where Mies Van der Rohe had established himself when he came to this country.

The work I did in preparing this paper would help me as I became involved in store design and, later, faced up to design questions related to the traditional English home we purchased from Peggy's folks and lived in very comfortably for twenty years.

Architecture, being large and heavy-impact sculpture, has great influence on all of our lives. To understand and appreciate it is both stimulating and extremely helpful in life. Applying the concepts and interpretation in specific building situations is very satisfying. From the time I prepared the paper to the present, architecture has been one of my avocations. The personal relationships with Minoru Yamasaki, Yoshinobu Ashihara, Louis Redstone, and William Kessler have been most satisfying.

At about the same time as the study group was operating, I became

Stanley with Peggy (to his right), Andra and Margi (to his left), Roger (far left), and Andra's son Alan Barr (front) the night Stanley received the Butzel Award, 1979.

involved in fund-raising in both the Jewish and the general communities. In both cases, it was Jimmy Wineman who came to me and asked me take on a leadership role in the Mercantile Division of the Jewish Welfare Federation and, later the same year, for the United Foundation. I was also invited by Sidney Shevitz, then president of the Jewish Community Council, to join the Community Relations Committee of that organization.

Many years later, in 1979, I would receive the Butzel Award, the highest annual award of the Jewish Community.

And so it was, in 1948, that I began to do as I had pledged to do following that meeting in 1946 with Herman Camp in San Francisco. I was further motivated by my perception of a business need, that I had an obligation to give back something to the city in which we were doing business. While my father and uncle felt that community involvement, especially with social problems, could antagonize customers, both men generally respected and supported my position.

It was—and is—my belief that active participation in the community is not only desirable but essential to the long-term health of the city and our customers, if handled with discretion. I have never had reason to regret my commitment and involvement.

I have never had a negative letter or telephone call in regard to my community activism. Peggy did receive one negative letter in the 1970s when she appeared in a *Detroit News* photograph with Jean Hudson in connection with Planned Parenthood. Perhaps that was a very mild precursor of today's hysteria over abortion.

Religious Perspectives

The word *religion* evokes both positive and negative reactions in people. On the one hand, religion plays a very positive and essential role in the lives of many individuals and families. Religion defines a particular way of life, a system for living that provides a standard of behavior as well as appropriate ritual. Religion can also answer the ultimate questions of why we are here and what the future, beyond life on earth, may bring. For those committed to the orthodox traditions of Catholicism, Islam, or Judaism, a major benefit is peace of mind.

On the other hand, we all recognize religious conflicts and the damage

Stanley receiving the Butzel Award from Mike Zeltzer (left) and Alan Schwartz (center) at the Jewish Welfare Federation Annual Meeting, 1979.

they continue to generate. In Roman times, Christians were executed. Later, the Crusades brought death in the name of Christianity. Then came the Spanish Inquisition in the late fifteenth century, with death for those who were not Christian or who would not convert to Christianity. Solyman the Magnificent conquered most of Europe in the name of Islam in the sixteenth century.

Today conflict rages. There has been one positive development with the cease fire in Northern Ireland between Protestants and Catholics, although it is still on very shaky ground. In the Arab countries of the Middle East, Islamic extremists challenge many governments. Islamic extremists control Iran. At the same time, the Orthodox Jewish leadership of Israel has outlawed the more liberal Conservative and Reform movements in which the chief rabbi of Israel is on record as calling for the death of Conservative and Reform Jews.

The hot and cold war between Israel and its Arab neighbors has been reduced significantly by peace agreements with Egypt and Jordan. Yet the conflict between the Palestinians and Israel continues relatively unabated, punctuated by terrorist attacks despite the "peace process."

These examples do not reflect the religious concept of love for one's neighbors. They reflect the very opposite of love, which is hate.

And yet religion has the potential, if practiced according to the principles that organized religions espouse, to be a very positive humanizing force. That is possible if the radical right of Christianity, of Islam, and of Judaism are willing to become part of a broad consensus based on mutual respect.

This is not likely to happen during my lifetime, since we are currently witnessing the growing polarization of American society based on politics, economics, and the political involvement of the Christian right. Businesses are adding to this polarization by emphasizing the immediate bottom line rather than taking a longer-term view.

On a more personal level, religion is, and has been, very important in my life. I have developed a strong commitment to Judaism and, more specifically, to Reform Judaism since the end of World War II.

Our faulty religious education at Temple Beth El in the 1930s ignored the fundamental issues of the day: Zionism and Israel. There was an emphasis on English in the liturgy rather than Hebrew. For all practical purposes, the Reform Judaism as practiced by Rabbi Leo M. Franklin at Temple Beth El in Detroit was assimilationist in character. It followed the pattern of Reform Judaism as it developed in Germany in the mid-nineteenth century.

My wartime experiences in California as well as my study of group dynamics, and especially the book *Resolving Social Conflicts* by Kurt Lewin, in the late 1940s helped to establish my direction. My firm commitment to Reform Judaism developed when I embraced the basic social action responsibility that is inherent in prophetic teaching.

In 1948, Harry Truman and then most of the civilized world recognized the State of Israel. It was a time of great rejoicing in Jewish communities around the globe. The absolute horror of the Holocaust had given rise to the reality of a Jewish State and homeland.

Israel became the ultimate destination for hundreds of thousands of refugees and survivors of Nazi terror as well as for hundreds of thousands of Zionists who were committed to becoming a part of this new country and making it successful despite the violent hostility of its Arab neighbors.

During that same year, as a member of the Jewish Community Council's Community Relations Committee, I was present for a great debate before an audience of seven hundred fifty members of the Jewish Welfare Federation and the Jewish Community Council with respect to the Federation's control of the Council budget. The immediate issue was a Federation proposal for line-by-line budgeting of the Council. The meeting was rancorous, with a much deeper and more significant negative overtone.

While Federation leaders and financial supporters regarded the Federation as *the* Jewish community, the leaders and members of the Community Council regarded the Council as *the* Jewish community. From a historic point of view, the Federation was there first and was composed of the givers as well as the planning and budget leaders of the community.

The Jewish Community Council was formed in 1936 on the initiative of Jewish Welfare Federation leaders for two purposes. The most immediate purpose was the need to establish an organization that would counter the anti-Semitic mutterings of Father Coughlin and other rabble rousers such as Gerald L. K. Smith. The second purpose was to involve those Jews of eastern European origin in the organized community. Federation leaders at the time were of western European origin.

The Council was regarded as the more democratic institution by its founders and board members, having as its constituency all of the Jewish organizations in the community, including synagogues, schools, health and welfare agencies, and the *vereins* and *landsmanschaften* that were secular and Zionist.

The ultimate authority of the Council was the delegate assembly composed of the designated representatives of the member organizations—hence the claim that the Council was *the* Jewish community and not subject to the discipline of the Federation budget process, despite the fact that its entire budget came from the Federation. The facts indicated that both organizations were perpetuated by nominating committees proposed by the officers, so that, in reality, neither organization was truly democratic in practice.

Since I was an integral part of both organizations, I was faced with the dilemma of reconciling the two positions. Ultimately, my answer was relatively simple.

I concluded that it was the two organizations together that constituted the Jewish community, not one or the other. My mentors in these days were Isadore Sobeloff, the executive director of the Federation, and Isaiah Minkoff, the executive director of the National Community Advisory Council in New York.

Sobey was a tremendous fund-raiser, community organizer, and Federation zealot. Minkoff, on the other hand, was an immigrant from the old country who had a marvelous humanistic perspective, a broad democratic philosophy, and an understanding of the dynamic processes of community organizations. He had a folksy approach coupled with great insight into human nature.

My involvement with the Jewish Community Council illustrates that I was already committed to social action through the council's activities in the field of community relations in the late 1940s. The 1954 biennial of the Union of American Hebrew Congregations (UAHC), the umbrella organization for the Reform movement, provided additional impetus to my direction.

A resolution of that convention called for each synagogue to establish its own social action committee. I recognized this as an opportunity for me as a young leader. I began discussions on the subject of a social action committee for the temple with my dentist, Leo Greenblatt, who happened to be the president of Temple Beth El's Men's Club and a member of the board of trustees of the temple. Leo Greenblatt proposed that the board establish a social action committee and that I be named its chairman.

Al Vorspan, the director of the UAHC Social Action Committee, and Rabbi Eugene Lipman had published the book *Justice and Judaism*, which laid out the philosophical base for social action. I was profoundly moved by the book and its quotations from the prophets. What could be simpler and more direct as a religious imperative: "What doth the Lord requireth of thee? But, to do justice, to love mercy, and to walk humbly with thy God." The prophets—Isaiah, Hillel, and Jeremiah—all made similar statements. It was Hillel who asked, "If I am not for myself, who will be, but, if I am only for myself, what am I?"

For me, this was the relevance for which I had been searching. My experiences with the community council and with the Beth El Social Action Committee formed the base for a lifelong devotion to social action. My business associates would wonder aloud, "Why can't you be involved with nice, safe activities like the Chamber of Commerce?"

For several years, I provided leadership for the Beth El Social Action

Committee until many of its individual members had become more involved in broader community efforts in Detroit.

In 1961, Detroit's new mayor, Jerome B. Cavanaugh, appointed me to the City of Detroit Community Relations Commission. This gave me the opportunity on a citywide level to stimulate positive changes in city policy. I viewed this as the prophetic teaching of Judaism being applied to practical social problems of the day, especially those related to racism, such as police brutality toward blacks and discrimination in employment, housing, and education.

By 1954, Peggy and I had became involved in the Young Married Group of Temple Beth El, and Peggy was elected vice president. The Young Married Group became the breeding ground for changes in the congregation. Leonard Simons, the president of the temple, was wisely encouraging us in subtle ways.

Leonard was also looking for a new rabbi to replace the excellent Rabbi B. Benedict Glazer, whose relatively short tenure ended with his sudden death. In the interim, Leonard had hired Rabbi Minard Klein to be the assistant rabbi. Minard was the perfect choice, a young man but very mature for his age. He was able to kindle strong feelings of religiosity in Peggy and me.

It was about this time that I suggested organizing a religious retreat. This idea was adopted by the Men's Club, and the first Men's Club retreat took place, with me as chairman, in the spring of 1954. The retreat was exhilarating. The quality of the discussions was extremely good, and the inspirational quality of Rabbi Klein came through admirably. What Minard may have lacked as an inspirational speaker, he made up for with his sincerity and philosophical logic.

After searching for many years for a concept of God that I could accept personally, it was easy for me, having been trained in science and math, to embrace the cosmological view. The concept of God as the creator of the cosmos was very meaningful, while the concept of a personal God was less appealing to me at the time. Today, I have an affinity for both. Many brilliant individuals I have known over the years have seemed to me "lost" with their agnostic views and lack of an emotional anchor. Albert Einstein's *Out of My Later Years* delineated the great scientist's commitment to the existence of God as the first cause in the universe.

My interest at Temple Beth El began with my commitment to social action. With my growing sense of religiosity and exposure to reconstructionism, I became involved in efforts to strengthen ritual practices, and my participation grew rather quickly as I was soon elected to the board of trustees.

Peggy's role as vice president of the Young Married Group found her chairing several lectures by prominent guests. The first was Eleanor Roosevelt, the widow of FDR. Eleanor was a brilliant, gracious, and committed

Peggy with Eleanor Roosevelt, Rabbi Minard
Klein (left), and Rabbi Richard Hertz (right), 1955.

woman and very effective at reminding Americans of the validity of the
American dream for all citizens and their duty to the downtrodden in this
country, a leadership message that is all but nonexistent as we approach the
new millennium.

Eleanor Roosevelt called Peggy when she arrived in Detroit to ask if
she could bring a friend along to the small dinner we were hosting at the
Standard Club before her lecture. Her friend turned out to be Pearl Mesta,
"the hostess with the mostest," a legendary democratic party fund-raiser
and former ambassador to Luxembourg. The discussion at dinner was most
stimulating as we covered the political waterfront of the day.

On the way to the temple, Peggy was practically speechless with excitement as I enjoyed small talk with our guests. The lecture drew a large crowd
in the main sanctuary. The comments of Eleanor Roosevelt were very well
received. One year later, at the Jefferson-Jackson Dinner of the Michigan
Democratic Party, Eleanor recognized Peggy by name and recalled the
earlier event with pleasure.

On two subsequent occasions, Norman Cousins, the editor of the *Saturday Review* and one of the great intellects of the day, was the guest lecturer.

We developed a friendship with Norman and corresponded periodically with him until his death.

After leaving the *Saturday Review*, which foundered on financial rocks, Cousins spent his remaining years at the Center for Democratic Studies in Santa Barbara, California. Suffering from a critical illness and close to death, Cousins used his positive attitude and sense of humor not only to sustain himself but also as a significant factor in his recovery. He went on to write a fascinating book about his "miraculous recovery."

Within the Young Married Group, there grew a substantial feeling that major changes were needed in the religious school and in the ritual practices related to prayer and the order of the Sabbath services.

When Rabbi Richard Hertz arrived on the scene, he changed the order of the service so that his sermon came at the end. We felt strongly that this was a mistake and that the sermon should be where it had been for many years: before the Kaddish prayers and the tribute to the honored dead of the congregation. We believed that the rabbi's preference reflected his ego and the desire that the congregants carry his message away from the service, rather than the prayers for those who had died. Eventually, the sermon was restored to its traditional position.

Since Rabbi Hertz was the son-in-law of Chicago's Rabbi Mann, it is probably not surprising that his orientation to Reform Judaism was just slightly more liberal than that of Rabbi Franklin. His tendency was to follow the pattern of Temple Beth El's history, although he did embrace the fundamental importance of Israel.

Rabbi Hertz was unprepared for the challenges he would face regarding ritual. The issue of bar mitzvah became a focal point for change.

For a number of years, I had subscribed to the *Reconstructionist*, the monthly periodical of the Reconstructionist movement led by Rabbi Mordecai M. Kaplan. The mission of the Reconstructionist movement was to reconstruct Conservative Jewish practices to make them appropriate for today. As a result of my reading of Kaplan and his son-in-law, Rabbi Ira Eisenstein, the editor of the *Reconstructionist*, I began to challenge Reform Jewish practice and to express the need for increasing the amount of "appropriate" ritual at Temple Beth El.

We, as members of the Ritual Committee, read the two volumes by Rabbi Solomon Freehof on *Reform Jewish Practice*. We noted that Reform ritual practice, at that time, varied from keeping kosher at one extreme to having Christmas trees at the other, with all gradations in between.

The obvious conclusion was that questions of ritual practice were determined by the rabbi and the board of trustees of each synagogue, working together through a ritual committee.

In the case of Temple Beth El, the Young Married Group and the Ritual

Committee pushed hard on the issue of bar mitzvah. We were successful, after considerable effort, in having the reading of the weekly portion of the handwritten Torah (first five books of the Old Testament) read by the bar mitzvah at the Sabbath service of the congregation on Saturday morning.

Bar mitzvah at Temple Beth El became the reward for learning Hebrew, with the ceremony taking place at the Sabbath services closest to the boy's thirteenth birthday. (The analogous bat mitzvah ceremony was opened up for girls many years later.) The ceremony did not mean that the boy or girl became an adult member of the community on that occasion. That status would come with the group confirmation ceremony (for both boys and girls) upon completion of nine years of religious education at age fifteen or sixteen. Confirmation took place during the month of June on the holiday of Shavout.

When we were having dinner together recently, Rabbi Hertz told me that he recalled being hired as the result of the recommendation of a search committee chaired by the former treasurer of General Motors, Meyer Prentis. About six months after his hiring, the rabbi told me, he asked Prentis to meet again with him. At that meeting, Rabbi Hertz advised Prentis that he was having difficulty with three of the younger members of the congregation, one of whom was Stanley Winkelman. Prentis's reply was, "My job was to hire you. You're on your own with this one."

Our relationship was actually much better than the tension surrounding ritual matters would indicate. I had great respect for Dick's broad involvement in the general community and for his strong commitment to social action. Indeed, we were friendly toward each other.

My experience as a member of the board of trustees was generally a positive one, and gradually I moved up in the hierarchy to first vice president. Friday night services were not well attended. Bar mitzvah, as a part of that service, would not be initiated until some years later. When bar mitzvah and then bat mitzvah were scheduled on Friday nights, attendance improved substantially.

Martin Butzel, the president at the time I was elected first vice president, suffered a stroke and was unable to continue in office for a second year. I realized that there was no way I could manage my responsibilities at Winkelman's and take on additional responsibility as the president of Temple Beth El.

I declined the presidency and chose instead to continue as first vice president. I did conduct the annual meeting that year as Aubrey Ettenheimer was elected president.

In the early 1970s, the board decided to erect a new building in the suburbs, outside the city. The migration of temple members out of Detroit had accelerated following the riots of 1967.

To be replaced was the Temple building at Woodward and Gladstone designed by the great architect Albert Kahn. It was truly magnificent. This was the second Albert Kahn building for Temple Beth El. The first one, also magnificent for its time, became the Bonstelle Theater and is now a part of Wayne State University.

For several years, the congregation owned a triangular piece of property of about ten and a half acres on the site of the present Prudential Center at Evergreen and Northwestern Highway in Southfield. In the course of debate, this was deemed to be too small, and a larger area was purchased in Birmingham at the corner of 14 Mile Road and Telegraph, the present location of Temple Beth El.

The debate centered on two questions: the need to move and, later, the choice of architect to design the building.

The desire to retain and/or expand membership led to the decision to build a new synagogue, despite my own personal reluctance. Having reviewed the history of Temple Beth El and other Jewish institutions, I was extremely disturbed by the tendency to rebuild our community facilities in almost every generation.

There were two factors in the movement of the Jewish population. The first was the desire to live in better neighborhoods, including those that had been all but closed to Jews by anti-Semitic restrictions. The second factor was the Jewish brand of racism, whether in the demeaning language of employing "shwartzas" or in the urgency of moving away from Detroit as black penetration of Jewish residential areas accelerated with open occupancy.

Open occupancy was a new reality for which I had been working as a member of the City of Detroit Community Relations Commission and, later, on the board of New Detroit, the urban coalition begun in 1967 following the riots of that summer. My first direct experience with open occupancy took place in 1961, when Governor George Romney participated in an open occupancy meeting sponsored by Detroit's religious leaders in order to generate pressure for change. Episcopal Bishop Richard Emrich, Catholic Archbishop John Dearden, and Alan Zahn, the head of the Detroit Council of Churches, were present, as were Rabbi Hertz and I (as president of the Jewish Community Council) representing the Jewish community.

The problem of open occupancy did not get solved in 1961, with the result that members of New Detroit would fly to Lansing in the fall of 1967 aboard three aircraft owned by GM, Ford, and Chrysler to lobby legislators under the auspices of the Michigan State Chamber of Commerce. It was a heady experience in which you couldn't tell the players without a score-board, because everyone was playing a different role from his usual one. Open occupancy legislation was passed in that session of the legislature. It

Stanley with Governor George Romney (center), Bishop Richard
C. Emrich (left), and Archbishop John Dearden (right), 1961.

was an important symbolic victory, with the hard work of implementation
still ahead.

The discussions of the Temple Beth El board regarding the architect for
the new building focused on Minoru Yamasaki, the most prominent architect in Detroit at the time. It was natural that Yami would be considered,
if only because of his work for the Center for Creative Studies and the
buildings he was doing for Wayne State University and for the Michigan
Consolidated Gas Company headquarters in downtown Detroit.

Personally, I was opposed to Yami getting the commission, although
Peggy and I were good friends of Yami and his wife Terri. Yami had built a
house for Ben Goldstein, my associate at Winkelman's, in the early 1950s
that was an absolute inspiration. However, Peggy and I had visited the North
Shore Temple in Chicago that Yami had designed. We found it lacking in
warmth as a synagogue. To us, it seemed sterile compared with the new
Congregation Shaarey Zedek in Southfield or Temple Israel's new building
in West Bloomfield. When the question of Yamasaki as architect for the
new temple was put to a vote, I was one of only two people voting in the
negative.

The edifice that resulted turned out to be a monument to Richard Hertz and is today one of the most inefficient synagogue buildings ever erected. Visually, however, it has great contemporary beauty with its huge tentlike structure.

The main sanctuary is connected by a long glass-enclosed hallway to the simpler two-story structure for the religious school—the small Maas Chapel, which does have great warmth and charm and incorporates the ark from Woodward and Gladstone, and Handleman Hall for special occasions. Because of the orientation of the *bema* (pulpit) at the eastern end of the sanctuary, there is no access to it except by the long walk from the entrance. The bright lights, high overhead along the center line of the top of the tent and shining down on the congregation, are annoying to those of us who enjoy looking up during the service.

Most difficult of all is the lack of energy efficiency involved with heating and cooling the big tent and the long hallway to the religious school. Conservation of energy was not a consideration in the construction, but in a very short time, it became very important with the Arab oil embargo and the sharp increase in the cost of fossil fuels that resulted.

My role as an officer of the temple was to be short-lived, since it was not very long before the board decided that Rabbi Hertz was not performing well and should be terminated. The result was a confrontation with the rabbi that happened to take place one week before our oldest daughter, Andra, was to be married.

Aubrey Ettenheimer did not provide strong leadership in the situation, except for his negative (and, in many cases, justified) feelings about the rabbi's performance. Fortunately, I had done my homework, including a formal appraisal of the rabbi's performance. My evaluation involved a detailed examination of each of Rabbi Hertz's responsibilities in relation to his performance.

When the meeting between the officers and the rabbi had concluded, Hertz suggested that I would not want him to officiate at Andra's wedding. I reassured him that we did want him to officiate. He suggested that he and Mary Louise would not stay for dinner. Again, I insisted they would stay for dinner and enjoy the evening.

Our confrontation with the rabbi led to a counterattack by the UAHC, with the officers being asked by Max Fisher and Nate Shapiro, to meet with them along with Rabbi Maurice Eisendrath, president of the UAHC, and Rabbi Nelson Glueck, president of the Hebrew Union College in Cincinnati.

We were told bluntly that we would not prevail. As a direct result of that meeting, the officers—including Aubrey Ettenheimer, Alan Schwartz, Walter Shapiro, and me—decided that we should not run for reelection at the annual meeting of the congregation, which was just a few weeks away. It was our view that Rabbi Hertz should have the opportunity to work with new, more sympathetic officers as he attempted to create a stronger leadership role for himself.

In fact, the rabbi's performance did improve significantly. As for me, today I have feelings that the confrontation should never have taken place. Had I been able to become president, I am confident that somehow Rabbi Hertz and I could have worked out a better solution.

I also recognize at this point in my life that a rabbi's job in a large congregation is difficult at best. The requirements for pastoral visits to the ill and the grieving alone—not even counting weddings and funerals—could take up all of his time in a large congregation. Add to all of this the preparation of sermons, teaching, and some scholarly work, to say nothing of community participation, and it becomes easy to see that doing an effective job as the senior rabbi of a congregation of sixteen hundred families is impossible.

And yet Rabbi Daniel Syme, who became the rabbi of Temple Beth El in 1996, is doing—through superhuman effort—an unbelievably good job, to the point that we are concerned about his stamina, his health, and his ability to retain the pace of his work.

Social Action

Prophetic teaching and the book *Justice and Judaism* by Al Vorspan and Eugene Lipman provided my thrust into the establishment of the Social Action Committee of Temple Beth El in 1954. What could be more basic to religious teaching than the admonishment of the prophets, "What doth the Lord requireth of thee, but to do justice, to love mercy, and to walk humbly before thy God?" I had been involved with the Jewish Community Council since 1949 through my developing relationship with Sidney Shevitz, the president of the council, in the study group we had joined.

My father-in-law, Sidney Wallace, owned the Arrow Manufacturing Company and believed that fair and honest dealings with people should be his watchword. Hence, he named his company to reflect that all dealings would be "straight as an arrow." At one time when he was faced with a sit-down strike, he told the workers on a very cold Friday night as he was about to shut the plant for the weekend that if they wanted to stay for the weekend, it was all right with him. But there would be no heat. However, if they wanted to leave for the weekend, they could do so and resume their strike positions on Monday. They did leave, and on Monday he permitted them to return to their strike positions as the new week began.

As part of my commitment to the Jewish community, and the commitment to the general community that I had made before my separation from the navy, I had become involved in the United Foundation (now United Way) and the Allied Jewish Campaign in 1948.

I became chairman of a division of the United Foundation campaign responsible for 10 percent of the successful $15 million effort in 1949 and a co-chairman of the mercantile division along with Al Sklar, a furniture retailer, about the same time. In each case, the professional staff members—Clay Howell at the United Foundation and Sam Cohen at the Jewish Welfare Federation—later became the professional leaders of their total respective campaigns.

While the fund-raising efforts were systematic and straightforward, as well as universally approved, social action programs were, necessarily, much less structured, less measurable in terms of results, and more complex, to say nothing of being subject to question on political grounds.

The tension between the Jewish Community Council and the Jewish Welfare Federation regarding which organization was the Jewish community has been mentioned earlier, as has my conclusion that the two organizations together constituted the Jewish community.

The tension between the Council and the Federation did not reflect opposition to the Council's social action program. However, it was not until the 1967 civil disturbance in Detroit that conventional wisdom and the general community fully supported these efforts. In fact, it was not until 1967 that the community relations work that I had been engaged in for many years became respectable.

The Supreme Court ruling in *Brown v. The Board of Education* in 1954, in which separate but equal educational facilities were declared to be inherently unequal, laid the groundwork for the civil rights movement of the 1960s. That 1954 decision became the basis for opening up all white schools to black students and for busing programs to help in the integration of black and white children. Social research at that time indicated that black children in integrated schools did better than black children in all-black schools. That research appears to have been discounted in recent years for reasons that remain obscure to me.

While I was involved with the Jewish Community Council since 1948 and the chairman of the Social Action Committee of Temple Beth El beginning in 1954, it was not until late 1960 that my involvement with the general community intensified.

In the late 1950s, I was appointed to the Commission on Social Action of the Union of American Hebrew Congregations. Working with Al Vorspan, the executive director, was exciting, especially because the book he and Rabbi Eugene Lipman had written, *Justice and Judaism*, had proved so influential in my life. Al and I would talk frequently by telephone and

Original New Detroit Board of Trustees, August 10, 1967.

get together in New York on my monthly merchandising trips there. Unfortunately, I was able to attend very few commission meetings because of my Winkelman's work schedule, and I left the group after about two years.

In December 1960, a meeting took place at the Park Shelton Hotel in Detroit. As president of the Jewish Community Council, I was asked to attend. The meeting's purpose was to put pressure on Mayor Louis Miriani to put a halt to the police practice of "Stop and frisk on the street" immediately. The meeting was effective; the stop-and-frisk practice was stopped within a few days. It was at that meeting that my close relationship with Arthur Johnson began to develop.

In the intervening years, Art Johnson and I have been close friends and have worked together on many community projects. In August 1967, we were both named as charter members of New Detroit. Art was later appointed vice president for community relations at Wayne State University, where he did an outstanding job until his retirement in 1997.

Art has been an outstanding spokesman on the subject of racism, with an incredible ability to articulate its manifestations. One of his primary objectives in life has been to be treated as a man, not just as a black man.

Art eventually came full circle from his position as executive director of the NAACP (National Association for the Advancement of Colored People) when he was elected president of the Detroit chapter. He was a close friend of Mayor Coleman Young and an adviser to the mayor during his four administrations and sixteen years in office.

It was also at that December 1960 meeting at the Park Shelton that my great admiration for labor leader Walter Reuther began. We had met before, but this was my first direct exposure to his leadership skills and his effectiveness in influencing the political process.

The other participants in that meeting were leaders of the Catholic and Protestant communities with whom I had worked previously in various community relations activities.

The Winkelman's salesman for White Stag Sportswear, Lou Gordon, was at that time a television reporter who was emphasizing the poor performance of Mayor Louis Miriani. Lou was a good friend with whom I would discuss Detroit policies on his visits to our sportswear buyers. Lou and I agreed on the need for political change in Detroit.

Lou was a significant factor in the election of Jerry Cavanaugh, a political unknown, as the mayor of Detroit. Following Cavanaugh's election in the fall of 1961, Lou recommended that Jerry appoint me to the City of Detroit Commission on Community Relations. The commission did a great deal of pioneering in attacking racial discrimination at various levels in the community. We were particularly active with George Edwards, the new police commissioner, with whom Peggy and I had been friends since 1948.

George Edwards had left his relatively secure position as a justice on the Michigan State Supreme Court at the request of Cavanaugh to become police commissioner of Detroit. George had previously been president of the Detroit City Council and before that a judge in the Probate Court.

George, following in his father's footsteps, had become a socialist at an early age. In the environment of the Socialist Party, he met the Reuther brothers—Roy, Victor, and Walter—with whom he later became involved as an organizer for the United Auto Workers. While his reputation was that of a flaming liberal, George Edwards was simply looking for a way to preserve our system in the depths of the Great Depression when the outlook was very bleak.

Edwards knew the city of Detroit, and he knew the problems of the police department. The Commission on Community Relations had two concerns with the department: we were deeply disturbed by the small number of black policemen, and we were also very much distressed by the instances of police brutality against black citizens along with the widespread feeling in the black community that the police were an army of occupation. Edwards was committed to dealing with both issues, while at the same time trying to

Stanley (far left) with Judge George Edwards, former State
Supreme Court Justice Ted Souris, former Governor
G. Mennen Williams, and Ted Sachs, attorney for the UAW, 1990.

reorganize the department and root out corruption. Progress was slow, but, in time, more blacks were recruited, and the incidents of police brutality decreased.

With respect to corruption, George Edwards was concerned with the influence of the Mafia within the police department. Perhaps the best illustration of this was the method he used to raid the Gotham Hotel, which stood across from Harper Hospital on John R Street. In order to protect the secrecy of the raid, Edwards worked closely with the one man in the force whom he knew he could trust, Vince Piersante, the chief of detectives. They handpicked a busload of policemen, and only after they were on the bus headed for the Gotham Hotel did they brief the men on the objective of the raid. When the police arrived at the hotel, they found all kinds of illicit activity, from numbers and other forms of gambling to prostitution, in full swing and operating openly. There were many arrests and a corresponding impounding of equipment. Eventually, there were prison sentences and a cleanup of the police department.

The Gotham Hotel was ultimately demolished. Later, George Edwards would testify in Washington about Mafia influences in Detroit at the hearings conducted by Senator Estes Kefauver's Committee on Corruption.

Two years after the stop-and-frisk meeting, the Reverend Martin Luther King Jr.'s marches and his "I Have a Dream" speech took place first in Detroit in June, 1963, and then in Washington, in August 1963.

It was at this time that Joe Hudson, the relatively new president of the J. L. Hudson Company, called me to discuss possible appropriate roles for him in community relations. Joe became a member of the Urban League board. He told me that I should call him if I felt the need to bring together a group of black leaders and white leaders to discuss community tensions.

Joe Hudson and I organized a meeting of black leaders and corporate leaders in my home in Sherwood Forest where a confrontation took place between black accountant Dick Austin and Louis Seaton, vice president for industrial relations at General Motors. Austin asked if Seaton was aware that no black accountants were employed by GM. Seaton replied that he was not aware of the fact that there were no black accountants employed by GM but vowed to employ black accountants at General Motors immediately if he found Austin's charge to be true. Among others at that meeting were Martin Hayden, managing editor of the *Detroit News;* Lee Hills, publisher of the *Detroit Free Press;* Bob Surdam, chairman of the National Bank of Detroit; Art Johnson, executive director of the NAACP; Ed Turner, chairman of the NAACP; and Damon Keith, at that time president of the Detroit Housing Commission.

About one week later, I joined labor and political leaders in the Reverend Martin Luther King Jr.'s march down Woodward Avenue in a most exciting yet peaceful demonstration in support of human rights.

Much later, Otis Smith, a prominent black jurist and former state Supreme Court justice, became the vice president and general counsel of General Motors. In addition, the Reverend Louis Sullivan, an outspoken black clergyman, was elected to the board of directors of GM.

In the mid-1960s, Bishop Richard C. Emrich, Episcopal bishop of Michigan, working with the Reverend Hubert Locke, a very talented young man, as his professional staffer, established the Equal Opportunity Committee. The committee was composed primarily of corporate executives and lawyers dedicated to pressing businesses to provide greater opportunities for blacks in executive positions. We met for breakfast once a month and succeeded in making significant impact by achieving commitments from corporations to hire or promote black executives.

Because of my personal commitment and the support of the officers and division managers of Winkelman's, we were leaders in developing black store managers and buyers. We stayed in close touch with Francis Kornegay, the executive director of the Detroit Urban League, who referred a number of good candidates to us. Later, we were recognized by the Urban League for our initiatives and commitment.

As a result of my work in connection with the 1967 riots, I received three awards, the Liberty Bell Award from the Detroit Bar Association, a

Stanley with Ben Hooks, national president of the NAACP, and
Tom Turner, secretary/treasurer of the Michigan AFL–CIO, 1975.

Community Relations Award from the University of Detroit, and the Amity
Award from the American Jewish Congress.

In the late 1970s, Andrew Young, Assistant Secretary of State for African
Affairs during the Carter administration, was traveling around Africa and
making what appeared to be anti-Semitic comments. This spurred much
debate and concern. I called Federal Appeals Court Judge Damon Keith to
discuss the issue. We agreed to call a meeting of six black leaders and six Jewish leaders to air our concerns. The meeting was held at the Detroit Club,
where, ironically, none of us could have been members a few years earlier.

Among the participants were Horace Sheffield, the head of the Trade
Union Leadership Council; Dennis Archer, before he was appointed to the
state Supreme Court and well before he was elected mayor of Detroit; Bill
Haber, University of Michigan professor of economics and the international
head of the Organization for Rehabilitation and Training; Art Johnson, vice
president for community affairs at Wayne State University; Tom Turner, an

officer of the AFL-CIO; Alan Schwartz, a leader in the Jewish and general communities; and Federal Court Judge Avern Cohn.

The most difficult issue taken up during that evening was that of university quotas. It was addressed thoroughly and successfully by Bill Haber, to everyone's satisfaction. All present also agreed that close relationships between the black community and the Jewish community were essential.

There is a great and continuing need for open dialogue and candid expression on a variety of issues that are important to both communities. For the most part, our two communities have had a common agenda with respect to civil rights, and while from time to time we may have differences on such questions as quotas, we should not lose sight of our common interests and combined political power to influence public policy.

We regret that the younger generation in both communities does not have the same close associations as we have had. I am proud to say that my son, Roger, has been very active with the black community, going far beyond his father's footsteps in his direct involvement with community leaders on an assortment of issues.

On the education front, my first major community experience came with the so-called Romney Committee established by the Detroit Board of Education with Superintendent Samuel Brownell in the late 1950s. One of the major results of that effort was the recommendation that property taxes be increased to provide more money for public schools.

Until that time, the Chamber of Commerce usually took a shortsighted negative position in opposition to any tax increases. This time, the increase was approved by the voters despite the Chamber's opposition.

A few years later, when Dwight Havens took over as president, the philosophy of the Greater Detroit Chamber of Commerce changed markedly. Under Havens's leadership, the Chamber began to recognize that what was good for the community was good for the Chamber and its members, and that a single-minded opposition to all tax proposals was not in their best interest.

George Romney's leadership of the Romney Committee, when he was chairman of American Motors, led to his initiative in generating the Michigan Constitutional Convention that proved to be the last organized effort to modernize the state constitution. As a result of his experience in the convention, Romney decided to run for governor.

My own experience on the Romney Committee led to my being invited to serve on other evaluations of the school system over the years. These included the Northern High School Study Committee in 1966, established following a series of unfortunate racial incidents at that high school.

Damon Keith, who would later be appointed to the federal judiciary by President Lyndon Johnson and still later to the Sixth District Court

Stanley receiving the American Jewish Congress Amity Award from
Professor Harold Norris (right) and the president of the AJC (center), 1968.

of Appeals by President Jimmy Carter, was appointed one co-chairman of
the Northern High School Study Committee. Ed Cushman, at that time
vice president of industrial relations for American Motors and later vice
president of Wayne State University, was the other co-chairman.

I became chairman of the School-Community Relations Committee.
That committee developed an idealistic but impractical answer to the
burning issue of integration. Our impractical but logical recommendation:
establish a series of high schools on the outskirts of the city, and bus both
white and black children to those schools from the city and from the suburbs.

Over time, busing became an impractical solution to Detroit school
integration, because the city had such a huge proportion of black students.
In connection with the integration of the Detroit schools, I was appointed
to the Federal District Court Monitoring Commission by Judge Robert
Demascio. I served on it for about two years but never had the feeling that
we were making any significant progress.

Ultimately, the Monitoring Commission effort was terminated with no
obvious success. At the same time, public opinion was turning against busing
as an effective means of achieving integration in the public schools.

Neither the black community nor the white community responded
well to busing as the answer to public school integration. And yet to

me, the integration of schools in the Detroit metropolitan area remains a significant public issue. In these days of multiculturalism, exposure of black and white students to each other in an educational setting is more important than ever.

Between the effects of multiculturalism and the concurrent weakness in the Detroit public school system, we are in the process of creating in the city of Detroit another generation of dysfunctional adults. Charter schools and other proposed or experimental schools will not produce the level of general education necessary for some measure of success for the adults of the future, no matter how successful they may be individually.

The people of Michigan have chosen to put huge sums into building prisons to incarcerate our misfit citizens, rather than going to the source of the problem, our system of education, that breeds massive unemployment of young people in the city. Broken homes are another aspect of the problem. Is it really surprising that young people turn to the high-paying drug business and other crime when they can't get honest jobs?

Somehow, society must resurrect the public schools in the city and succeed in providing a quality of education that is meaningful in today's world. This obviously means that school administrators and teachers accept accountability and that the system provide the resources, including retraining teachers and administrators, that are necessary to get the job done. The system of governance is a major problem urgently requiring change.

The revolution in communication technology and advanced computer systems can provide entirely new and more productive pedagogic approaches. These possibilities are beginning to be explored. Stronger leadership for public education must be provided by our universities' schools of education, which seem unusually quiet while the conventional wisdom seems to be that we need an alternative to public education. "Schools of choice" seem nothing more to me than a great cop-out and a vastly oversimplified cliché.

I can only hope that the takeover of Detroit schools by the City of Detroit in 1999, with the appointment of a strong, competent board by the mayor, will have the same positive result that similar action appears to be having in Chicago, where the concept has been in effect for about two years.

The leadership role of New Detroit, and especially of its president, Bill Beckham, has been outstanding in bringing about this change.

At a monthly meeting of the New Detroit, Inc., board while Bill Patrick was its president, during the time when I was filling in for Bill Day as chairman, an emotional argument was taking place. As the discussion became more heated, one of the radical members of New Detroit ran across the room and was about to jump over the table at which we were sitting to get at Bill Patrick. It was a very real crisis!

Without hesitation, I said loudly, "This meeting is adjourned." A remarkable quiet settled over the room, and every one of the thirty or thirty-five members attending the meeting walked silently out of the room. That was the one and only time in my life, in my capacity as chairman of a meeting, that I took such a drastic action. Much to my surprise, it worked. A month later, our deliberations resumed on a more civilized basis.

This incident illustrates the intensity of feelings within the board, the candor level of the discussions, and the emotional desire to fulfill our mission. Unfortunately, the creation of Detroit Renaissance, Inc., in 1970 damaged the effectiveness of New Detroit. The CEOs of the major corporations attended fewer and fewer meetings, and the candor level of the corporate leaders along with the genuine commitment of those leaders to New Detroit were severely damaged.

There were exceptions, including Lynn Townsend, chairman of Chrysler, and Dick Gerstenberg, chairman of GM, both of whom became chairmen of New Detroit; and Tom Murphy, successor to Gerstenberg at GM, who attended some meetings and was particularly articulate when the subject of doing business in South Africa became an issue at New Detroit. Their presence and hands-on participation ensured that the real issues were being addressed.

Bob Dewar, chairman of Kmart, has continued to be very much involved with Detroit while active at Kmart and after his retirement.

Father Malcolm Carron, president of the University of Detroit, became a close friend as well as a colleague during the many years of our association with New Detroit. On one occasion in 1972, he asked me to chair a large fund-raising banquet for the University of Detroit. It was a great privilege and honor for me to do so, particularly since the honorees that evening were Stanley Kresge, Lowell Thomas, and Carl Rowan.

My first task as chairman of New Detroit was to urgently address the question of replacing Bill Patrick, who had informed me that he would be leaving to become a vice president of AT&T in New York. I called a meeting of the business caucus and listened to the suggestions that were offered.

Not satisfied, I called Frank Judge, originally on loan to New Detroit by Ford but now back at Ford, to discuss the situation. Frank, whom I had worked closely with at New Detroit from the beginning, asked if I had considered Larry Doss. I answered positively but suggested he would not be accepted by the corporate leaders because of his leadership role in the Inner City Business Improvement Forum (ICBIF), which wanted no part of New Detroit. Frank advised me that Larry and Henry Ford II had a positive relationship.

That was all I needed. I called Lynn Townsend (of the Chrysler Corporation), the only auto company CEO who happened to be in town at the

Stanley, chairman of a banquet at the University of Detroit (far right),
with (from far left) university president Father Malcolm Carron and
honorees Carl Rowan, Lowell Thomas, and (seated) Stanley Kresge, 1972.

time. Lynn agreed to work with me in the interview process, if Larry would be interested in the job. I called Larry Doss and asked him if he would be interested. Larry deferred an answer until he talked with his ICBIF associates, and then called me back with a positive response.

Lynn Townsend and I were both impressed with Larry, who had just finished preparing guidelines for breaking the Detroit school system down into districts. In ten days time we completed the process so that Larry was named president of New Detroit prior to my departure for Europe on my semiannual merchandising mission. Hiring Larry Doss proved to be the best decision I made while I was chairman of New Detroit.

Complementing Larry was Bob Spencer, vice president of New Detroit. Bob had come in from the Greater Detroit Area Health Council and stayed on for many years until he was tapped as president of the new Detroit Economic Growth Corporation, whose goal was to expand Detroit's economic base.

Early in my tenure as chairman of New Detroit, after Larry Doss had become president, I worked with Robben Fleming, president of the University of Michigan, in setting up a meeting with all the deans of the university. We met at Inglis House, in Ann Arbor, to explore ways in which the strength of the university could be brought to bear on the problems of Detroit.

The meeting was extremely worthwhile. A number of ideas were discussed that could be implemented with the School of Social Work, the School of Public Health, the Law School, and the Survey Research Center. The meeting also had the effect of sensitizing the deans to the problems of Detroit.

The Survey Research Center conducted an annual attitude survey of residents of Detroit and residents of the suburbs and reported on the relation of the findings in each.

A number of years after this meeting, I tried to analyze the relationship of attitudes of black people in the city to the attitudes of black people in the suburbs, but the available sample was not large enough. I was convinced that black attitudes in the suburbs would be very close to white attitudes in the suburbs, just as black attitudes in the city were similar in many respects to white attitudes in the city.

My concept of community is based on *cultural pluralism*, which recognizes the need for individuals to identify with a group, as opposed to the *melting pot* ideal, which did not recognize the strong psychological need for group identification. Today, we are faced with *multiculturalism*, with its emphasis on individual cultures. To my mind, this becomes a kind of group nationalism that is not healthy for the United States. Without strong and continuous effort to develop and enhance broad national unity of mission and purpose, multiculturalism can balkanize our society.

If I seem unduly concerned about multiculturalism, it is because I believe that the term itself does not improve on cultural pluralism. Rather, it suggests a more militant relationship between groups without regard to the needs of the greater society.

It is my very strong view that we cannot survive as a society if we isolate ourselves by creating strong nationalistic enclaves rather than a series of groups representing their views while, at the same time, working together in the national interest.

During my year as chairman of New Detroit, Wayne County Community College (WCCC) developed very serious management problems. My response was to call together the presidents of the major universities in the state to discuss the problem and to develop possible solutions. We had a dinner meeting at the Standard Club to which we invited several trustees of the college including, especially, Don Thurber.

The presidents of Wayne State University, the University of Michigan, and Michigan State University were all present. When the evening ended, it was recommended that I talk to Al Pelham and request that he take over the management of WCCC.

Al had been one of the most competent individuals in Michigan on the subject of fiscal policy matters, and, in addition, he had a reputation as a most effective manager. We had known each other for a number of years. I persuaded Al to come out of retirement and become the interim president of WCCC.

Al Pelham was a fortunate choice. Before long, he had the college back on a constructive track, operating on a tight but balanced budget. In the process, Doris and Al Pelham became good friends with Peggy and me. That friendship was to grow stronger about a year later.

Lynn Townsend, who succeeded me as chairman of New Detroit in 1972, even as he continued on as chairman of the Chrysler Corporation, called me one day and asked if I would chair a new High School Study Commission that would be charged with solving the immediate problem of an $80 million deficit in the current fiscal year. In addition, the committee would be charged with evaluating the management of the system, the effectiveness of teaching, and ultimately the curriculum.

My wise answer was to turn down the chairmanship, because I did not have sufficient experience in dealing with the legislature. Instead, I suggested that I would happily accept the role of co-chairman provided I could prevail on Al Pelham to come out of retirement once again to be the other co-chairman.

Lynn Townsend accepted my proposal, and Al Pelham agreed to work with me. It was agreed that Al would be primarily responsible for the outside work, while I would work with the staff on the inside. The commission

Peggy and Stanley with Al Pelham at Stanley's fiftieth birthday reception, 1972.

began to function in December 1972. My confidence in Al was immediately justified when State Senate Bills 1 and 2 in 1973 funded the deficit. We were off to a remarkably good start.

In the beginning, the school board was very cool to the commission. We did have the support of Charles Wolfe, the superintendent, and Stuart Rankin, an assistant superintendent who worked very closely with us in providing competent advice and arranging for various meetings with administrators and teachers.

Art Jefferson, who had been involved with New Detroit and would later become the superintendent succeeding Wolfe, also worked closely with us. Aubrey McCutcheon, the assistant superintendent for personnel, was another major supporter. After an acrimonious beginning, the members of the Board of Education became much more receptive.

Money to support the work of the task force was an immediate problem, although New Detroit, the McGregor Foundation, and the Kresge Foundation provided help almost immediately. For our major source of funding, we focused on the Ford Foundation, which in those days had a separate Detroit Fund.

During the discussions and negotiations, I met with Jim Kelley in the Ford Foundation Building in New York on East 42nd Street. The building itself, with its huge atrium, provided a marvelous setting. We arrived at a figure of seven hundred fifty thousand dollars to fund the task force and, with the money in place, turned our attention to finding a very competent executive director. Jim suggested that we contact Vern Cunningham, the dean of the School of Education at Ohio State University.

Al Pelham and I talked with Vern Cunningham, and Vern met with a number of people in Detroit. In short order, we hired him and he resigned his position at Ohio State.

In the first year, we focused on the financial problems of the system and on its management. Charles Fisher, later to become chairman and CEO of the National Bank of Detroit, worked on finances with Pelham. In addition to getting the legislature to fund the deficit, the committee worked with the staff of the schools and the board to put in place a new financial management system and a new chief financial officer, Clem Sutton. Sutton was committed to the proposition that the schools would operate on a balanced budget and that he would provide close supervision of the budgeting process.

To chair the management committee, I called on Doug Fraser, the president of the United Auto Workers, whom I regarded as one of the best managers in Detroit. Of course, Fraser would have the kind of labor relations sensitivity that was desirable to keep Mary Ellen Riordan, the president of the teachers union, working in a constructive role within the task force and at the same time permit the questioning of all aspects of management. Since the administrators were also members of a union, Fraser's sensitivity was particularly important in looking into the entire management process.

It did not take long to realize that the management system contained a fundamental flaw. Excellent teachers were promoted to the position of assistant principal and then principal with no management training whatsoever. The result was the loss of excellent teachers and the appointment of incompetent managers.

In the second year of the task force, Dr. Ethylene Crockett joined Al Pelham and me as a third co-chair. Ethylene was a noted gynecologist and the wife of Congressman George Crockett. Her responsibility was curriculum and the effectiveness of teaching.

My primary role was to organize and then conduct the meetings of the steering committee (or executive committee) and the monthly meetings of the entire task force. This was an interesting challenge, especially because we were working with a very diverse group, in some ways similar to New Detroit itself.

More than twenty years later, the administration of the schools has unraveled once again with educational outcomes nowhere near the level required if we are to avoid approaches that detract from the real problems of public education. The only answer is to provide each and every child with a quality of education that will ensure preparation for jobs, today and tomorrow. Management by objectives must be embraced at every level of management with principals and teachers retrained to accomplish agreed-upon objectives.

Once again, the financial system and its controls have broken down with resulting significant deficits. Once again, New Detroit has ridden to the rescue.

Accountability on the part of administrators and teachers must be the basis of a new and more effective school system. At the same time, the quality of the Board of Education itself must be questioned for its failure to provide improved education within an agreed-upon budget.

Unfortunately, members of the Board of Education, and the board itself, have had the bad habit of interfering in the day-to-day operations rather than holding the administration accountable for resulting educational outcomes. Bill Beckham, currently the president of New Detroit, and the committee working with him have done an excellent job in a very short time. Their work, if taken seriously, will have a very positive result.

Working against the New Detroit recommendations is the historic weakness of the board and the lack of real reportability of the Board of Education to the city or to the state. The system of governance and the reportability of the board are archaic.

While it is possible under present law for the governor to "take over the system," it is not likely to happen, and even if he did, it is not clear that he could bring about needed changes. The education of our children is too important to be left to a single, autonomous, incompetent Board of Education.

Most recently, Governor Engler and the legislature have turned over the management of the schools to Mayor Dennis Archer who, in turn, has appointed a very strong board. With the selection of David Adamany as interim superintendent, bringing to the position very strong leadership skills as well as an understanding of complex management problems, I expect a very positive turnaround.

From the time that New Detroit was formed, I had always expressed my concern that many of Detroit's problems could not be solved without positive action by Lansing and/or Washington. A case in point is the drug problem, which was becoming very serious in the 1970–1972 period.

Lynn Townsend, believing as I did, organized a visit to the head of the Drug Enforcement Administration in Washington to press for more dynamic action on the part of federal authorities. Lynn and I, along with a few others, flew to Washington one morning aboard a Chrysler Corporation jet. We spent most of the day meeting various officials, including the leader of the Drug Enforcement Administration, and then flew back to Detroit. While we came away with the feeling that we had made some progress, it is obvious in retrospect that nothing significant resulted from our mission.

The incident does have a very positive aspect, since it reflected the commitment of time and money by Lynn Townsend and the Chrysler Corporation toward solving Detroit's problems.

The establishment of Detroit Renaissance, Inc., in 1970 led to the Renaissance Center. I was the CEO of a relatively small company, and Winkelman's was not invited to contribute initially, nor was I asked to become a member of the board.

Bob McCabe was brought in from New York to be the president and to manage the commitment to physically rebuild Detroit. Max Fisher, the chairman, and Henry Ford II were the primary leaders along with Al Taubman in this pioneering effort. Planning began almost immediately for the building of the Renaissance Center.

The choice of architect, John Portman, and the basic design turned out to be seriously flawed. The berms along Jefferson Avenue and the elevation of the ground-floor level above the street serve as barriers against people. The design created an environment in which the strong positive effect of this major investment in relation to the surrounding area was not realized in terms of economic growth.

The interior design was, and is, very confusing, and at the same time spectacular, with the huge atrium and green plants as well as the use of natural light. The sameness of the vertically rippled columns and building supports is boring, creating a tendency for people to get lost as they try to find their way among the four towers that surround the hotel.

From the beginning, I was skeptical of the retail space layout and the concept of having higher-priced boutiques that would draw hotel guests and more affluent customers from around the city. I was, however, convinced that Winkelman's could be very successful with traffic drawn from those who worked in the office towers.

With the Renaissance Center in the process of development, in 1972, Max Fisher asked me to become a member of the board of the Metropolitan Fund. Don Young, vice president for community affairs at Burroughs, was the president of the Metropolitan Fund, and Kent Mathewson was the executive director.

The Metropolitan Fund was started around 1970, when the president of Wayne State University, Clarence Hilberry, brought together the chairmen of the Big Three automobile companies and UAW president Walter Reuther to stimulate the birth of an organization that would do urban research geared to the metropolitan region.

Bill Day, the CEO of Michigan Bell, became the first chairman. He was succeeded by Joe Hudson, who was functioning in that role when the New Detroit Committee was formed in 1967. Initially, the New Detroit Committee was a committee within the Metropolitan Fund.

Before I joined the board, the Metropolitan Fund had given birth to SEMCOG, the Southeast Michigan Council of Governments, and also to SEMTA, the Southeast Michigan Transportation Authority. My duties were billed as relatively easy board responsibilities, but it turned out otherwise. The terms of Don Young and Tom Reid, the vice president of Ford who succeeded him, were for the most part routine.

During this time, Kent Mathewson proposed a pair of new towns, one within the city and one outside the city. It was an interesting exercise at a time when new towns such as Columbia, Maryland, were being built, but it went nowhere.

For many years, since I first began traveling to Europe in 1957, I had been concerned with the fragmentation of metropolitan areas in this country. European cities usually had greenbelts around them. When expressways were built, they took the form of ring roads around the cities. This, combined with strict land-use restrictions beyond the city limits, had the effect of confining development and preventing urban sprawl. More important, urban policy prevented the carving up of cities as has happened in the United States.

With my involvement in the Metropolitan Fund, I became very conscious of the more than seven hundred units of government in a six-county area that included Detroit. While at the Delos IX Conference on Urban Settlements in Greece in 1971, I questioned Constantinos Doxiades about this multiplicity of governmental units in a seven-county area in the United States in relation to the structure of European cities, which is much simpler. Doxiades' response was direct and revealing. The European cities were laid out based on how far a man could walk in an hour and how far a horse could go in a day. In Europe, the development of new cities was carefully controlled, whereas in the United States it was chaotic and ultimately related to car travel.

Detroit, with its multiplicity of governmental units, is in sharp contrast to the simple metropolitan government of Toronto. Despite the obvious inefficiencies resulting from so many governmental units, American society has been unwilling to consolidate governments as was done in Toronto. No one is willing to give up autonomy, and no one is willing to face up to the duplication of taxing authorities, police departments, fire departments, housing authorities, and school systems that the present system requires, and at a very high cost.

While I favored then, and still do today, a shift toward metropolitan government, I did not anticipate the strong community reaction against a proposal developed by Kent Mathewson and speaker of the Michigan House of Representatives, Bill Ryan, that, in reality, would have been a very small step toward metropolitan government.

Suddenly, the financial support for the Metropolitan Fund was put in jeopardy by politicians who felt threatened. I decided on a risky but necessary course of action.

Meetings were held with the Big Three and with the UAW. The purpose was to state that funding the Metropolitan Fund was not philanthropy but rather a contribution to an organization working in their interest to help the region operate in a more efficient manner. We were perfectly willing to close down the Metropolitan Fund if we did not find the level of support needed to continue.

At Ford, we met with Henry Ford II and executives with relevant responsibilities. Irv Rubin, who was working with SEMCOG and SEMTA at the time, and Will Scott, the vice president for community affairs, were among the six or seven individuals present. The discussion took about three-quarters of an hour. Henry was supportive and later responded by saying that the concept was valid and that we should persevere.

At General Motors, Tom Murphy, the chairman at the time, invited us to an early-morning meeting of the Executive Committee. All of the members were present except Pete Estes, the president. Since Tom Murphy was a close neighbor, I was able to dramatize my presentation by saying that I had followed GM's chairman downtown that morning. His driver had driven him twenty-five miles through sixteen different communities on his way east on Long Lake Road to Woodward Avenue and then down Woodward to the General Motors Building. I listed the names of all of the political entities and emphasized that each one had a separate school system, separate police and fire departments, and separate taxing authorities.

I pointed out that there was a great deal of cost duplication and that efforts for joint projects and especially consolidation could pay off handsomely. The objective would not be easy to accomplish, but without an organization such as the Metropolitan Fund to pursue it, a positive result was very unlikely. In our favor, but no guarantee of success, was the very tight budget climate of the 1980 recession, which we felt would cause pressure for structural change. After a few days, I received a call from Tom Murphy with an affirmative reply to our proposal that the Metropolitan Fund go through a process of reorganization to get away from the stigma of recent declining support and to reaffirm the purposes of the organization.

We talked in similar meetings with Chrysler and with the leaders of the UAW. After the meetings, the support was unanimous. If the Metropolitan Fund did not exist, we would need to create it in order to deal with a growing array of regional problems.

At the same time, we were advised that the Metropolitan Fund would not be able to immediately achieve the funding level that we proposed because of the recession. In addition, we were compelled to do something to get away from the impression that we were attempting to force a metropolitan government on southeastern lower Michigan. We therefore began a restructuring of the Metropolitan Fund and in the process revisited our mission.

Kent Mathewson decided to retire at this time and moved to North Carolina. Kent continued to be a member of the national umbrella organization for local groups devoted to regional research. He also participated in problem solving in his new local area.

Lou Zimmers, treasurer of Michigan Bell, became chairman of the Metropolitan Fund's Restructuring Committee. Lou did a remarkable job in helping us to sort out both our structure and our direction. Joe Bianco, who at that time was with Hudson's, also played a key role. And, of course, Mike Glusac, the executive director of SEMCOG, played a very important part.

Initially, we considered a tie-up with the University of Michigan-Dearborn campus, in the person of Bernie Klein. Then we considered Wayne

State University when Bernie moved there. Neither seemed quite appropriate at the time. Ultimately, the intriguing possibility of tying up with SEMCOG surfaced.

A SEMCOG tie-up would avoid the kind of conflict the Metropolitan Fund had already experienced. The key question was the matter of the independence of our new organization, which we named the Metropolitan Affairs Corporation (MAC).

After considerable debate, we decided to gamble on the association with SEMCOG. MAC would have no paid staff but would pay SEMCOG for providing the necessary services.

MAC would have the benefit of the SEMCOG perspective, and SEMCOG would have complete knowledge of MAC's plans and activities with the chairman of SEMCOG serving as a member of the board of MAC.

In fact, the arrangement has worked exceedingly well, in no small way because of the strong leadership of Mike Glusac and his successor as the executive director of SEMCOG and MAC, John Amberger. Mike left MAC after a year or two to become the vice president for community affairs at Chrysler, where he succeeded the late Harwood Rydholm. Amberger proved a worthy successor to Glusac. We worked well together and with Dan Murphy, who was the Chairman of SEMCOG at the time.

Harwood Rydholm was a good friend and one of my predecessors as president of the Metropolitan who died prematurely, probably from the strain of arranging the Chrysler bailout by the U.S. Congress. It was during the congressional debate about the Chrysler bailout that I arrived home in the evening to be told that I had received a call from a Bob Dole who asked me to call him at his hotel. Peggy questioned me as to the identity of Bob Dole. I told her that the only Bob Dole whose name I knew was the Senator Robert Dole.

I called the hotel and enquired as to whether Senator Dole was registered. When his presence was confirmed, I asked to be connected to his room. The dialogue was as follows when he picked up the receiver:

"Senator, this is Stanley Winkelman returning your call."

"Hello, Stan, I just arrived from Oklahoma City and have regards from a friend of yours." (He mentioned a name that I did not recognize.)

Embarrassed, I recovered enough to ask, "Senator, what brings you to Detroit?"

"The Chrysler problem," he replied.

"How do you feel about it?" I asked.

"I believe the legislation will pass," said the Senator.

Feeling a great sense of relief I said, knowing that he was the primary opposition up to that time, "If you think it will pass, I'm sure that it will."

He went on to ask if Max Fisher was in town. When I told him that by chance we were having dinner together that evening, he asked me to urge Max to call him, which I agreed to do.

It was in 1983 that John Amberger, Harold Shapiro (president of the University of Michigan), Sam Oakes (Community Affairs officer of GM), and I charted a small airplane to fly us to Mackinac Island so that we could attend the Annual Greater Detroit Chamber of Commerce Meeting.

One of the first issues to come before the newly constituted board of directors of MAC was involvement in economic development. The Greater Detroit Chamber of Commerce was deeply involved in that area, and the question of duplication of effort was thoroughly discussed, with Hans Gehrke (the chairman of First Federal) and Alan Schwartz both stressing the desirability of MAC, including economic development as an important part of its agenda. Their position emphasized that MAC was the only organization that included representatives of labor, government, and business on its board. Marc Stepp, vice president of the UAW in charge of Chrysler, was a vice president of MAC as well.

Very soon after the agenda for MAC was established, I asked Max Fisher to give me the opportunity to discuss MAC's progress with the board of Detroit Renaissance. I had previously reported to them in an effort to gain support for the reorganization.

I felt strongly that the Detroit Renaissance board was an appropriate forum, since all of the companies represented on the board had a stake in MAC. What's more, this was the one place where all of the CEOs met regularly. Max reluctantly agreed to the first meeting and then, more readily, to the second. By this time, I had become a member of the board of directors of Detroit Renaissance, Inc., myself. It was shortly thereafter that a photograph of the board appeared on the cover of *Fortune* magazine on April 21, 1980.

My initial comments to the board summarized the rapid growth of the region and the lack of growth in Detroit despite the efforts of Detroit Renaissance. This was followed by my suggestion that it was time for Detroit Renaissance to refocus its efforts and look to the region as well as the city. My comment was met by a glare from Mayor Young and the comment, "If you mean that building the addition on Cobo Hall will provide additional occupancy for the hotels in the suburbs, that's OK."

At that point, Phil Caldwell, the CEO of Ford, said, "I never could understand why, if Ford wanted to put up a new plant and could not find the right situation in Detroit, that Detroit Renaissance was not anxious for that plant to be located within the metropolitan area."

The substance of this discussion, along with concern for the fragmentation of chief executive time with our multitude of civic organizations, led to the strategic planning process.

The board of directors of Detroit Renaissance, Inc., shown here on the April 21, 1980, cover of *Fortune*. Stanley is standing in the top row next to Joe Hudson.

At that time, I was serving on the Long-range Planning Committee of Detroit Renaissance with Dave Easlick, the president of Michigan Bell, as chairman. We were all looking for ways to make Detroit Renaissance more effective.

We were also involved in coordinating the major nonprofit organizations, the Chamber of Commerce, MAC, the Convention Bureau, New Detroit, the Economic Growth Corporation, and the Economic Alliance for Michigan.

Detroit has a pattern of special-purpose organizations, each with its own board and mission. In many ways, this has been a good thing. At the same time, the failure to involve labor in the Chamber of Commerce process made the broader structure of MAC necessary in order to deal with regional problems.

The same was true of the Economic Growth Corporation in relation to Detroit Renaissance. Art Seder, the chairman of a pipeline corporation at the time, insisted that the Economic Growth Corporation be a separate entity. It would have been preferable to bring it under the umbrella of Detroit Renaissance, as difficult as that would be with corporate, labor, and government leaders involved in a situation analogous to the relationship between the Chamber of Commerce and MAC.

The Detroit Renaissance agenda had been dominated by the time spent on the annual Formula One Grand Prix automobile race through downtown Detroit and the annual Montreux/Detroit Jazz Festival. Bob McCabe did an excellent job of creating these special events, which resulted in very positive publicity about Detroit as well as the excitement of the events themselves. But then he continued to manage them instead of spinning them off, as has been done more recently.

During this time, as MAC was getting its sea legs, Bob Larson arrived on the scene as the vice chairman of the Taubman Company. I had met Bob Larson in Washington, in 1976, when he and Bob Taubman took me on a helicopter tour of that city as I was evaluating the advisability of opening Winkelman's stores in shopping centers around the city.

Larson was involved in a regional organization in the Washington area. When he arrived in Detroit, I asked him to join the board of MAC. His leadership impact on the organization was very strong as he set about to develop a list of urban issues of the 1980s and then, after he succeeded me as president, established committees of the board members to focus on those issues a few at a time.

One of the first urban issues pursued was venture capital, since there was, and still is, a lack of venture capital in Detroit. Joe Bianco chaired that effort with Professor David Brophy from the University of Michigan, a national authority on the subject, in the role of consultant. The result was a landmark study that emphasized the lack of venture capital available in Michigan and attempted to point out a more positive future direction.

After seven years as president of MAC, I was succeeded by Bob Larson, and I became president emeritus.

We had successfully transformed the Metropolitan Fund into the Metro-politan Affairs Corporation. It was now operating with a strong sense of purpose, with stronger monetary support from its members, and with substantially increased vitality that continues more than fifteen years later.

The Political Realm

As an admirer of FDR, as a humanist, and as a deeply concerned citizen, I was, not surprisingly, very much inclined toward the Democratic Party. From a business perspective, I felt strongly that what was good for Winkelman's customers was good for me personally.

In evaluating the two major political parties, I have long held the view that the Democratic Party has focused primarily on social issues and individual rights, while the Republican Party has focused primarily on business investment incentives and property rights. Republicans have usually been called conservatives or ultra-conservatives, just as Democrats have been called liberals. I find the labels inaccurate and confusing. They become code words for dismissing the thinking of thoughtful people whose only concern is what is good for our society.

The UAW has played a very important leadership role in America with respect to many important public policy issues, including the five-day work week, health insurance, and retirement benefits. At one time in the 1960s, I was proud to have my name on the letterhead along with several leaders of the UAW, urging support for universal health care. To me, it is a national disgrace that millions of people have no health insurance coverage.

In Michigan, the Democratic Party appeared to be dominated by labor during the 1940s and 1950s. This was not the case in other parts of the country, nor is it the case in Michigan today.

My first opportunity to vote came during World War II, in 1944, when Franklin Roosevelt was running for a fourth term as president. The implications of the 1944 election suggested to me that term limitations are a bad idea. It was urgent for the country that FDR be reelected for a fourth term at a critical juncture of World War II. A divisive political campaign was avoided, as were the problems of indoctrination of a new president. Vice President Harry Truman seemed an unlikely successor to FDR, especially with his relationship to the Pendergast machine in Kansas City in earlier years.

It is not hard to imagine the tone of Senate hearings if Truman were appointed to any important government office today, with the kind of personal vendettas that are all too much a part of the Senate's advise-and-consent role with respect to presidential appointments. Yet Truman succeeded FDR easily when FDR died in April 1945 because he was a part of the decision-making process and required very little time to get up to speed as president. Indeed, Harry Truman turned into a great president!

Victory in Europe was achieved within a few weeks. It was then, in late July, that Harry Truman made the difficult decision to drop atomic bombs on Hiroshima and Nagasaki in Japan. This was a high-risk effort to shorten the war with the Japanese and eliminate huge American casualties in the invasion of Japan. Since I was sitting on an LST at Ulithi, headed for that invasion, Truman's decision could well have saved my life.

It was only four weeks after the first atomic bomb in history was exploded at Alamogordo, New Mexico, in early July 1945, that atomic bombs were dropped on Hiroshima and, shortly after, on Nagasaki. The casualties were huge. The Japanese surrendered almost immediately. The war was over, and we would soon be able to return to civilian life.

The development of the atomic bomb was a miraculous scientific and technological breakthrough. It was most fortunate that our scientists and engineers were successful ahead of the Germans, who were frantically trying to build a bomb themselves. Fortunately, too, great scientists such as Albert Einstein, Enrico Fermi, and many others—alienated and subjected to persecution by the Nazi regimes in Germany and Italy—immigrated to the United States or Britain.

By 1948, I was well settled into a new career at Winkelman's, and, as a young activist, I ran for precinct delegate as a Democrat and was elected to my first political office.

My experience at the district convention, which I attended with Peggy Edwards, the wife of George Edwards, at Northwestern High School in 1948, was important and educational. I began to recognize the complexities of our political system and that it was a long, long way from precinct delegate to district chair.

I learned firsthand, at subsequent conventions, about the power of the well-organized UAW in controlling the district conventions where they had the numbers to do so.

There is no question that the Michigan CIO (Congress of Industrial Organizations, which in 1955 merged with the American Federation of Labor to form the AFL-CIO) put together a powerhouse under Gus Scholl's leadership that lasted for a substantial number of years while G. Mennen (Soapy) Williams was governor. Yet that power existed because there was no strong business caucus or other coalition of groups to challenge the CIO leadership. At the same time, Gus Scholl and Walter Reuther had frequent battles over policy and tactics.

While a number of us younger Democrats were elected as precinct delegates, the leadership of many districts was strong enough to keep us out of the decision-making District Executive Committee.

Over the years, I developed great respect for the UAW and warm friendships with many of its members, including the Reuther brothers, Leonard Woodcock, Irv Bluestone, Doug Fraser, and the indefatigable Millie Jeffries. Their strong leadership on the important issues of the day was an important factor in my personal perspective. In 1999, I received a recent photograph of Millie in a Winkelman's coat that she purchased some thirty years earlier and continues to wear.

A portion of my political activity came about through governors' appointments. I was appointed to Governor Williams's Fair Election Practices Commission on which I served from 1956 to 1958. Later, from 1963 to 1967, I was pleased to serve on Governor George Romney's Panel on Ethics and

Stanley and Peggy at a party given by Governor and Mrs. G. Mennen Williams, 1954.

Morals in Government. Both commissions tied in directly to my experience in social action.

There were several state commissions offered by governors that I declined. These include the Fair Employment Practices Commission (FEPC) by Governor John Swainson, the first Michigan Council for the Arts by Governor William Milliken, and the Southeast Michigan Transportation Association by Governor Milliken. In each case, I was concerned about the time commitment and my ability to do a credible job.

In 1986, my friends Roy Slade (the retiring chairman of the Michigan Commission on Art in Public Places) and Bill Kessler (the architect of the new Michigan Library, Archives, and Historical Museum), who was chairman before Roy Slade, twisted my arm to replace Roy as chairman as his term of office was expiring. After several discussions with Governor James Blanchard and his wife Paula, I accepted the appointment. It was fortunate for me that E. Ray Scott, executive director of the Michigan Council for the Arts, was transferred to the Commission on Art in Public Places. (Before Blanchard decided to run for governor, Roger and I met with him in an attempt to dissuade him, since we felt it important for him to keep his influential position in the House of Representatives.)

Ray was disappointed at being removed from the more prestigious Michigan Council for the Arts, where he had served from its conception. At the same time, Ray had committed the unforgivable political error of keeping a photograph of Governor Milliken on the wall of his office, instead of replacing it with one of Governor Blanchard. Because of the switch to a Democratic governor, Ray, an extremely competent executive, was being demoted to staff a commission that had worked informally and without staff during the commissioning and creation of the monumental Heizer sculpture on the plaza behind the Capitol Building in Lansing. Money for the Heizer sculpture was raised privately. However, with the need to provide important art for the new Michigan Library, Archives, and Historical Museum building, a small staff and budget were approved by the legislature. E. Ray Scott came on the scene to make it effective.

During my tenure as chairman of the commission, we decided that an inventory should be taken of all state-owned art and that a catalogue should be published that would serve as a tourist attraction possibly in conjunction with the AAA motor club. We received support from the legislature based on the realization that it had a fiduciary responsibility.

Diane Kirkpatrick, head of the Art Department at the University of Michigan, became the editor and I was prepared to raise the money for the catalogue's publication. In a meeting with the director of the Grant Committee at the Getty Museum in Los Angeles, I was told that the Getty had great respect for the Wayne State University Press and that the Getty would help with the funding. Unfortunately, after all of the work in preparation for the catalogue, including sending photographers around the state to photograph the works on site, it all came to naught with the election of John Engler as governor. Governor Engler replaced the commission and the project was dropped.

Having retired from Winkelman's in 1984, I looked forward to working with this commission and to jousting with Bob Naftaly, the budget director under Governor Blanchard. Naftaly had made a reputation for himself as "Dr. No." He and I were friends, however, which helped a great deal.

Over the years, most of my political activity was in support of candidates with small dollars and some work on their behalf, beginning with members of the city council in the early 1950s.

The Adlai Stevenson presidential campaigns of 1952 and 1956 were great intellectual exercises. Our leader was a man with tremendous intellectual capacity but insufficient charisma to be successful against General Dwight Eisenhower, the great World War II hero. The highlight of the 1952 presidential campaign for us was the art auction held at Ben Goldstein's Yamasaki-designed house in Birmingham.

By 1960, the Democratic Party leadership had moved toward the young and charismatic leader John Kennedy. Soapy Williams, from the more liberal branch of the party, created an unsuccessful rebellion of "young turks" at the convention that year in an effort to win the presidential nomination for himself. As a matter of fact, it was our friend Don Thurber who brought Williams and Kennedy together on Mackinac Island in an effort to work out a truce between them. The rebellion failed as Kennedy won the nomination and went on to win the election. Kennedy's assassination in November 1963 moved Vice President Lyndon Johnson immediately to the office of president.

I met Kennedy on only one occasion, at the Michigan State Fairgrounds as he was campaigning in Detroit. My son, Roger, was with me, and we shook his hand.

President Johnson, like Truman before him, rose to the occasion and took advantage of his experience as a congressional leader. While the Vietnam War was a disaster for Johnson, he will be long remembered for his success in having his civil rights proposals adopted by the Congress. The Vietnam War, which had been escalating quietly through the presidencies beginning with Eisenhower, turned out to be the Achilles' heel of the Lyndon Johnson administration.

During Johnson's presidency, the opposition to the war had grown to huge proportions as civil unrest, including the Los Angeles and Detroit riots of 1967 and the shooting of student war protesters at Kent State University in Ohio, created a political disaster. The Civil Rights Act, pushed through Congress by Johnson, was landmark legislation that continues to have a positive effect on American society. But this was not enough to offset the unpopularity of the war.

Johnson's greatest mistake, in retrospect, was his failure to fund the war effort. This failure led to significant inflation and began the process of increasing the national debt, something that was done on a much larger scale by President Ronald Reagan in the 1980s.

Hubert Humphrey, vice president during the Johnson administration and a great liberal leader as a senator, was now tainted by the war through his association with the president's policies. Humphrey was opposed to the war but unable to speak out against it. The result was that Richard "I am not a crook" Nixon was elected president in his race against Humphrey in 1968 after Johnson decided not to run for reelection.

Nixon ended the war in Vietnam. He worked hard to control inflation. And, best of all, he established relations with the People's Republic of China during his second term. Nixon was a strong, irrational anticommunist

Stanley with former President Gerald Ford in
Ford's office in Rancho Mirage, California, 1983.

in the 1950s, when he and Roy Cohn were the counsels for the Investigating Committee of Senator Joe McCarthy. Many careers and reputations were ruined by testimony and innuendo before that committee. Even President Eisenhower was attacked as being soft on communism.

If anyone else had recognized China, Nixon would have attacked them mercilessly. But Nixon was, above all, a pragmatist, and he realized that the time was right to act. He did so with great flair, and his action was widely applauded.

But in his heart, Nixon was a crook, and this was his undoing. Nixon's role in the Watergate affair violated the law and violated the sense of decency of most Americans. Nixon's growing paranoia and concern with his enemies caused him to be a part of the illegal break-in and theft from the Democratic Party headquarters. With impeachment action pending in the Congress, Nixon chose to resign.

Richard Nixon had come to Detroit in 1971 to hold a press conference at Cobo Hall with seven thousand people in attendance. Since I was chairman of New Detroit, I was given the opportunity to ask several questions. Nixon, in essence, evaded my questions regarding the administration's policy toward the cities, with well-rehearsed general answers that did not respond to the more specific issues I was raising.

After Nixon's resignation, Vice President Gerald Ford moved into the

Oval Office and did a good job until the election of 1976, when he was defeated by Jimmy Carter. Peggy and I have been friends of Gerry Ford since we met at Ramona Park, near Petoskey, when Ford was running for reelection to the House of Representatives in 1956. We have shared strong feelings of mutual respect, despite our political differences, and have met from time to time over the years, once at the Aspen Institute where Ford was on a panel discussing foreign policy. We met again in Ann Arbor when former Presidents Ford and Carter conducted a seminar on foreign policy. And we met yet again when Ford was co-chairman of the Campaign for the University of Michigan with GM chairman Roger Smith as the other co-chair. On that occasion, he suggested that we call him when we came to Palm Springs.

In December of that year, at President Ford's request, we called and met with him at his office in Rancho Mirage, California. We spent almost an hour together discussing recent history and especially President George Bush's political position in opposition to abortion. The Fords were good friends of Helen and Bill Milliken, our former Michigan governor, and we were told that they all (including Betty Ford) were pro-choice, as was Barbara Bush.

We also discussed the confrontation between former Governor Milliken and Governor John Engler at the annual Governor's Arts Award Dinner in

Stanley and Peggy with Senator Don Riegle in the senator's Washington office, 1977.

Detroit regarding state support for the arts, which Engler was in the process of eliminating.

At a later time, I asked Gerald Ford to become the honorary chairman of the Friends of the University of Michigan Library, a position he readily accepted.

Jimmy Carter had defeated Ford in the presidential election of 1976. I was invited to the White House in 1978 during the Carter administration to participate in a regional briefing on the Panama Canal. Sol Linowitz, who had been chairman of the Tennessee Valley Authority (TVA), was the president's point man on the subject. President Carter and Linowitz conducted the meeting in the State Dining Room. President Carter spoke about the pending transfer of the Canal to Panama and met each of us individually. J. P. McCarthy, the radio talk-show host, and Erma Henderson, president of the Detroit City Council, were also present. Peggy and I had visited Washington in 1977, at which time we met with Senator Carl Levin and Senator Don Riegle.

The next time I met Jimmy Carter was at a small breakfast meeting called by Henry Ford II to raise money to support the Carter Presidential Library after Carter was defeated by Ronald Reagan in 1980.

Reagan was nominated at the 1980 Republican Convention held here in Detroit, the Host Committee for which I, a Democrat, was a member. During the course of the convention, Peggy, Roger and I had the opportunity to meet many of the Republican dignitaries including Reagan, Al Haig, and Alan Greenspan, as well as a number of senators and representatives, at various receptions. We also had marvelous seats for the convention sessions.

The Reagan presidency was a great victory for the radical right, the "ultra-conservative" wing of the Republican Party. The arms buildup against the Soviet Union worked well with the collapse of the Soviet state in 1989. The Reagan tax cuts, benefiting primarily the wealthy, created huge deficits as a consequence of his unwillingness to pay for the increase in armaments. The extraordinarily large deficit caused reductions in important social programs that all but obliterated the so-called safety net that had protected our less fortunate citizens since the time of President Franklin Roosevelt fifty years earlier.

With the 1984 election in the offing and Walter Mondale the front runner for the Democratic Party, Senator John Glenn, who had gained fame as the first astronaut to orbit the earth (and would do so again in 1998 as the oldest astronaut), announced his candidacy in April 1983. Peggy and I were attracted to John Glenn as an alternative to Mondale, whom we felt could not be elected. We were in touch with Glenn's staff and at their request organized a meeting in the inner city of Detroit so that Glenn would have an appropriate forum to highlight the failures of the Reagan administration

Erma Henderson, Irving Bluestone, Stanley, and Mayor Roman
Gribbs at the White House for a hearing on the Panama Canal, 1979.

and discuss his proposals for revitalizing cities. The luncheon that day with
Peggy sitting next to John Glenn was an exciting affair, as was the meeting
at St. Patrick's High School across Parsons Street from Winkelman's main
office. Unfortunately, Senator Glenn did not become the Democratic Party
nominee, and, of course, Reagan was reelected.

While I felt that each administration had made at least some small
contribution to the betterment of American life, there were some highlights,
both positive and negative, in addition to those already mentioned.

President Truman's recognition of the State of Israel in 1948 had a profound and positive impact on Jews and Judaism. Israel would provide a home
for the refugees and survivors of the Holocaust. Israel would also provide a
focus for Jewish people around the world, many of whom had been victims
of anti-Semitism. In the United States, the anti-Semitic ravings of Father
Charles Coughlin, Henry Ford, and Charles Lindbergh were put behind us.

In connection with Israel, President Eisenhower moved much too
quickly to counter the invasion of the Suez Canal by the French and British.
The course of history in the Middle East would, in all probability, have been
more positive for Israel had he delayed his response to their action for just
a few days.

Jack Kennedy had his disaster in the failed Bay of Pigs invasion of Cuba.

Peggy and Stanley with Technion honoree Bill Davidson and General Al Haig, 1984.

On the other hand, Kennedy's handling of the Cuban Missile Crisis was salutary. His firmness and resolve under fire can only be admired. Only recently has Robert McNamara, Secretary of Defense under Kennedy, expressed doubt about his role in expanding the Vietnam War during the Kennedy administration.

No one else has had the courage to face up to the fact that it may have been possible to negotiate with Ho Chi Minh and thereby avoid the disaster that would seriously polarize the United States and intensify an already unpopular war. The "domino theory" that was the conventional wisdom of the day emphasized that the U.S. position in Asia would be seriously undermined if we were to lose Vietnam.

More important, the domino theory stated that the collapse of one country would necessarily lead to the collapse of others, like a line of standing dominoes being pushed from one end. It was later realized, after thousands of lives were lost in a war we could not win, that communism was not, in fact, monolithic and that each communist country was to some degree independent of the others. This new thinking made the domino theory obsolete and brought into question the entire Vietnam strategy, beginning with Eisenhower in 1954.

Yet, even today, almost forty-five years later, it is difficult to believe that Dwight Eisenhower would not stand up to Senator Joe McCarthy's hysterical anticommunism. Public opinion, as well as the opinions of the leadership in the United States, visualized Soviet Russia in a position of control over all of the communist nations in the world at that time. This attitude prevailed until the mid-1980s as the position of Soviet Russia began to collapse when faced with the huge U.S. arms buildup generated by the Reagan administration.

As successor to Ronald Reagan, George Bush was a bland leader whose "Read my lips, no new taxes" was his downfall. George is a fine man but not a charismatic leader. As far as taxes are concerned, we need the taxes that will support the government programs that the people of the United States want supported. The phrase "no new taxes" is a cliché designed to generate an emotional response rather than a thoughtful one. It goes along with "deregulation," a code word that avoids the question of "appropriate" regulation.

Closing out the century in the White House, we have the brilliant, very charismatic, and at the same time stupid Bill Clinton. President Clinton is the product of our political system that makes it difficult, if not impossible, for those who would be the best candidates. The system, unfortunately, brings into focus all of the personal weaknesses and mistakes made by candidates and those elected to office. Clinton, unfortunately, betrayed the public trust with his sexual escapades. On the other hand, he has done a brilliant job with the economy, and overall he has been effective both domestically and overseas as well. Bob Rubin, his Secretary of the Treasury, has done an outstanding job.

I feel a major concern for the polarization of American society and the acceptance of hypocrisy as a fundamental social value. At the same time, nothing could have been more shocking than the actions of President Clinton in terms of his sexual activities over many years and the lies that he used to cover them up.

It is symptomatic of the times that support for Clinton's presidency has been at an all-time high despite the fact that he was impeached by the House and then wisely cleared by the Senate. The hypocrisy on the part of the Republican members of the House was unbelievable as they attempted to make his personal behavior meet the constitutional grounds of high crimes and misdemeanors. In addition, the media overplayed the situation to the detriment of everyone—all of which made the United States look foolish to our friends around the world.

As for the new millennium now upon us, and the long-term future, it should be obvious to everyone that confidence in our elected officials must be restored and that trust must be a fundamental value if the United States is to survive.

On the local scene, I have worked to support many candidates for mayor, beginning with Jerry Cavanaugh in 1961. Only one of the candidates I have supported was not elected, and that candidate was Dick Austin. I felt strongly that it was time to elect a black mayor in Detroit in 1969. The best candidate, black or white, in my opinion, was Dick Austin. I worked hard for Dick and made several speeches on his behalf. Roman Gribbs, the sheriff of Wayne County, ran against Austin and won the election by a narrow margin. It was a bitter disappointment for me. But, for Dick Austin, defeat was a blessing. At the next state election, he was elected secretary of state, a position to which he was reelected five times along with both Democratic and Republican governors. Austin was finally defeated by Candice Miller.

Four years after Gribbs was elected, Coleman Young, a state senator who grew up in Detroit's Black Bottom, was elected mayor. Coleman Young was a charismatic man of the people, and especially of his people, the African-American community. I not only worked for Coleman's election, but we became good friends during his first two terms as mayor. Coleman had the guts to stand up to the abusive Senator Joe McCarthy during the senator's hearings on communist involvement in government, the entertainment industry, and in society generally.

In his first two terms, Coleman was fabulous. He worked hard and had a competent, well-qualified staff that included both black and white members. Coleman did everything a white mayor would have tried to do, but he did it better and with solid citizen support. Coleman Young balanced the budget and worked closely with Max Fisher, Henry Ford, and Al Taubman in the development and building of the Renaissance Center. He created a positive environment in the city of Detroit. The police department was no longer the army of occupation. Under the leadership of Police Commissioner George Edwards, the police were dedicated to working with the people who lived in the precincts in an effort to control crime.

Years later, after George Edwards had completed a distinguished career as a judge on the Sixth Circuit Court of Appeals, in 1980, I was in Lansing for a meeting of the Michigan Commission on Art in Public Places when a portrait of George was being hung in the Supreme Court chambers.

The mayor's primary mistake from the beginning of his tenure was his failure to reach out to the suburbs as a statesman in an effort to create one metropolitan community. This mistake became more apparent in his third and fourth terms. By that time, the quality of Young's staff had deteriorated, and the mayor appeared complacent in his job, more like an absentee landlord than the mayor of a great city.

During the Carter presidency, Coleman Young worked closely and productively with the White House and the Michigan delegation to the Congress. But with the election of Ronald Reagan and Reagan's neglect of the cities, the situation turned from positive to negative in Washington.

Stanley talking with Kathy and Mayor Roman Gribbs
and an unidentified man (shaking Kathy's hand), 1972.

Coleman Young had the capacity to become a truly great man, but somehow he lacked the vision and the desire to achieve that status. Coleman was charming. Coleman was capable. But Coleman failed to rise to the occasion and to use his strong leadership ability to unify southeast Michigan and then go on from there to higher political office as governor or senator.

We are most fortunate and filled with great pride to have our son, Roger, deeply involved in the community and in Democratic Party politics, where he is currently the treasurer of the party. Roger has a strong commitment to social justice and to bringing people together, Jews with gentiles, whites with blacks, Jews with blacks, and Jews with Arabs. Roger has worked with Coleman Young, with members of the Detroit City Council, and with Coleman's successor, Dennis Archer. In addition, Roger has been involved with elected and appointed officials at every level and with all three branches of government in the state.

Dennis Archer, elected to succeed Coleman Young in 1993, has a much broader vision. Dennis's attitude, when I first met him at one of the black and Jewish leadership meetings that Judge Damon Keith and I had put together, came across as quite militant. His outlook broadened as his leadership role grew from state Supreme Court justice to mayor of Detroit.

Dennis Archer today is a broad-gauged man who recognizes the need to bring Detroiters together no matter where they live. Roger and I met with Dennis prior to his election to talk about the problems of Detroit and our perspective in relationship to them.

Under Archer's leadership, the climate of the city has changed for the better, and investment dollars are flowing into the city, whether through the federal Empowerment Zone or from private sources.

The move of the General Motors World Headquarters into the Renaissance Center, along with the purchase of the RenCen by GM, will revitalize not only the Renaissance Center but also the entire waterfront.

At the same time, Chrysler has invested more than $6 billion in revitalizing its Detroit plants. Bob Eaton, CEO of Chrysler, has been providing strong leadership for Detroit Renaissance. Bob's strong personal, public commitment is unique on the part of corporate leadership and sets an example that has been sadly lacking. About two years ago I wrote an op-ed piece in the *Birmingham Eccentric* newspaper urging greater personal participation by our corporate leaders and praising Eaton's contributions in the city as though I were his press agent. Unfortunately, the merger of Chrysler and Daimler-Benz with headquarters in Germany will, in all likelihood, if history is any guide, bring an end to Eaton's participation. I hope that my prediction is in error.

Over at the Detroit Economic Growth Corporation, Bob Larson, who succeeded me as president of the Metropolitan Affairs Corporation, has recently retired as chairman. Larson has been providing strong support for the mayor and attempted to break through the red tape and roadblocks that the Archer administration has experienced with city employees in its economic development activities.

Casinos and stadiums do not fit with my conception of a "New Detroit." Casinos create the wrong environment for a progressive city. Because it appeared that casinos would become a reality, I did testify at a Gaming Commission hearing that although I am opposed to casino gambling in Detroit, the commission should ensure that a substantial portion of the profit would be committed to community development.

While I have no quarrel with a new stadium or two, I do object strenuously to investing public money in them, since they add very little to the economy, while, at the same time, they add immensely to the financial wealth of the owners. It has been a long time since sports were sports and entertainment was a separate field. Today sports are entertainment, with unrealistically high salaries and little if any sportsmanship.

Because of the dominance of television as a medium for entertainment and, in many respects, its ability to provide intricate detail and analysis of sporting events in slow motion through instant replay, teams are able to pay huge amounts to their key players. This situation is exacerbated by the power of strong agents and unions representing the players. While I have no objection to the players getting all that they can get, I do object to the astronomical amounts of money involved, while at the same time—to cite but two examples—teachers and university faculty members are grossly underpaid. Society's values are all mixed up.

The dominance of television is also a major factor in exacerbating the problems of our political system. Television is responsible in a major way for the exorbitant costs of political campaigns as well as the plague of negative attack ads associated with them.

Expensive slogans and sound bites are the order of the day, with little substantive debate along the way. While the polarization of our society cannot be attributed to television, the mass media are a major factor in exaggerating political differences as they trumpet the extreme political positions of various factions. Civility, a treasured and satisfying aspect of life, has all but disappeared.

The many millions of dollars of so-called soft money raised in the 1996 presidential campaign, in spite of laws limiting contributions to individual political candidates, illustrates dramatically the lengths that both political parties have gone to in order to win the election. Soft money, raised by both parties, has supposedly become essential to meet the high cost of television advertising.

All too frequently, soft money has wound up supporting individual campaigns, with personal attack ads at the core of most political campaigns. Just as bad are the efforts of businesses, lobbyists, and wealthy individuals to buy influence at every level of government.

The entire legislative process is being perverted by the extreme, uncompromising positions of antihumanist forces of the extreme right. There are loud cries to turn political power back over to the states, countered by national legislation controlling personal decisions on issues such as abortion. The inconsistency is, to say the least, confusing.

With partisan politics so predominate, the concepts of civility and statesmanship are much too rarely utilized in the "debate" on various issues. Lobbies carry too much power and manage to buy votes through their support of particular candidates.

Meanwhile, the strong pressures for deregulation from conservative Republicans fly in the face of increased need for regulation, whether it be the inspection of fish and chicken, fees for the use of ATM machines, or fraud in Medicare.

Our society continues to require law enforcement officers to keep honest people honest, including areas of white-collar crime. Doing away with regulation will result in chaos and a gigantic increase in fraud and other crime.

The focus should not be on the code word *deregulation* but rather on *appropriate* regulations that meet today's needs.

What regulations are needed for cyberspace, one of the newest and most revolutionary technological developments with huge future potential? The cry for "no regulation" will prove to be absurd. But, again, what would be appropriate regulation? Should there be regulation with respect to pornography? Fraud? Should there be taxes on cyberspace transactions?

Airline deregulation was supposed to increase competition, but what has resulted is the development of monopolistic airline hubs that limit competition and keep airline ticket prices high. The question is not regulation or deregulation. Once again, it is a question of appropriate regulation.

Recently, I was asked by newspaper columnist Hugh McDermit about the Fair Campaign Practices Commission and the Guidelines for Fair Campaign Practices that I was associated with when G. Mennen Williams was governor of Michigan. It is a good question! The lack of civility and the polarization of society militate against such guidelines. Yet society desperately needs to improve the quality of debate on the important issues and to eliminate personal attacks carried out through television sound bites.

Without substantial improvement in the control of campaign finance and elimination of personal attacks as a fundamental part of political campaigns, we are doomed to seeing the continued deterioration in the quality of political candidates. The most capable individuals will not subject themselves to this demeaning process.

Given my frame of reference, it is easy enough to understand my concern for the effects of twentieth-century technological developments on the quality of life. Today we have problems of drugs and guns that were barely present, if at all, in the 1950s. We have witnessed the breakdown of the family with a huge divorce rate and a lack of personal commitment to making marriages work. We have seen the enormous increase in illegitimate births. And even more important to the future of the country, we have seen our education system deteriorate so that now we have at least two generations with a substantial underclass in our cities coupled with chronic unemployment that feeds the drug distribution system and adds substantially to crime statistics.

The United States has chosen to build more and more prisons and paid only lip service to more and better education that is essential today in our technologically advanced society. We know that per-pupil education costs are substantially less than the cost of incarceration. Yet, despite the din of philosophical alternatives that would further undermine public education, nothing of consequence is happening to mitigate this disaster.

In the face of inflation and higher costs for police—for salaries, equipment, and operating expenses—we have been victimized by cuts in budgets for many years. More recently, we seem to be relearning the lesson that more police on the streets will reduce crime. I was always appalled by the willingness of corporate leaders and Mayor Coleman Young in Detroit to accept lower levels of police protection on the premise that budget cuts were essential.

Yes, indeed, there are gigantic problems related to public finance, to taxation, and to equity in the system. Corporate America now supplies its own policing. The public and especially our poorer citizens cannot do this.

Inflation has taken a terrible toll. It began with Lyndon Johnson, who failed to increase taxes to pay for the Vietnam War. The Arab oil embargo heightened the problem and caused a major devaluation of the dollar.

But it was Ronald Reagan who did the most damage by insisting on huge armament expenditures to protect us from the evil, monolithic communist enemies, without an accompanying tax increase to pay for it. Yes, the Democratic Congress did not provide a balanced budget by cutting the guts out of programs that most Americans considered essential, and Reagan would not agree to increased taxes. As a matter of fact, at the beginning of his administration, President Reagan had pushed through Congress a substantial tax cut that gave huge benefits to the wealthy, hurt the vast middle class, and added significantly to the number of those whose incomes are below the poverty line. It was as if Reagan were purposely trying to undermine the social fabric of the country for the benefit of the wealthy. Trickle-down economics that didn't trickle down was the name of the game.

In 1997, the situation was much worse, with conservative Republicans and the religious right trying to roll back the clock to the days of Herbert Hoover and the Great Depression of the 1930s. Humanism, commitment to the health of the broader society, and civility are all but dead.

Turn government back over to the states but at the same time insist on a constitutional amendment to prevent abortion and establish a national policy that would permanently involve the government with religious doctrine? The philosophical inconsistencies are all too obvious for those who care to see them. These inconsistencies are appalling.

In addition, these same conservative politicians would have us create a new amendment to the Constitution that would require a balanced budget each year despite the human, social, and economic consequences.

And, above all, with great sarcasm I add that access to the President, the White House, the Congress, and the federal bureaucracy should be available only to those willing to pay a very high price. My feelings of sarcasm and cynicism relate to both political parties and to the political process. They are all very disturbing.

6

Culture's Call

Books, the Arts, and
Other Treasures

Jewish culture, Christian culture, Islamic culture, Shinto culture, Buddhist culture, Nok culture, and Benin culture all have been of interest to Peggy and me at various times in our lives.

As Jews, the 5,800-year history of our people occupies a very important and special place in our minds and in our hearts. The development of the Bible with its incredible history and direct ties to the finds of modern archaeology are most exciting.

Bibliophiles

Following Peggy's bent as a bibliophile, member of the AIB in Paris and the Grolier Club in New York, we have viewed many manuscripts, beginning with the Dead Sea Scrolls in Jerusalem. In Vienna, we examined the Joshua Scroll produced in Cairo in the tenth century. In Copenhagen, we were privileged to view a magnificent, illuminated twelfth-century manuscript by Maimonides.

In addition, we have examined many Haggadahs, including the Rylands Haggadah at the John Rylands Library in Manchester, England, as well as several others from Spain and Portugal at The British Library. With the AIB, we have attended meetings in many places including Stockholm, Copenhagen, Manchester, Istanbul, Los Angeles, San Francisco, Prague, Budapest, Paris, and The Hague. At the same time we have made many friends with whom we meet on our visits to Europe and with whom we meet whenever possible in the United States.

Among those friends are Mirjam Foot, in charge of all the books in The British Library, and her husband, Michael, a noted military historian. We arranged for Mirjam to lecture to the Friends of the University of Michigan at the Hatcher Library and for Michael to meet with the history faculty at the university when they stayed in our home one January a few years ago.

In Paris, we stay in close touch with Dr. Andre Morel, whose lovely wife Janine died recently; with Antoine Coron, the director of the Rare Book Reserve at the Bibliotheque de France; and with Marie Bullion, who has retired from the Bibliotheque de la Arsenal. Fred Adams, former president of the AIB and retired director of the Morgan Library in New York and his wife Mary-Louise are another couple we see in Paris.

Other London friends are Jean and Anthony Rota; Anthony was the president of the International Association of Booksellers. They, too, stayed in our home during the visit when Anthony lectured to the Friends of the University Library at the University of Michigan, based on an invitation that we had also arranged. The Rotas' devotion to opera provided the opportunity for us to meet them in Santa Fe in the summer of 1993. Peggy and I arrived a few days earlier to visit the nearby pueblos and Los Alamos. The experience and our two brief meetings for dinner and opera were marvelous except for the fact that the night before their arrival, I fell into the dirt on the grounds of one of the pueblos and spent the evening in the hospital. It was fortunate that my former competitor, Ernie Schwartz, former president of Albert's stores, insisted on taking me to the hospital. He was marvelous! His sense of humor kept us in stitches as he waited with us while I was cleaned up and sterilized. He even insisted on taking us to a pharmacy and then back to our hotel at 1:10 in the morning.

In terms of Jewish religious objects, during the 1960s we were privileged to see the collection of Chinese-Jewish religious objects from Kai-Feng-Fu at the home of Oxford University Professor Cecil Roth, the famous historian. The Scroll of the Book of Esther was spectacular, with the calligraphy in Hebrew and Chinese illumination surrounding the text. The scroll dates back to the early nineteenth century. A synagogue attributed to the "lost Jews" of Kai-Feng-Fu was built there in 1652.

We had lunch with Cecil Roth at a restaurant on the Oxford campus prior to visiting his home. His books on Jewish history and Jewish art speak for themselves, while his speech at lunch was practically unintelligible because of his soft-spokenness and mumbling with a pronounced accent, aggravated by the background noise of the restaurant.

On a more contemporary basis, we own a copy of the Old Testament that was printed in German and Hebrew in 1863. It is illustrated by the French artist Gustave Dore and was probably printed for Reform Jewish congregations.

The Reform Jewish movement developed in Germany in the last half of the nineteenth century as German Jews began to use the vernacular in their ritual and to think in terms of assimilation. What a rude awakening and shock they received from Adolf Hitler! Two and three generations after many Jews embraced Christianity, they were rounded up by the Gestapo and sent to concentration camps for extermination.

In addition to the historic Haggadahs we have seen and the facsimile of the Rylands Haggadah that we own, we use twentieth-century Haggadahs illustrated by Ben Shahn and Leonard Baskin in our home for the Passover seder. While neither of us can read or speak Hebrew because of our neglected education at Temple Beth El, we do have a keen interest in Hebrew and also in Yiddish.

Yiddish is in danger of becoming extinct as a result of acculturation in this country and in Europe, although efforts are under way to increase its vitality. Our British friends Betty and Sidney Corob have funded a chair in Yiddish at the Oxford Center for Jewish Studies at Oxford University.

My experiences with the members of the secular Vereins and Landsmanschaftens, Yiddish-speaking social organizations, when I was president of the Jewish Community Council from 1959 to 1962, were a marvelous education for me.

I had a firsthand glimpse of the decline of Yiddish in the United States when its use was almost entirely confined to the older generation of immigrants who were gradually dying off. The younger generation was studying Hebrew with a focus on the relatively new State of Israel.

My relationship to Christianity has evolved from the time of the comparative religion course in the Temple Beth El High School in the late 1930s. Most recently, it has come from exposure to books that Peggy has collected along with visits to many libraries and churches.

Religious manuscripts dating from the eighth to the fifteenth centuries at the cathedral in Cologne, Germany, in the Baroque Library at St. Florian Abbey in Austria, at Westminster Abbey in London, and in the Vatican Library shown to us by its director, Father Leonard Boyle, are the most memorable.

The cathedral at St. Denis, outside Paris, has an extraordinary collection of manuscripts and bindings from the days of Charlemagne. As an exciting byproduct of these church visits, I have had the opportunity to photograph many of them.

Peggy has a remarkable Christian religious book, illustrated with many engravings, printed by the Soncino Press, a Hebrew press in the small Italian town of Soncino. *Decachordum Christianum* ("The Ten-String Lyre of Christ"), the greatest masterwork of the press, was published under the privilege of Pope Julius II in Fano, Italy, in the year 1507. The Soncino Press was established by a Jewish family of jewelers named Soncino in 1483 after they were forced to leave Germany and then made their home in Soncino, Italy. In 1488, the Soncino Press printed the first Hebrew Bible—just thirty-four years after the Gutenberg Bible was printed in Mainz, Germany. While the Soncino Press paid homage to the pope and had his support, it was nevertheless forced to move every few years because of anti-Semitism. In 1988, the city of Soncino celebrated the five-hundredth anniversary of the printing of the first Hebrew Bible with an exhibition of all of the books printed by the press at the Sforza Castle. A four hundred-lira postage stamp featuring the first words from the book of Genesis ("In the beginning") printed in Hebrew was issued by the Italian government in honor of the event.

We heard about the exhibition when we visited the Palatina Library in Parma in the spring of 1988. Back in Detroit, Peggy asked so many questions through the Italian consul that the mayor of Soncino wanted to know, "Who are those Winkelman people who are so interested?" The mayor invited us to have dinner with him and his wife in Soncino on our next trip to Italy. Little did he know that we would plan to be in Soncino at the time of the October pret-a-porter openings in Milan in the fall of that year. The hospitality of Mayor Fabamoli and his wife was very warm. Because we were there at noon, rather than in the evening, after a visit to the mayor's office, they took us to lunch at an excellent restaurant. Afterward, we walked to the Sforza Castle, where copies of much of the material that had been on exhibition were still on display. We were given gifts of a page of stamps, copies of first-day covers, and a bronze medal struck to commemorate the five-hundredth anniversary of the Soncino Press.

It was later on this same trip that we met David Vaisey, the Bodleian librarian at Oxford University, and Richard Judd, the man in charge of the Hebraica Collection. Vaisey showed us some of the great treasures of the Bodelian and Judd showed us some of the Hebrew Treasures, including a five-volume series of books printed by the Bodoni Press in Parma by the Catholic clergyman, De Rossi, on the subject of De Rossi's lectures on the old testament. De Rossi had assembled the largest collection of Hebrew books outside of the Vatican, which was purchased by Marie-Louise, then Duchess of Parma, and given to the Palatine Library in Parma.

The technology of printing in 1488 was primitive compared to the computerized typography and printing of today. But the quality of the paper was infinitely better in the fifteenth century, with the result that books from the early days of the printing press are in better shape today than those of the late nineteenth and twentieth centuries despite all of the advances in photolithography and printing methods.

Most of the books of the last one hundred fifty years will disintegrate into dust unless there is very extensive and expensive restoration to rid the paper of its acid content. It has only been in recent years that books have been printed on acid-free paper.

Martin Luther has been of particular interest to us, despite his virulent anti-Semitism. Luther, in his fight with the Catholic church, was the first individual to use the printing press for political purposes. We have a good friend, Maria Von Katte, a librarian at the great Herzog August Library in Wolfenbuttal, Germany, who has made the focus of her career researching and writing about Martin Luther.

A few years ago, we arranged for Paul Raab, the director of the Herzog August, to lecture to the Friends of the University of Michigan Library at the Hatcher Library in Ann Arbor on the subject of the remarkable collection of his library.

John Calvin is another Protestant leader whose career has been of great interest to us, as he compromised some of the extreme positions of Martin Luther and built a much larger and more popular branch of Christianity.

Religious Conflicts

For those who can believe and practice orthodoxy, whether it be Jewish, Christian, or Islamic, there is great peace of mind. At the same time, orthodox political practices have created very negative policies because of the practitioners' beliefs that they, and they alone, have the true path to God.

In Israel, Reform rabbis cannot perform marriages, and Reform Jews, generally, are not regarded as Jews. The fight between the Catholics and Protestants in Ireland and the less toxic arguments between Catholics and Protestants in Quebec are further cases in point.

As for Islam, one need only look at the militant history of Iran since the deposition of the Shah. The attempts of Islamic fundamentalists to impose their orthodoxy on other believers in Allah are but another example of the intolerance of orthodox beliefs.

On a broader basis, religious wars have been all too frequent. Romans against Jews in the first century and the Christian Crusades from the tenth to twelfth centuries are early examples. Battles between Catholic and Protestant countries in the days of the Reformation and the sheer horror of the Spanish Inquisition in the last years of the fifteenth century related not only to anti-Semitism but also to a desperate attempt to reestablish the Catholic church as the only legitimate church. The anti-Jewish pogroms of the Russian czars and the antireligious attitude of the Russian Communist Party in this century are both examples of religious persecution at its worst, whether by believers or nonbelievers. Ideally, religions, in the contemporary world, should generate mutual respect in keeping with the principle they preach of "love thy neighbor as thyself."

The new technology that made warfare easier to wage and killing opponents more efficient has had a very negative influence on humanity, although for more than fifty years since World War II, no one has used an atomic weapon except in testing and development.

We were better off with the spears, bows and arrows, and crossbows of the first millennium than we are today with the great weapons of mass destruction, despite our claim of being more civilized. Technological discoveries and advances are not always friendly.

While wars are still being fought with conventional high-explosive weapons, the great fear today is that a rogue nation or group will blackmail the world by exploding or threatening to explode an atomic bomb or by using deadly biological weapons.

Once again, advances in technology have compounded the risks to humanity and added great tension to life at the end of the twentieth century. While these risks do not relate just to religion per se and the cultures it has generated, they do threaten all religions and all cultures everywhere on earth at a time when religious teaching is being ignored or perverted.

Our exposure to the great religions of Asia, the religions of tribal Africa, and those of Native Americans has come with our visits to Japan, China, Taiwan, Singapore, and Thailand in Asia; Senegal, the Ivory Coast, Nigeria, and Dahomey in West Africa; and the Southwest region of this country.

Of particular interest to us in Africa were our visits to Senefu villages four hundred miles north of Abijan in the Ivory Coast and the Nok culture centered in Ife, Nigeria, dating back almost two thousand years. The Benin culture, from the Nigerian city of the same name, produced the fantastic bronze sculpture in the eighteenth century that has been widely publicized. However, that work was greatly influenced by the Portuguese traders of the time and was not absolutely indigenous, as was the much earlier Nok culture.

Royal Patronage

For more than five thousand years, governments and rulers have been a major source of artistic sponsorship, the alternative to, or perhaps the companion of, religion as a source of cultural development, whether in the visual arts, in crafts, or in the performing arts.

A visit to the tombs of ancient Egypt conveys the cultural impact of the pharaohs of the Old Kingdom and the excitement of the unique artistic talent of that day, whether in tomb wall paintings or in the amazing array of artifacts buried there.

The splendors of ancient Greece and then Rome came almost three thousand years after the early Egyptians. Breathtaking beauty and artistic creativity abound from the days of Charlemagne, some six to seven hundred years later.

And then came the Renaissance patrons, the Medicis, who commissioned some of the greatest paintings and sculptures the world has ever seen. From Palladio in architecture to Michelangelo in sculpture, to Leonardo da Vinci in painting, the quality of life was being greatly enhanced with much of the art being made available to the public.

Henry VIII was a patron, too, when he brought Hans Holbein to England to be a painter in his court.

Manuscripts, with their magnificent illumination and calligraphy, gave the writing of the times a special cultural stamp, from the papyrus records of Egyptian times up to and beyond the birth of printing in the mid-fifteenth century.

The Greek library at Ephesus on the coast of Turkey consists of the remnants of one of the greatest libraries of the ancient world. Ephesus is just one of the many magnificent archaeological sites along the coast of Turkey that Peggy and I have had the opportunity to visit.

The Laurenciana Library, designed by Michelangelo and commissioned by Lorenzo da Medici in Florence, is probably the most beautiful library built during the Renaissance. The manuscripts were hung on chains in front of tables and chairs where one could read them. The reader was brought to the particular manuscript, which was located within the appropriate language section. From the front of the library, the language sections began with Greek manuscripts, followed by those in Hebrew and then Latin.

Before it was common for commoners to know how to read, libraries were very exclusive. Security at the Laurenciana was a definite problem, as even kings were known to have stolen valuable manuscripts.

Fine Art and Fashion

The relationship between the fine arts and fashion design has always fascinated me. While there is no direct cause and effect as a generality and the influences are quite subtle, in some cases, such as the Mondrian-related dress designs of Yves St. Laurent, there is a direct connection.

Beginning with an interest in purely contemporary art, Peggy and I have traveled the route back through history to the arts of ancient Egypt and China with a growing interest in all that is in between as well. As a matter of fact, we have become highly skeptical of the lasting influence of most contemporary art and artists. At the same time, we stand in awe of the great masterpieces of many artists who were a part of the intervening cultures.

The highlights of our explorations of Egypt, Rome, Persepolis, Luristan, Troy, Israel, Istanbul, China, Taiwan, Japan, Korea, and Thailand have already been mentioned. Having been educated as a chemist, I found that my education in history and the fine arts was lacking. But our travels and curiosity have enabled us to learn a great deal and to gain a wonderful perspective, not only about history but also with respect to the arts associated with that history.

Joys of Collecting

Peggy became a trustee of the Detroit Institute of Arts in 1962, where she developed and operated the Museum Shop in its early stages with the guidance of Bill Woods, the director of the DIA. Woods suggested to Peggy that while she was with me in Europe, she should buy some French limited-edition illustrated books, known as *livres d'artiste*, for sale in the Museum Shop. While the books did not sell easily or well, Peggy fell in love with them and eventually bought several as they were being removed from the stock of the shop and sold at auction. This was the beginning of her rare book collection.

Peggy's collection began with the *livres d'artiste* from the very late nineteenth century to the early twentieth and included signed limited editions by some of the most important French artists—such as Bonnard, Picasso, Matisse, Toulouse-Lautrec, and Leger. The major book dealers in Paris would comment that Peggy was the only woman they knew who was looking for books while her husband was looking for fashion. While Peggy speaks French fluently, I do not, and I was always asking why she bought only books written in French; I was hoping she would find some that I might be able to read.

I became very interested in the English caricature artists of the late eighteenth and early nineteenth centuries, including Thomas Rowlandson, George Cruickshank, James Gilray, and, later in the nineteenth century, "Spy," who worked for *Vanity Fair* magazine. Their visual commentary on their life and times is absolutely fascinating to me.

A growing interest in illustrated English books led Peggy to William Hogarth, who in the mid-eighteenth century wrote the definitive book on the aesthetics of the time, entitled *Analysis of Beauty.* There are two large, magnificent engravings folded into the book that illustrate the aesthetic standards of the day. Peggy bought that first edition for her collection.

A short time later, in London, I found a copy of the first Italian edition, published some fifteen years after the first English edition, that had exactly the same plates, engraved on the identical paper.

We also bought a number of William Hogarth's eighteenth-century engravings in the "Rake's Progress" series when we were at the Stratford Shakespeare Festival in Stratford, Ontario.

For many years each summer, we went to Stratford, Ontario, with Leonard Leone, an Elizabethan scholar who was the director of the Hilberry

Peggy and Stanley with Bert and Dr. Leonard Leone, Director of Theatre at
Wayne State University, on the banks of the Avon River in Stratford, Ontario.

Theatre at Wayne State University. Along with his wife Bert, an artist, we
would picnic along the Avon River and discuss the play that we were about
to see.

While Hogarth, Gilray, Rolandson, and Cruickshank were English artists with a great deal to say about the politics of the day, the French caricature
artists—such as Honore Daumier—also had a great deal to say about the
politics of the day.

Our friend Jim Cuno, who is now the head of all museums at Harvard
University and who was previously associated with the Wight Gallery at
UCLA, put together an Exhibition of French Caricature Art in connection
with the bicentennial of the French Revolution. We were privileged to see
the exhibition at UCLA and again at the Bibliotheque Nationale in Paris.

Peggy's book collecting and my knowledge of history are closely tied
together. This is especially true in connection with incunabula, books
printed between 1454 and 1499, such as the *Nuremberg Chronicle* published
in 1493 that reviewed all of recorded history from the creation of the world,
with three pages left blank for future history. It is also true of a myriad of

other books in Peggy's collection as well as for the hundreds of books and manuscripts we have been privileged to view, and in many cases to peruse, in libraries all over Europe and in the United States.

Musical Notes

Music in the forms of symphonies, chamber music, operas, and jazz have also been important factors in our development. There is little new technology with these forms of live music aside from the amplification of sound, which in many cases I find objectionable.

Technological development, on the other hand, has been an extremely important factor for the recording industry, where the recent introduction of digital sound provides the opportunity for better sound quality than the "high fidelity" quality of the recent past. While the pursuit of ever higher quality may be important for professionals, it is probably not worth the expense to those of us who are looking for excellent quality of reproduction, but not perfection.

For many years Peggy and I went to Milan for the pret-a-porter press openings and to shop the boutiques on and off the Via Monte Napoleon. We would often have dinner with Ken Scott, the American designer of printed banlon knit dresses, which were sold by the ton at Winkelman's. Ken moved to Milan, where he designed higher-priced ready-to-wear as part of the pret-a-porter collection. Ken had probably the best sense of color of anyone I have ever known. His assistant in the years before he died was the niece of Louise Nevelson, the American artist.

Opera at the famous La Scala Opera House in Milan is always a fairy-tale experience. For our first opera in that legendary setting, we heard Maria Callas sing Rossini's *La Sonambula*. Two other outstanding opera experiences at La Scala were the Brigitte Nielsen and Franco Corelli gala performance of *Turandot* and the hundredth-anniversary Gala performance of Rossini's *Siege of Corinth*.

The atmosphere of La Scala—from the formally dressed Milanese opera lovers to the elaborate decor of the many tiers of boxes, and especially the Roman numeral clock centered high above the stage—is not duplicated anywhere.

For the gala performance of Turandot, I had called ahead from Florence to arrange the tickets and, knowing that black tie was in order, stopped as we drove into Milan to buy a black tie to wear with a dark business suit as I had done on a number of previous occasions.

The four of us—Peggy and I with two of our merchandise managers—walked in with the crowd. As our tickets were being taken, I felt a hand on my shoulder preventing me from entering. I insisted that the others in our party go ahead and be seated.

Meanwhile, as I waited in the lobby with two or three others who, apparently, had the same problem of not being properly dressed, I could hear the members of the orchestra tuning their instruments. Finally, a guard in elaborate regalia complete with a long sword led us up the stairs to what I thought would be the highest point in the theater. We climbed and we climbed and we climbed.

Finally, as the orchestra began playing the overture, we came out in a room with a very high ceiling that looked down directly on the stage. I, along with the few other improperly dressed ticket holders who had been apprehended, was seated in the royal box, where we were confined for the duration of the performance. At intermission time, Peggy and our guests came up to visit with me.

After *The Siege of Corinth*, we went next door to the Biffi Scala restaurant, where we had supper and talked with Thomas Shippers, the conductor from the Cincinnati Symphony, and with Beverly Sills and Marilyn Horne. What a remarkable evening that was!

By the way, for all other gala performances at La Scala, my black tie and dark business suit worked extremely well.

Aida, in the stadium at Vicenza, was another spectacular experience, with elephants and camels as part of the Grand March. The only discordant note that night was the noise from soccer fans as they passed by the stadium, celebrating Italy's victory in the World Cup.

Almost as spectacular were the opera performances in the Festspielhaus in Salzburg and at the Garnier Opera House in Paris.

In addition, Borodin's *Prince Igor* by the Warsaw Opera at the Theatre Des Champs-Elysees in Paris and Igor Stravinsky's *Rakes Progress* at the Theatre de Chatelet in Paris were both outstanding by virtue of the music, the dancing (Prince Igor), the sets, and the costumes.

Salzburg was another very special experience. With my retirement in May of 1984, I was able to plan a trip to attend the Salzburg Mozart Festival in August. Until that time, my August activities were concentrated on planning Christmas advertising.

We flew to Munich where we spent time in the library as well as the two great museums, the Alte Pinakothek and the Neue Pinakothek. In the Alte Pinakothek we had the opportunity to study the works of Albrecht Altdorfer, the contemporary of Albrecht Dürer at the end of the fifteenth century.

Altdorfer became our focus of study as we prepared for the trip based on a retrospective exhibition of his work that we had seen in Paris some years earlier. Having skipped Germany for almost thirty years because we were uncomfortable with German attitudes following the Holocaust, I had suggested to Peggy that this would be a good time to visit Germany since the strength of the German culture was of interest to us despite the murder of six million Jews during World War II. The Paris exhibition included two engravings of a synagogue, so we decided to study his work with a positive approach.

At the Metropolitan Museum of Art Library in New York, we found a book entitled *Four Hundred Years of Altdorfer Criticism*, which included works that Altdorfer had inspired by Pablo Picasso, Chaim Gross, and a number of other contemporary Jewish artists. Altdorfer's greatest masterpiece is located at St. Florian Abbey, near Linz, Austria. One of the photographs shows an engraving by Picasso, the subject an almost literal interpretation of one of Altdorfer's St. Florian paintings.

From Munich we drove to Regensberg, Altdorfer's birthplace, where he worked as an architect and served as a member of the city council. Our great disappointment came when we discovered that the reason he had done the synagogue engravings was to record the building as an historical record just before it was burned down in 1494 at the time of the Spanish Inquisition.

Salzburg, for us, was an inspirational musical experience with opera, chamber music, and recitals in a town that has an abundance of facilities— from the Mozarteum, to the two Festspielhaus auditoria, to its many churches.

We took side trips to St. Florian Abbey and to two other libraries within a fifty- to one hundred-mile radius. St. Florian itself is a remarkable early gothic series of buildings within the village of the same name. The composer Anton Bruckner is buried under the organ in the church.

We took the tour that included the room containing the fourteen paintings by Altdorfer and the magnificent baroque library. Not satisfied because of the crowd, Peggy made an appointment for us to come back and meet with the librarian.

When we arrived the next day, the librarian, who was also a priest, took Peggy behind the open library and spent a great deal of time showing us tenth-, eleventh-, and twelfth-century manuscripts. When Peggy inquired as to whether they had all been catalogued, the answer came back, "No. No time."

When we asked to see the Altdorfer masterpieces again, the librarian took us to the room and pulled out a huge bunch of keys, such as St. Peter might have carried. After opening the door and turning on the lights, he locked us in the room with the fourteen Altdorfer paintings, which depict the martyrdom of St. Sebastian and scenes of the Passion, while he did something else for the next twenty minutes. There we were, Peggy and me and my camera, alone with fourteen priceless and inspirational Altdorfer paintings. Salzburg had become for us an outstanding center of art as well as opera.

After Salzburg we drove to Melk, the site of another great church and library along the Danube, before driving on to Durnstein, on a beautiful site overlooking the Danube, where we would be staying for several days while we visited Vienna just a few miles away.

In Vienna, Peggy had arranged for us to meet with the world renowned manuscript specialist, Otto Mazal, at the National Library. Mazal showed us many early manuscripts, the most important of which, to us, was the Joshua Scroll, written in Hebrew in Cairo during the tenth century.

While in Vienna we also attended a Mozart opera and a Richard Straus folk opera, and of course we ate our share of Sachar Torte (a special cake originating in Vienna at the Hotel Sachar).

Back at home, for many years, we enjoyed the Metropolitan Opera performances at the Masonic Temple in Detroit each spring, along with the many social events connected with them. We participated as part of the leadership supporting the Met. One year, Peggy and I invited about forty guests to our home for dinner and arranged for a bus to take us to the Masonic Temple for the opera, then back to our home afterward for the afterglow.

Today, the marvelous new Detroit Opera Theater, home of the Michigan Opera Theater, is a technological marvel in terms of reconstruction, refurbishing, and acoustical engineering. It is a monument to the tireless effort of David DiChiera, the director, and the lay leadership headed by Bob Dewar, the former chairman of Kmart.

Many years earlier, in 1970, Paul Ganson, first-chair oboist in the Detroit Symphony Orchestra, set out to save Orchestra Hall. This acoustical marvel, built in ninety days in 1919 for the new Detroit Symphony conductor Ossip Gabrilovitsch, had lain fallow for many years. It did enjoy a brief comeback as the Paradise Theater in the 1950s, featuring such great jazz musicians as Duke Ellington.

The conventional wisdom of the day was very simple: Detroit did not need another symphony hall. Ford Auditorium, which was built as a civic auditorium, was good enough. At the same time, the members of the orchestra understood the vast acoustical difference between Ford Auditorium and Orchestra Hall, even if the corporate leadership did not.

Ganson made his move in 1970 just as a wrecking ball was about to tear down Orchestra Hall to make way for a Gino's restaurant. Fred Campbell, who owned the medical building directly across Woodward Avenue from Orchestra Hall, called to ask me to talk with Ganson regarding his objective to "save Orchestra Hall."

Paul and I met in my office, and I asked him why he thought Orchestra Hall had been abandoned for so many years. His reply was that no one had really tried to save it. Next, I asked why he felt he could save it. Again Paul's answer was direct: he said that he would do whatever was necessary to save it. With that, I promised that Winkelman's would match the first $7,000 he could raise.

In 1974, Frank Stella, who had been an early supporter, became chairman of the Friends of Orchestra Hall and vice chairman of the Save Orchestra Hall Committee, with George Gullen, then president of Wayne State University, as chairman. With the untimely death of Gullen, Stella took on the chairmanship.

An Orchestra Hall—Paradise Theater publication by Save Orchestra Hall dated July 1976 declared that Orchestra Hall had been saved and that it was being reborn. It noted that Orchestra Hall's good neighbor, Winkelman Stores, Inc., "became the first to contribute to the $900,000 goal when Stanley J. Winkelman, President, announced the company's $7,000 gift to Save Orchestra Hall, Inc." While Peggy and I were both members of the Save Orchestra Hall Committee, my personal effort was devoted primarily to working with the neighborhood leaders in creating the Parsons Street Oasis.

This same publication showed a photograph of Fred Campbell with

Stanley with Leon Atchison, governor of Wayne State University; Tom Angott, president of Melody Farms; community leader Frank Stella; and Detroit councilman Jack Kelley, caucusing outside a meeting in 1980.

Paul Ganson and two others as they were rolling out felt in preparation for installation of the new roof. Concerts began on May 23, 1976, with a performance of Bach's "Mass in B Minor" by Detroit's Schola Cantorum. The Chamber Music Society of Detroit and many other groups began using the hall in the fall of 1976.

At the end of 1978, Peggy became involved as co-chair of the "Adopt a Seat" program for Orchestra Hall. The other co-chair of this very successful effort was Gordon Staples, concertmaster of the Detroit Symphony Orchestra.

Fortunately, Paul Ganson was indefatigable in his effort to overcome the huge inertia of conventional wisdom. As Paul began to show progress in getting donations and established the Save Orchestra Hall Committee, he and I took the initiative to begin discussions with Marion Lundy, president of the League of Catholic Women, at the far end of what came to be known as the Parsons Street Oasis, along with Father Duffy from St. Patrick's Church next door and Sister Mary Watson from the St. Patrick's High School building, then a meeting place for the aged in the neighborhood.

As an extra contribution of Winkelman's, I offered the use of the Winkelman's parking lot if Orchestra Hall would provide the necessary supervision and insurance. Winkelman's would provide the lighting. A year after the hall reopened, I asked how much income the parking had generated and was disappointed to learn that a parking fee had not been collected. From that point on, parking fees were charged and more than $10,000 of income yearly was generated by this contribution of Winkelman's.

The city council agreed to changes we had proposed. The city would provide new lighting, and Winkelman's would pave the part of the parking lot that was unpaved, provide a high level of lighting for the parking lot, and create a park area between the curb and a two-foot-high brick wall to separate the park area from the parking area. We provided grass, shrubbery, and park benches in front of the low brick wall, along the street from the alley behind Winkelman's to the last existing house at the end of the block near Cass Avenue. Indeed, working with the city we had created the Parsons Street Oasis, which would stand until the very commercial-looking parking deck was installed after the Winkelman's main office and distribution center was torn down in the late 1990s.

As chairman of the Save Orchestra Hall Committee, Frank Stella provided strong and dedicated leadership that was slowly generating broader community support. The banks were notable for their absence, as were almost all of the corporate leaders in this critical period. It is more than a little ironic that at the dedication of the very beautiful Louise Nevelson sculpture in 1998, Peter Cummings paid tribute to the banks for their role in the construction of the new Detroit Symphony Orchestra Building that now stands where Winkelman's main office and distribution center had stood for fifty years. The banks, so highly praised in 1998, were absent from the Save Orchestra Hall effort.

With Orchestra Hall being slowly resuscitated and improvements being made along Parsons Street, one day in late 1979 or early 1980 I was sitting in my office, which looked west along Parsons Street and north along the alley between the church and Orchestra Hall, when I noticed what looked like smoke pouring out of the north end of Orchestra Hall. I called in the fire alarm and watched as fire engines filled up Parsons Street in a desperate effort to save the hall. As it happened, the fire provided instant urban renewal to the two-story building adjacent to Orchestra Hall and provided room for the amenities, park, and fountain that now fill the space.

It was strictly good timing and luck that permitted the fire department to save Orchestra Hall from being consumed by the blaze. The dilapidated roof, full of holes, allowed firefighters to easily pour water into the building and save it. The consequence, however, was a substantial flood in the orchestra area.

As the renovation continued slowly, once the roof was covered, activity within picked up. An annual ball was held on a platform that extended out over the orchestra seats, with Mitch Miller, a great attraction, helping to raise money as he conducted the Detroit Symphony in what was to become its new home.

I arranged to conduct Winkelman's seasonal store manager merchandise meetings from the stage of Orchestra Hall. This was a great thrill for all of us.

When I had offered the use of Winkelman's parking area, my sole request for my effort was that I be permitted to buy seats in a mezzanine box on a continuing basis if I wanted to buy them.

It should be noted that Leon Winkelman served on the board of directors of the Detroit Symphony Orchestra for about ten years before his death in 1958 and that he was succeeded on the board by my mother, Josephine Winkelman, who served until her death in 1975, following which Beryl Winkelman was elected to replace her.

With the Detroit Symphony Orchestra back in its home at Orchestra Hall and with Winkelman's taken over by Petrie Stores, I felt that I should take the initiative in stimulating Milton Petrie to give the building to Orchestra Hall once Milton had decided to move Winkelman's main office and distribution center out near Plymouth.

My retirement from Winkelman's was somewhat acrimonious from Petrie's point of view because I had successfully challenged the manner in which he was dealing with Winkelman's executives and told him that his credibility with those executives was zero. I therefore decided to call Sam

Frankel to suggest that he call Jerry Schostak, whom Petrie had installed as
chairman of Winkelman's upon my retirement. The result was a gift of the
Winkelman's building to Detroit Symphony Orchestra Hall.

While I have not sought credit for my role or Winkelman's role with
respect to saving Orchestra Hall and being the catalyst for the gift of the
Winkelman's building, it was a source of great embarrassment to me and
other members of the Winkelman family to have the site of the Winkelman's
building referred to as "the site of a bankrupt department store" in the
remarks of Detroit Symphony chairman Al Glancy during the Nevelson
sculpture dedication.

My comments in no way deprecate the role of Peter Cummings, who did
a remarkable job in planning the new facilities in a manner that will provide
financial support for the orchestra, and Lew Spisto, who has operated as
president of the Detroit Symphony Orchestra in a very professional manner.
At the same time, I regret that there is no understanding of the Save
Orchestra Hall Committee and the role it played in providing the symphony
with its home. In addition, I regret that there is no understanding of how
the Winkelman's building happened to be given to Orchestra Hall. Yes, I
do believe that there should have been, and should be, some recognition
of the role of Winkelman's and members of the Winkelman family in the
history of Orchestra Hall and as a part of the Detroit Symphony Orchestra.

The site of a bankrupt department store, indeed! It is always a question
of "What have you done for me lately?" Peter Cummings did arrange for
hanging the bronze relief portraits of I.W. and L.W. on a hallway in the
new Detroit Symphony building. The reliefs were the work of prominent
sculptor and longtime friend Walter Meidner, the head of the Center for
Creative Studies. I had commissioned them and placed them in the lobby
of Winkelman's main office, where they hung for more than twenty years
as a tribute to the co-founders of Winkelman's.

While we enjoy symphonic music in general, and the Detroit Symphony
in particular, we have tended to favor chamber music since the days of the
Stanley Quartet that played at the Rackham Auditorium. Next came the
Chamber Music Society of Detroit, led by Karl Haas until he moved to
New York.

"Tiny" Konikow, a dentist, followed Karl and moved the performances
to Orchestra Hall, almost before the rebuilt hall had its new roof. Tiny had
a marvelous rapport with the musicians. He loved them, and they loved
him. Tiny put together an inspiring program for many years, but then, in
failing health, he moved to Florida.

Location changes and timing problems became more severe each year
after the Detroit Symphony moved back to its 1919 reconstructed home.
We retired from the board of the Chamber Music Society and dropped

our season tickets. Now we rely on the Great Lakes Chamber Series, the Detroit Oratorical Society, and the Detroit Chamber Winds.

The Associated Artist Series was performed at Kingswood for many years. Our good friend, Joann Shwayder Clayman, herself a prominent pianist, was the organizer of these concerts as well as a participant in them.

We enjoy the intimacy and the individual performances of chamber music. One of my pet peeves over the years has been attending symphony concerts where all we could see was a row of violins on one side and cellos on the other, plus the sides and feet of those players, and the back of the conductor.

Once the Detroit Symphony had moved to Orchestra Hall and our seats were in a box located almost over the stage, we could see all of the players and observe them as they performed in that optimal acoustical environment.

Jazz, too, has been a source of great pleasure to us, beginning with Dixieland, where the banjo and tuba were important instruments. The banjo has long since been replaced by the amplified guitar, a technological improvement. We were fortunate to be in high school and afterward at the University of Michigan during a time when the outstanding swing bands of the 1930s and 1940s were in their prime. Artie Shaw, Benny Goodman, Glenn Miller, Tommy Dorsey, Count Basie, Duke Ellington, and many others were part of our lives.

The bands were big, and the music is still exciting to us. But it couldn't last because of increasing costs. Gradually came smaller groups led by personalities such as Jonah Jones, Oscar Petersen, King Oliver, Louis Armstrong, and Lionel Hampton, who played great jazz and in some cases are continuing to play great jazz.

Unfortunately from our point of view, the amplification of sound—particularly that of modern rock, heavy metal, and other manifestations of pop music—is highly objectionable because it damages the hearing of those who listen to too much of it.

In addition, we find young people dancing almost by themselves rather than with each other. There is a kind of blatant sensuousness with many of the groups, but the romance is gone.

The sound level of the music, even at the pret-a-porter designer press presentations in Europe, is much too loud. At the same time, I find little satisfaction in or stimulation from it. Rap is the one contemporary form that I do find of interest as long as the lyrics are not violent or vulgar.

Chaotic Times

To me, the chaotic state of contemporary art, architecture, and popular music reflects the pressures and vicissitudes of the times in which we live.

The 50 percent divorce rate dramatically illustrates the breakdown of the family. Because of the high rate of inflation in the last thirty years, in a great many instances it has become necessary for both partners in a marriage to work in order to maintain a decent standard of living. The American dream has become mostly a nightmare in all too many families. On the upper end of the economic spectrum, the wealthy find it easier and easier to increase their wealth and pass it along to future generations.

The high price of both husband and wife working takes its toll on their children. Children in families where both husband and wife are working suffer because of the limitations on the parents' time (regardless of income). They also suffer from the lack of quality day care, to say nothing of the risk of violence with improper day care.

While there has been close to full employment, standards of living and real wages have not increased in recent years. The stock market has done extremely well as corporation after corporation has reorganized and down-sized operations to be more competitive in the world economy, pushing thousands and thousands out of work or into early retirement. While the strong economy has provided job opportunity, many of the displaced middle managers were forced to accept lower-paying jobs.

Corporate pension plans have, in many cases, been changed to 401(k) plans that provide no fixed retirement benefit, adding to the insecurity in the lives of white-collar workers and executives who rely more and more on the stock market. Meanwhile, compensations, at the top of the business pyramid and for those executives who are still a part of it, are out of sight.

The disadvantaged in our society are living a continuing disaster. The verdict is still out on welfare reform, although there appear to be more people with jobs as a result of it. One question that remains concerns the number and status of those who cannot find work or are unable to work.

As this book is being written, many in Congress are attempting to eliminate all federal government support for the arts. This would be a severe blow to the spiritual quality of life. It was different in the days of great royal patrons who provided public art and helped to support struggling artists of the day. Democratic societies must provide government support to the arts, and they do.

The bottom line is that for the members of the middle class, technology has hurt, and not helped, their economic position. From a caring society, we have become one in which the only important value is to beat last year's profit and thereby perpetuate the stock market boom.

For the stock market itself, technology has been a great boon with instantaneous on-line communication providing thousands of mutual funds specializing in many different aspects of the economy with the ability to be valued at least once each day. The Internet and cyberspace are contributing positively to this technological revolution.

Despite new technology, however, without a continuing increase in profitability the Dow Jones Industrial Average, the S&P 500, and the Nasdaq indices can fall substantially with disastrous results for people and especially for retirees. Indeed, the volatility of the financial markets, aggravated by economic disasters in Asia and South America, is becoming more pronounced, jeopardizing the retirement prospects for millions of people.

For the uneducated underclass in our cities, the picture is even more dismal, with poor-quality education from which it is all too easy to drop out. The extremely high unemployment rates among this segment of the population, and the ready availability of drugs, provide easy money to those who are tempted. To make matters worse, transportation is sadly lacking to take people to available jobs. There is no answer for the chronically unemployed except to become involved in criminal activities such as drugs and other crime.

This is the unhappy state of American culture as we close out the twentieth century, a glorious period in the history of the United States and its people. All of the scientific breakthroughs and all of the great technological advances that have built our manufacturing industries and thriving economy have little meaning to about forty percent of the population. Despite substantial improvement in the quality of life during the twentieth century, we find ourselves now with the quality of life in jeopardy for a large segment of our citizens.

7

The Forces of Change

Looking Ahead

Accelerating and ever more rapid technological change has characterized the seventy-five years of my life. In many ways, living in the 1920s was simpler and less stressful than today. Of course, the Great Depression of the 1930s took its toll on many people, as did World War II, the Korean War, the Vietnam War, and the Cold War.

At the same time, each of these events gave rise to significant changes in American society and in our value system. These changes were in many cases triggered by technological changes related to these same events. While the Great Depression affected mainly our political and societal values, the other events triggered much of our new technology.

World War II was the harbinger of jet aircraft, rocket-powered missiles, radar, and—perhaps most profound of all—the gigantic force of nuclear energy. The war set the stage for nuclear electrical generators, commercial jet aircraft, and new communications systems. It also saw the development of punch-card accounting systems, which in turn led to the early vacuum tube computers and to the unbelievably sophisticated computer-chip systems of today.

Nukes

Nuclear power was the astounding development that ended World War II. The basic theoretician and the man who pushed President Roosevelt to set the high priority for scientists and resources to build the atomic bomb was Albert Einstein, a Jewish refugee from Nazi Germany. When the first two atomic bombs, ironically developed by a team of scientists that included many refugees from Germany and Italy, were exploded over the Japanese cities of Hiroshima and Nagasaki in August 1945, the Japanese immediately surrendered.

Nuclear power plants built since the war have been successful in supplying large amounts of electricity. However, substantial safety risks have emerged that have caused huge cutbacks and a preference today for oil- or gas-fired electrical generators. The Russian Chernobyl disaster was the most spectacular nuclear accident to date, with substantial loss of life and exposure to deadly radiation.

In this country, the meltdown of the atomic pile at Three Mile Island served to create a negative climate for the use of atomic energy to generate electrical energy. While a controlled hydrogen bomb reaction without radioactive atomic waste is feasible for the generation of electricity, it is a long way in the future.

Huge amounts of atomic waste, the byproduct of atomic reactions, are important threats to our safety, with burial sites scattered around the country and great potential for leakage and seepage into the water table. Congress has seen fit to avoid facing up to this very dangerous situation. Concentrated research to find answers has been sadly lacking.

There are, of course, important medical advances that utilize radioactive elements created in atomic reactions. Radioactive cobalt for the treatment of certain cancers is a case in point.

The greatest future danger from nuclear energy lies with the possibility that rogue governments will acquire access to the atomic bomb and use it for blackmail to accomplish their political objectives.

Weapons

At a much more elementary level, armaments advanced exponentially during World War II with automatic weapons and rockets of tremendous firepower. At the same time, individual ownership of guns since the end of the war has skyrocketed. The easy availability of guns has led to many murders—premeditated, emotionally driven, and accidental—that have made our society a very violent one.

When will we learn that human values are more important than the right to bear arms? Regardless of the words that seem to provide implicit approval within the Constitution, and regardless of the power of the gun lobby, the availability and the use of guns must be curbed. Today, children carry guns to school, and shootings in schools have become almost commonplace. When will we learn?

Space

With the announcement that the Russians had launched their first Sputnik space capsule carrying an astronaut into orbit in 1962, the United

States, under President John F. Kennedy's leadership, immediately launched a massive space effort that resulted in Neil Armstrong's "giant leap for mankind" when he stepped down from a spaceship onto the surface of the moon in 1969. Subsequent space flights have sent other astronauts to the moon and have sent cameras and other sensors to most of the planets in our solar system. Together with the deep space discoveries of the Hubble Space Telescope and other scientific satellites, these space journeys have broadened and enriched our understanding of our place in the universe.

Electronics

Electronics and telecommunications have already been mentioned in relation to the use of the Internet. They represent broad fields of amazing change during my lifetime, from being practically nonexistent in 1922 to dominant forces by the end of the century.

The cellular telephones and satellite communication systems of today provide for unbelievable availability, consistency, quality, and speed of communications that seem like a dream come true. The ultimate personal communication will be available soon. It will use satellites and permit a single telephone with one's own personal number to be used anywhere in the world.

This all contrasts with the difficulties of making overseas telephone calls fifty years ago, when highly variable radio transmission was the only medium available. While underseas cables were a vast improvement in transmission in the 1950s, they nevertheless were subject to occasional problems and suffered from limited capacity. More recent satellite communications have excellent quality, consistency, flexibility, and capacity.

From no television at all before World War II, another miracle of scientific and technological development is the televisions of today with large screens, quality color, and stereo sound. Direct broadcast television is being replaced by cable networks that are available as another utility cost. Later, cable may well give way to direct broadcast through satellites with the capacity to handle many simultaneous transmissions, including telephone calls and data of all kinds.

The cable networks offer unlimited potential in the number of stations available, but at a price. At the same time, the availability of the free TV stations is gradually being jeopardized, limiting access of the lower economic groups to this important medium. In any event, we are at the beginning of another new and fascinating era of technological changes that will provide new opportunities in communication and in entertainment that hopefully will be available to all people.

Perhaps the greatest sin in connection with new technology is the congressional mandate for a shift to high-definition television transmission (HDTV), which will make all current TV receivers obsolete and require a major expenditure in a few years by everyone who wants to watch television.

It is incomprehensible to me that Congress did not insist on some kind of compatibility, so that present TV sets can continue to be utilized with a picture that is at least very good, if not the ultimate in quality. If one uses audio radio receivers as an analogy, all of the advances in sound quality including the major advance from AM to FM, with a huge increase in fidelity, along with the more recent availability of digital radio transmission and receivers, are available to those who are willing to pay the price, but without compromising the earlier AM and FM receivers.

I know of no precedent for the congressional action comparable to the legislation that makes current television sets obsolete within a few years. The battle cry of Congress, on the one hand, is "Give power back to the states!" On the other hand, Congress has established a national policy on video transmission standards that will be costly to all taxpayers.

The advent and ever-accelerating pace of the computer revolution is probably the single most important influence on our lives today and a major factor in the postindustrial revolution. The first computers, in the early 1950s, were huge vacuum tube calculators with limited or no memory capacity. The invention of the silicon computer chip, with ever-growing capacity and speed, provided the replacement for the limited-capacity, fragile vacuum tube computers. The silicon chip has led the way to large mainframe computers with huge memory, constantly increasing speed, and rapidly decreasing memory costs.

The large mainframes became the data processing work horses of medium and large businesses, including Winkelman's. With IBM, Remington Rand, and Burroughs as the leaders, each year there were continuing improvements in speed, capacity, and capability along with cost reductions.

Programming mainframe computers was expensive and very time-consuming. Large staffs of expensive programmers were essential, and even then there were special problems created by different programming languages as companies upgraded their data processing systems.

But then two new developments occurred that affected the computer business in very positive ways. The first was the development of the Microsoft DOS operating system that set the stage for the desktop, laptop, and even smaller portable personal computers of today and tomorrow. While Microsoft DOS was designed for IBM desktop computers, there was some parallel development with Apple computers.

Bill Gates, a true genius and giant of the computer era, has made possible through his company—Microsoft—the development of an unlimited variety of software that provides the average individual with programming and capability that can meet almost every requirement of the individual or small business, without involving high-priced programmers.

More recently, with the development of larger-capacity and faster chips by Intel as well as Microsoft's introduction of its Windows 95 and now Windows 98, new multimedia operating systems have been created.

Networks of desktop computers have made the mainframe obsolete for many businesses. Desktop computers provide quick communication and access to the database. In some cases, desktop computers are tied into a mainframe. In other cases, they are tied together as very efficient networks.

Simultaneously with these latest developments, on-line services have been established that make possible instant updating of information and email through the use of a modem connected to a telephone line. And now there is the Internet, with its practically unlimited potential for expansion in cyberspace, providing a world of information and communication at the click of a mouse.

While cyberspace potential is unlimited, on a more limited basis—and with huge potential for tremendously increasing our knowledge of the universe—the Hubble Space Telescope is one the most exciting technological developments of recent years with a long list of discoveries since it started to operate. Even the process of repairing it in space was exciting.

Business Effects

For businesses, most of these innovations are very positive in terms of improving efficiency and providing actionable data and control of manufacturing production on a most timely basis. For individuals, that is not necessarily the case. Many middle-management positions have been eliminated, and, while many new jobs have been created, the remuneration for those new jobs is often at a lower level of pay.

There is a tendency in individuals to waste time on the Internet exploring the World Wide Web, which is often time-consuming and unrewarding. Email, on the other hand, can be very productive for interpersonal and business communications because it is direct, inexpensive, and immediately available to those who keep an eye on their computers.

For me, the personal computer has been a godsend. I did have substantial experience in the development, management, and design of the electronic data processing system at Winkelman's. However, it was not until I retired in 1984 that I developed hands-on capability with the PC.

I use the PC for bank accounts, for tracking investments, and for word processing. I used it to design the software program Library-Master, for the control and analysis of Peggy's library. A young specialist did the actual programming for Library-Master, which resulted in a copyright for the Library-Master program.

The fax machine, or, more properly, the facsimile machine, is another development in technology that is a major factor in the speed of communications today. How exciting it is to be able to write or type a message, possibly including photographs, that is instantaneously transmitted to the addressee and instantaneously acknowledged as having been received.

For me, all of this new technology has brought personal excitement and pleasure to my activities since my retirement in 1984. Writing this book, by way of example, would have been impossible for me without word processing software and the capability to put individual chapters together into a total document.

My business activity in retirement has been closely tied to technology that became available, principally, in the last twenty years. In the main, it has been jet aircraft and innovations in communication that have been so beneficial to me. But it is also the availability of new business facilities, such as Kinko's Copies, that supplement my personal ability to get a job done.

One major negative is the telephone system—or, more accurately, systems—with which we must cope today. Yes, capacities have been increased through the use of microwave relays, fiber optic cables, and satellites. Costs have come down, and there is developing competition. But the fragmentation of area codes and the inability to locate telephone numbers because telephone books have been segmented beyond belief are leading us rapidly toward chaos. And then, to top it off and add insult to injury, the telephone companies have increased the charge for "information" calls even as these same telephone companies have created much of the problem by fragmenting printed directories to smaller and smaller geographical areas.

It is all but impossible to talk to AT&T, Ameritech, or MCI personnel directly without long waits on the phone, hoping to hear a live human being rather than another recorded menu designed to waste my time and shield the people from me. Is this progress?

Retirement Views

Since retiring, my life has been absolutely fascinating. My office at the top of the very beautiful Fisher Building for ten years was an inspiration with its view of downtown Detroit and Canada on the south and the Ambassador Bridge and the Ford River Rouge Plant toward the west. I was perched on the southwest corner of the twenty-seventh floor in an office originally occupied by Charles Fisher, one of the Fisher Body Fishers who were the builders of this important Albert Kahn masterpiece.

Despite all of the pressures on, and polarization of, society today, I have been able to continue working on various community projects as I have been doing management consulting work during my retirement. My knowledge of strategic planning, marketing, product design, and human resources management provided the skill base from which I have worked. The computer and the fax machine have become the new tools of my trade.

In addition, I have spent time with many new executives, community leaders, and politicians providing perspective on the history of the nonprofit organizations in the Detroit Metropolitan Region and their relationship to each other. In more recent years, my son Roger has arranged for lunch meetings because he felt I could provide some insight into some aspects of their work.

Early in my retirement, I had a strategic planning assignment to develop a proposal for generational change at the architectural firm of John Greenberg Associates. It has worked out so successfully that John Greenberg Associates has become a leading design firm for the retail industry.

My association with Allen Rosenstein, professor of electrical engineering at UCLA and president of Pioneer Magnetics, led me in 1985 to a USAID project in the Caribbean and to a two-and-a-half-year consulting role with Coopers & Lybrand as a part of President Reagan's Caribbean initiative.

Allen's brother-in-law, who was under contract with USAID through Coopers & Lybrand, suggested that I could be of help with the company's project of increasing the amount of labor-intensive apparel manufacturing in the former British colonies from Grenada on the south to Antigua on the north.

The leader of the project came from Coopers & Lybrand in London and was working out of the Washington office as a part of the USAID Caribbean project. I went to Washington for briefings and then went to work contacting and meeting with apparel manufacturers, some of whom I already knew, to urge them to consider these islands for factories.

The key to success for the project was the "807" provision of the U.S. Customs Regulations, which permits the cutting of piece goods in the United States, shipping to a Caribbean country where the fabric is sewn into garments, and then shipping the garments back into this country with duty only on the value added.

The "807" regulation was apparently designed as a protectionist measure for American textile manufacturers, since it provided them with a significant outlet for fabric that otherwise would have been purchased overseas. At the same time, it provided American apparel manufacturers the opportunity to utilize the cheap labor that was available in the Caribbean islands and to avoid the high-cost labor in this country.

In May 1987, it was time for me to visit the countries involved. I had arranged visits to the area by those U.S. manufacturers who had shown an interest in contracting for assembly of their garments in the Caribbean. My tour of the area began in Barbados, where we met with USAID officials working in that part of the world. Peggy accompanied me on this trip, as she had done on all of my European and Asian trips previously.

In each country, we met with the head of the government to discuss our objective and to evaluate the process for U.S. companies to become established. Licensing regulations, customs regulations, taxes, training programs for workers, labor laws, and a host of other subjects were covered.

Our first stop was Grenada, which was still recovering from the U.S. invasion a year earlier to oust a left-wing government. Grenada is a beautiful island with an excellent harbor and marvelous beaches.

We visited several plants where we met with the owners to assess the environment for building factories as well as the quality of the labor force and the physical facilities. Telecommunications, damaged by the invasion, were being repaired and improved by a Canadian firm, with much of the work remaining to be done.

Our routine was similar in each of the countries we visited: St. Lucia, Nevis, St. Kitts, Montserrat, Dominica, and Antigua.

Several facts became obvious to me as we flew from island to island. First and most important was that labor costs were higher than in other Caribbean countries such as San Salvador, Haiti, or Guatemala. Second, the red tape in most of the countries was excessive. Third, the leadership of the countries in some cases had a reputation for corruption. Fourth, timely shipping was often a problem.

From an American manufacturer's point of view, it was obvious that competent local management in combination with an American manager was most important in the successful plants I visited.

Most of the factories I visited were sewing jeans or intimate apparel. There was one good plant making blouses in Grenada, but that was the exception.

Some of the most successful American operations in these countries were computer data entry installations of large American firms that found it much cheaper to perform this operation in the Caribbean islands, rather than on American soil.

It was later in 1985 that I attended the International Conference of Retailing in Zurich, Switzerland. There, I met Sir Terence Conran, who spoke on the subject of store design. Terence had sold Habitat Stores, of which he was the founder, and was now devoting his time to design. Before long, he bought Del Epostrophe, at Butler's Wharf, across the Thames from the Tower of London. This became a major urban redevelopment project where he built the Design Museum on the water front and an excellent restaurant, Le Pont de la Tour.

While in Zurich, Peggy and I visited Max Bill at his studio in Zurich. We had been friends for a number of years, since the days when we would vacation in Crans-sur-Sierre and then drive on to Zurich. Max, a student at the Bauhaus in the 1930s, was the head of the Bauhaus Archives in Berlin, which we visited in 1986.

Peggy and I would meet Terence periodically on our trips to London. Terence had a growing chain of restaurants, and we would lunch together at one of the establishments and talk about the state of the world, and especially the art world. One day, as we were lunching at Bibendum, he introduced us to Francis Bacon, the artist, who was also having lunch there. Quaglino's and Mezzo are two other of his restaurants where we lunched with Terence or took friends to dinner.

In 1986, Jack Robinson, chairman of the board of Perry Drug Stores and also on the board of Entertainment Publications, Inc., suggested me and Brod Doner, the head of the advertising agency bearing his name, as members of the board of Entertainment Publications. Both Jack and Brod had been on the board of Winkelman's.

The next five and a half years were fascinating as Hughes and Sheila Potiker, the founders of Entertainment Publications, developed their business. Jack, Brod, and I had the continuing challenge of reminding the Potikers of their obligations as the leaders of a company that had recently sold stock to the public.

Hughes Potiker was always looking beyond the successful, growing business and, in the process, brought in a Chicago investment banker from Paine Weber as a board member.

Originally, the capital raised by the sale of stock was to be used for acquisition. However, after a number of false starts, Hughes began pursuing a recapitalization that would keep the Potikers in control but at the same time provide a major distribution of cash. To me, the ethical problems of using the shareholders' money in this way were significant.

As chairman of the outside directors committee established to evaluate the proposal, I hired Ira Jaffe, a very competent Detroit attorney, to represent the committee on which Jack Robinson and Brod Doner also served. I also hired Shearson Lehman as investment banker to evaluate the deal in terms of the minority shareholders as a part of our due-diligence effort.

It wasn't long before I had to report to Hughes Potiker, on behalf of the committee, that the proposal was unfair to the minority stockholders. For the next thirty days, I was regarded as the enemy.

In the end, the problem was resolved by a merger with CUC International in which all of the shareholders received an excellent price for their stock and the Potikers walked away with $100 million.

It was several years after the merger of Entertainment Publications with

CUC that CUC was acquired by Cendant, and, within a short time, that fraud was discovered in the CUC operation. The fraud, however, was in no way related to Entertainment Publications. At this writing, there is talk of Cendant selling off Entertainment Publications.

A Photojournalist

In 1987, I became a photojournalist covering the European pret-a-porter designer press presentations in March and October for the *Observer & Eccentric Newspapers* of Michigan. This has been a series of very exciting experiences for me.

Since I continued to follow fashion developments after my retirement from Winkelman's, being part of the working press had many advantages for me, not the least of which was the opportunity to develop a more interesting writing style to replace the pedantic business style that had become a part of my personality. I had often dreamed of doing some writing, perhaps a book.

For ten years, I covered the pret-a-porter showings twice each year as a photojournalist. The *Observer & Eccentric Newspapers* published my evaluations of the new collections and printed my photographs of the highlights of Paris, London, and Milan in color each season. These trips to Europe provided Peggy with the opportunity to attend the annual congresses of the International Association of Bibliophiles as well as to visit with book dealers and our many friends in the United Kingdom, France, and Italy.

The year 1987 was also when Gil Silverman recommended to Dick Elsea, owner and founder of Real Estate One, that I become a member of the advisory committee to the company. The committee met three times a year until October 1997 and then was discontinued when Dick Elsea turned the management of the business over to his two sons.

I had known Dick Elsea since we worked together in the 1960s on the Detroit Commission on Community Relations. Dick operated with a strong entrepreneurial style in the management of the largest residential home brokerage firm in Michigan. He was not receptive to strategic planning. Like Winkelman's and Perry Drug Stores, Real Estate One had attempted growth outside Michigan with less than satisfactory results.

This same objective, of expanding outside of Michigan, has ultimately led to efforts for Real Estate One to intensify expansion within Michigan with corresponding increases in share of market along the way.

In 1989, I received a call from Eugene Miller, the chairman and CEO of Comerica Bank, asking if I would join the board of the bank's new mutual fund family that a short time later became known as the Ambassador Funds.

This became another fascinating and broadening experience as we were the overseers of a new multimillion-dollar financial institution.

The chairman, Chuck Elliott, treasurer of the Kellogg Company at the time, had been a partner in the Chicago office of Peate Marwick, the national accounting firm. We had a compatible board, and the relationship with George Eshelman, the senior vice president responsible for the investment of the funds and their management, was a very good one.

The latest technology plays a critical role in mutual fund management both in the analysis and execution of investments and in the monitoring of the fiduciary aspects of those investments. On-line communication of pricing and execution of investments is a fundamental part of successful investment today. Mutual funds would not exist, and certainly would not be growing as rapidly as they are, if it were not for the capability of computers and now the Internet to provide instantaneous information.

The situation was a little tricky, since the board of the Ambassador Funds was put together by Comerica. Yet the Ambassador Funds became an independent corporation that hired Comerica as the investment adviser to the funds. This produced, in my mind at least, a potential and inherent conflict of interest if the board were going to truly look out for the best interest of the shareholders.

While the fiduciary aspects of the job were exceedingly important, I felt it was the responsibility of the board to formally review the performance each year. If we were to find the performance unsatisfactory, I would have chosen to resign. But I did not expect that to happen.

Because Ambassador Funds was a start-up operation, I expected the going to be slow in the beginning. Nonetheless, I felt it important to set financial objectives for the funds, however modest, so that the board would have guideposts along the way and be able to measure progress toward those objectives. It did not happen.

In the end, Comerica recognized the weakness of the mutual funds results and chose to work out a joint venture with Lee Munder and his family of mutual funds, The Munder Funds. Unfortunately, because of my age, it was necessary for me to retire from the board just as the joint venture became effective.

In the early 1990s, Frank Stella called me to request that I look over some Russian apparel samples from a "large clean plant in Belarus." Ron Leonetti, former officer of Winkelman's and a good friend to both Frank and me, brought the samples to my office. I looked them over and concluded that the workmanship was good but that the styling, fabrics, and colors left a great deal to be desired. I recommended that Frank send them over to Kmart and ask his friend, chairman Joe Antonini, to have them evaluated.

Ron and I took them to the buyer designated by Antonini and found the evaluation to be the same as mine. The buyer then gave us several samples, which we sent off to Belarus and requested counter samples plus fabric and color swatches. In the meantime, I was expressing my concern with our lack of facility with the Russian language.

Then, one day, I received a call from Jerry Chazen, former merchandise manager of Winkelman's and more recently one of the founders and CEO of Liz Claiborne. Jerry told me that a mutual friend, dress manufacturer Mort Schnapp, had asked him to call me to see if I could help get his girlfriend a visa in Milan so that she could come to the United States. I told Jerry that it was a little bit out of my line, but that I would see what I could do.

My call to Frank Stella was a request to "the coach" as to whether it was feasible for me to respond to Jerry's request, and if so, how I should go about it. Frank's response was positive. I should call the U.S. consul in Milan and request that he approve the visa. The result of an exchange of telephone calls was negative.

I called Frank—my "coach"—to update him and to request further guidance. He suggested that I call Morty Schapp and ask to provide guarantees of Schnapp's girlfriend's return to Milan. As if by magic, within thirty days, the young lady arrived in New York and Morty Schnapp called to thank me for my help and to ask Peggy and me to join him for dinner on our next trip to New York, which we did.

Morty had the young lady with him when we met. We were in for a surprise. She had been born in Russia and spoke Russian fluently. This could be our answer to the supervision of the Belarus plant manager, a dress manufacturer with an "associate" who could speak and read Russian. I asked Morty Schnapp to meet with Leonetti, Stella, and me in Detroit to discuss the possibilities.

The meeting took place and a possible working relationship developed. However, and unfortunately, the project fell through because the plant in Belarus did not have satisfactory piece goods sources.

Postretirement

One of the most gratifying aspects of my retirement has been the development of my son, Roger, into a broad-thinking man, deeply involved in Detroit and the region, both locally and at the state level as well. His commitment to assist in solving community problems goes beyond my own participation and commitment.

I have particularly enjoyed the opportunity to meet with Roger and many community, political, labor, university, and business leaders to discuss their approaches to various problems.

As a direct result of my various consulting assignments, exposure to the workings of a number of companies in different fields as a board member, and also my continued involvement with nonprofit community organizations, my postretirement education has continued at a rapid pace.

At the same time, Peggy's library and her memberships in the Grolier Club and the International Association of Bibliophiles have provided me with a marvelous education in printing, bindings, paper, and publishing. These exposures have also provided me with a perspective on world history that is very exciting.

Peggy has literally saved my life with her wonderful care while, at the same time, providing stimulation and support. She has been a true partner in all I have done.

Facing the Future

Despite the euphoria that exists in the United States today, the condition of the American people is quite depressing when one focuses on the quality of life for a huge number of our citizens. This is especially true when we place their condition in the context of a buoyant economy, the dizzy height of the stock market, and the amazing material progress that has been made since the end of World War II.

Within the Jewish community, I have great concern regarding the shift to the right and away from historic positions that in my view relate to prophetic teaching. Affirmative action is a recent case in point. If Jews do not feel and act with compassion, how will positive leadership be sustained? And what will be the long-term social consequences of "me too" on the right? The negative code words have been provided by the extreme right.

Within the community at large there is an important question: "Is technology a significant positive factor at this time?" The answer is both yes and no.

While technological advances have been miraculous in my lifetime, in many cases they have been offset by economic and political pressures that negate, in whole or in part, the benefits of the scientific advances.

Since 1980, the conservatism of Ronald Reagan, the increasingly bold and strident positions of the radical right, and the influence of some irrational, ultra-conservative members of Congress have managed to polarize American society.

As a result of this political polarization and the economic changes that have taken place, the strength of the dominant middle class has been severely eroded, and the number of those below the poverty line has increased dramatically. At the same time, the number of those individuals with very high incomes and extremely high incomes has grown substantially.

The trickle-down theory of economics was the modus operandi during the Reagan presidency. If the economy was strong, then the benefits to the wealthy would trickle down to the workers. But this did not happen. Instead, until recently, real wages actually declined in the intervening years, with very little current growth as the end of the century approached.

Not only have real wages for workers declined, but, in addition, corporate reorganizations, made possible by new computer and robotics technology along with strong global competition, have taken their toll on middle-class and upper-middle-class executives by reducing their numbers significantly. We have entered a new era in which fewer middle managers are required to supervise first-line managers. Thanks to the computer and the exception reports it produces in prodigious quantities on a very timely basis, and to computerized robotics controls of production, the span of control of middle- and higher-level executives has been markedly increased.

All of this has been accomplished to prepare the United States for the emergent global economy in order to ensure competitiveness and greater profitability for the shareholders in this shrunken world. Meantime, the rich get much richer and the poor get poorer, at a time when there is no national policy, except laissez faire, to buffer these changes that are affecting large numbers of people adversely.

A February 1998 survey of five thousand households by the Conference Board, a nonprofit business-sponsored research organization, published in *Business Week* magazine provided very revealing results to the question, "Are you better off financially today than you were in 1990?"

Significantly, 77 percent of the respondents felt that high-income families were doing better than in 1990. But, more significantly, less than 45 percent of the households surveyed felt that their own families were better off than they were in 1990. At the same time, 37 percent of those questioned felt that young adults were worse off than they were in 1990, and only 17 percent said that the middle class is better off than it was in 1990.

Sadly, there is no national policy that calls for an increase in taxes on those who have benefited enormously. Congress must help society cushion these traumatic changes. Instead of sensitivity to the needs and problems of citizens, opposition to big government is rampant with no significant debate about what could or should be done.

For those two-wage-earner families with young children, and there are many of them today, there is very little quality to their lives. What's more, their children are in jeopardy. Quality child care is not readily available at affordable prices to help shape the lives of the next generation. For the multitude of children living with only one parent, conditions are much worse.

While there are many reasons for women to work, many feel compelled to do so in order to maintain a stable family financial position. But the big question is, how does society help ensure the health and education of their children while their parents are trying to earn a decent living to support them?

"Eliminate regulation" is the loud cry from so-called conservatives, rather than deciding, on a continuing basis, what national regulations are appropriate for the United States today. Where would we be without regulation of pollutants from automobiles? Bank regulation? Stock market regulation? Air transport regulation?

Which is the better way to conserve the American system? Is it by doing away with regulation? Or is it by examining the need for regulation and making sure that whatever regulation is decided upon is appropriate, on a continuing basis, to the particular regulatory problem? Who can be opposed to regulations that ensure the safety of the food we eat and the water we drink?

American industries and professions have had very limited success in policing themselves, and, even then, "policemen" are required to catch the cheats and thieves. If for no other reason, human nature demands policemen (by whatever name the regulators are called) to keep honest people honest.

The notion of self-policing is great in theory, but it requires a discipline that does not exist. The theory of individuals taking the responsibility for their own destiny is also a great theory, but it breaks down when there are sudden and/or significant changes in society, because of major technological advances, or because of other changes in the society such as the huge number of corporate reorganizations in the last fifteen years.

The question is not liberal or conservative in the political sense, but how can we preserve this miraculous political and economic system for our children and our children's children? In my day, the answer was: Vote Democratic, and live like a Republican.

Today, I don't feel that either party is facing the real issues of the day. We have moved from one end of the political spectrum, the left, with communists challenging our democratic system in the 1930s, to the other end, with the influence of conservative Republicans and the religious right, both of which would, if they could, do away with the very elements of public policy that have made the United States so successful in the intervening sixty-odd years since the depths of the Great Depression in the 1930s.

Humanity and compassion, most important to our success as a nation, are being eroded at an alarming rate. Civility in today's political climate is almost nonexistent, while hypocrisy reigns supreme.

The weaknesses in our political, economic, and social structure should be obvious to anyone who wants to think about them in human terms. In this framework, I want to examine some of the major scientific advances in my lifetime, beyond the earlier discussion, for their effect on my life as well as on the human condition.

Starting with medicine, I have witnessed fantastic breakthroughs in the treatment of numerous diseases. My father, who died at the age of sixty-three in 1958, could have lived many more years if there had been an effective treatment for high cholesterol at that time.

As for me, I wouldn't be alive today if it were not for relatively new and very effective treatments for severe asthma, diabetes, and eosinophilic pneumonia. Steroids, all by themselves, save lives every day. Dr. Charles Kirkpatrick, at the National Jewish Center for Respiratory Disease, literally saved my life with his practical advice for managing my asthma during the 1980s. And we continue to talk by telephone every month or two regarding some aspect of my complicated medical problems.

For me, cortisone has been very important in the control of the asthma and the pneumonia, though the potential side effects are a cause of great concern. In time, a better treatment will be developed that will avoid the potential side effects of glaucoma, kidney disease, circulatory difficulties, and osteoporosis.

But these personal examples are only a tiny sampling of the spectacular advances in medicine. The Salk vaccine has all but eliminated the terror of polio that reached epidemic proportions in the 1930s.

AIDS is a modern-day epidemic affecting some thirty million people around the world. Medicine's ability to counteract the disease is moving faster than early predications, but it is not fast enough. In the United States, the growth in the number of AIDS patients is being slowed with improved drugs and drug therapy that help to ease the misery of many, while in Africa the AIDS epidemic runs rampant.

Microsurgery and laser surgery have improved significantly the success of operations on various parts of the human anatomy. Oncology and radiation for the treatment of cancer, along with the development of advanced diagnostic tools, such as the CAT scan and the MRI machine for advanced diagnosis, have made the probability of control and cure of cancer much higher today.

For heart disease, the combination of new drugs and new surgical techniques, including open-heart surgery and angioplasty, has increased substantially the prospects for survival and recovery.

The spectrum of dramatic medical and scientific innovations is mind-boggling. People are living longer and more productively.

More recently, genetic research is generating a whole new field of utilizing genes for treatment of many illnesses. It is also leading to a new generation of pharmaceuticals. We are on the leading edge of medical treatments utilizing genetic engineering.

What a contrast there is in just the last fifty years between the use of sulfa drugs during World War II and the breakthrough with the antibiotic penicillin. Today there exists a whole range of antibiotics for use in combating specific illnesses.

But that is only the positive part of the story. Costs of health care have risen to the point of jeopardizing the health care system itself. Many people have no health insurance. They can't afford it. In addition, a new problem has arisen: the growing resistance of bacteria to antibiotics.

While society in general and our political leaders in particular are recognizing these problems, solutions are very slow in coming because the political climate is negative. True quality of life is only available to those with relatively high incomes. With reference to the more unfortunate among us, the word "compassion" has all but disappeared from our vocabulary.

The trend toward health maintenance organizations (HMOs), or managed care as it has more recently been named, is great in concept but severely lacking in execution. I was co-chair of the health committee of the Economic Alliance for Michigan when, as a group of union leaders and corporate executives, we proposed the use of HMOs and PPOs (preferred provider organizations), and then, after they were approved by the full board, worked for passage of enabling legislation.

The media have emphasized that, in general, more than half of the people are satisfied with their lives. But what about the more than 40 percent who are not happy? The fact is that the disparity between those with high income and those with low income has increased substantially in recent years.

Not only do we have a large underclass today, but we also have lower-middle-class and middle-class populations that can barely make ends meet. The health care system, while in many ways the best in the world, is a major factor in "the safety net" for the nation. Unfortunately, that safety net has a serious hole in it for the lowest economic group, which is outside the network for those who cannot afford insurance. The same is true to a lesser degree for the vast middle class who belong to HMOs, where cost control and bottom-line profit are primary and "health maintenance" is secondary.

Is the quality of health care today substantially better than it was in 1922, the year in which I was born? The answer is a resounding "Yes!" The medical advances in the last seventy-five years are almost beyond belief. Yet the availability of health care for those in the lower-income half of the population has been severely eroded. Even for the elderly, where Medicare has been a marvelous source of support, the system is being threatened by the tax-cutters and expense-reducers in Congress.

Politically, the cry is "Reduce taxes, and reduce federal expenditures." To me, the 1997 tax cut was a mistake of serious proportions along with the "Balanced Budget Act of 2002." If there had been no tax cut, the 1998 budget would have been in balance. Besides, there is no guarantee that with the "balanced budget agreement" the budget will be in balance in 2002, although 1998 showed a projected budget surplus of about one hundred billion dollars.

The wealthiest segment of the population does not need a capital gains tax cut as an incentive to invest. The economic development record of the last fifteen years attests to that. On the other hand, the health care system and the social security system do need urgent attention.

The same is true of education, the most important place where support and incentives are needed if the future quality of our population—in both economic and human terms—is to be ensured. The quality of American society has, for the most part, been built on a great system of public education.

Public education is in trouble today for many reasons. Yet that is no reason to abandon the system, as many would like to do. On the contrary, it is imperative that we provide the opportunity for a quality public education for all of our children. The competence and accountability of teachers and administrators have been urgent issues for many years. However, there is no sign at the city, state, or national level that the political leaders are responding except with lip service and proposals to move away from at least a minimal enforced standard of education for all children.

K–12 education must see major improvement if, as a society, we are to arrest the decline that has already taken place. Politics aside, we must set national standards for reading, math, science, and language, as well as for computer literacy, if the next generation is to meet the challenges of its day.

We cannot afford to waste another generation! Leaving education standards to the states and/or local school boards is out of the question if our place in the world is to be retained. It is the future of the United States that is at stake, not just that of individual cities or states.

With the availability of, and access to, knowledge on the Internet so abundantly present, the earlier young people can learn to utilize that knowledge, the better. It should be obvious that every student should be able to enjoy the excitement of this new technology and, in the process, enhance his or her own individual skills and understanding of the universe.

Community colleges and universities are already taking advantage of the new technology by facilitating the opportunities for research and exposure through Internet connections to research libraries and other sources of information.

The new Undergraduate Library at Wayne State University is a marvelous example of what can be done to enhance the learning process through the incorporation of hundreds of computers and work stations into a library setting.

But, once again, there are serious problems relating to on-line connections in general and Internet connections in particular. Security is a special challenge that comes with being on-line, whether through the spreading of viruses by malicious individuals or by the invasion of privacy by hackers.

Pornography is present, or even rampant, and con artists are out in force, giving rise to calls for regulation. In addition, there is the potential for wasting a great deal of personal time—including a growing problem of Internet addiction—as well as a growing risk of criminal activity.

Can these problems be resolved? Yes, of course they can be resolved! But it will not happen through a laissez-faire or self-policing approach.

The bottom line today in the United States is a mixture of both positives and negatives. Yet there is a very positive outlook for the future if we can overcome the obstacles by working together as a society devoted to the common good rather than for the selfish, politically, or economically powerful few.

It is apparent to me that the degradation and decline of America is well under way. Deregulation and laissez faire will only hasten that decline and further undermine our society.

It is possible, however, that with a strong emphasis on human values, appropriate regulation of society, and constant vigilance with respect to world security, a glorious future is possible for our children's children. The key to a positive future is strong leadership dedicated to improving our whole society.

This memoir would not be complete without a reference to my wonderful children and grandchildren. We love them dearly. I am very proud of each one of them and regard each as very special. Fortunately, all of our children live within six miles of our home, so that we are able to be together with some frequency.

Andra, our oldest daughter, was mentioned earlier in terms of her arrival just as I was leaving the country during World War II. Today, she has two wonderful identical twin grown daughters, Pamela and Tracey.

Pamela earned her bachelor's degree at the University of Michigan and has just completed her first year of rabbinic study in Jerusalem at the Hebrew Union College, to be followed by four years at the Hebrew Union College in Cincinnati.

Tracey, her twin sister, is committed to helping people whether at the Crisis Center in Ann Arbor as a volunteer or in her studies at Schoolcraft Community College to become a nurse. In addition, Tracey works a regular schedule as an assistant manager at a McDonald's restaurant. We are very proud of her commitment to working her way through school.

Pamela and Tracey spent many summers at the National Music Camp at Interlochen. In addition, Pamela spent her high school days at the Interlochen Arts Academy where she developed great skill with the viola.

Meantime, Andra continues her work as a teacher of children, teenagers, and young adults with learning disabilities. She and her husband, Bruce Soble, are a fine couple enjoying their life together as Bruce continues his work at the GM Engine Plant in Romulus.

Margi, our younger daughter, and her husband Donald Epstein have two daughters. Lilly and Lena are lovely, brilliant young ladies who are currently attending Harvard University. They both have very broad interests. Lena demonstrated a strong religious commitment in leadership roles at Temple Beth El High School. Lilly spent one summer as an intern for the Joint Economic Committee of the Congress, where she did currency research and was present for the meetings with Alan Greenspan.

Since the unfortunate death of his brother, Donald has taken over the management of Vesco Oil and is doing a superb job after being a lawyer in the firm of Sommers, Schwartz, and Silvers for many years. Margi practiced law for a number of years before retiring to devote her time to her family. Donald is an excellent golfer, although his game time is currently suffering because of his business commitments.

The community activities of our youngest, Roger, have gone substantially beyond the level of my activities. He is working with numerous nonprofit and community groups as well as with many individuals in the corporate world. His deep involvement in the political process has resulted in his being elected and then reelected treasurer of the Michigan Democratic Party. Roger—a lawyer in the firm of Couzens, Lansky, Fealk—and his wife Linda, an accountant with Blue Cross, are raising two delightful young ladies, Jackie, age twelve, and Julie, age nine.

Roger and Linda enjoy traveling with Jackie and Julie, and they attend many special community events together. Linda is a very warm, committed, and competent woman. With her responsibility for her work at Blue Cross, for the children, and for their home, Linda has her hands full, as does Roger by the nature of his community commitments that tend to run both day and night. Roger is also associated with me in Stanley Winkelman Associates, my management consulting business.

Peggy and I have been fortunate to spend time with Jackie and Julie and to watch them grow under the watchful guidance of their parents. Needless to say, what comes out of the mouths of these two bright girls often surprises us in terms of their awareness; their sophistication continually amazes us.

Peggy and I have been very fortunate to have been able to travel together on many occasions with our children and grandchildren to the Florida Keys, to Palm Desert, and to Scottsdale.

Peggy, Stanley, and Roger on the shore of Lake Superior near Saulte Ste. Marie, 1957.

Peggy and Stanley with daughter Andra Barr and her twin daughters, Pamela and Tracey, at Rancho Las Palmas in Rancho Mirage, California, 1990.

Stanley with Pamela and Tracey near Sedona, Arizona, 1972.

The entire family, except for Lilly Epstein, on their way to the Amtrak station in Dearborn to board the train for Ann Arbor for Stanley's seventieth birthday party, 1992.

Lena and Lilly Epstein (far end of table) and Jackie Winkelman (to Peggy's left) help their grandparents celebrate their fiftieth wedding anniversary in Hawaii, 1994.

In 1961 we took Andra, Margi, and Roger to Europe, where we toured Switzerland in a Volkswagen microbus and spent additional time in Paris, London, and Amsterdam as well.

I stay in touch with my brothers, especially Fred and his wife Carol. Hank and I stay in touch by telephone and email. He and Judy live in Scottsdale. Their children are a source of joy to us. Jack, Fred's twin brother, lost his wife, Sharon, a few years ago. He flies back and forth to San Diego to visit his daughter, Leslie, and her family.

Pamela and Tracey, with their mother Andra and grandparents, standing in front of the Ark, holding the Torah at their B'not Mitzvah, 1976.

Andra with husband Bruce Soble (center) and Andra's
twin daughters Pamela (left) and Tracey (right), 1995.

It was in early 1979 that I gave a surprise party for Peggy at the Perigord Park Restaurant in New York. Our children flew in, as did many Detroit friends, for that event. Gaby and Milton Bluestein, Milton and Carol Petrie, and Stanley Goodman were among the guests. This was the second of three surprise parties I gave for Peggy.

The first surprise party was at the Ponchartrain Hotel in Detroit, and the third was in Palm Springs on her seventieth birthday. At the Palm Springs surprise party, which took place at Le Vallauris restaurant, I presented Peggy with a 400-photograph photobiography that I managed to prepare without her knowledge. I almost cracked up as we listened to Saturday night "big band music" on the drive to the restaurant. The song being played was "You Can't Pull the Wool Over My Eyes."

We have also done some traveling with our grandchildren, depending on their ages and availability at the time. We explored Chicago with Tracey; Paris and London with Pamela. For our fiftieth anniversary, we took Lilly, Lena, and Jackie with us to Hawaii.

We have had a very full and productive life, for which we are very thankful.

Stanley with brothers (from far left) Jack, Hank,
and Fred ready to depart from Escanaba, 1980.

Stanley and Peggy in Palm Springs, California, 1996.

Index

References to illustrations are set in italics

Titles in the Great Lakes Books Series

Detroit Images: Photographs of the Renaissance City, edited by John J. Bukow-
czyk and Douglas Aikenhead, with Peter Slavcheff, 1989

Hangdog Reef: Poems Sailing the Great Lakes, by Stephen Tudor, 1989

Detroit: City of Race and Class Violence, revised edition, by B. J. Widick, 1989

Deep Woods Frontier: A History of Logging in Northern Michigan, by Theodore
J. Karamanski, 1989

Orvie, The Dictator of Dearborn, by David L. Good, 1989

Seasons of Grace: A History of the Catholic Archdiocese of Detroit, by Leslie
Woodcock Tentler, 1990

The Pottery of John Foster: Form and Meaning, by Gordon and Elizabeth
Orear, 1990

The Diary of Bishop Frederic Baraga: First Bishop of Marquette, Michigan, edited
by Regis M. Walling and Rev. N. Daniel Rupp, 1990

Walnut Pickles and Watermelon Cake: A Century of Michigan Cooking, by Larry
B. Massie and Priscilla Massie, 1990

The Making of Michigan, 1820–1860: A Pioneer Anthology, edited by Justin
L. Kestenbaum, 1990

America's Favorite Homes: A Guide to Popular Early Twentieth-Century Homes,
by Robert Schweitzer and Michael W. R. Davis, 1990

Beyond the Model T: The Other Ventures of Henry Ford, by Ford R. Bryan,
1990

Life after the Line, by Josie Kearns, 1990

*Michigan Lumbertowns: Lumbermen and Laborers in Saginaw, Bay City, and
Muskegon, 1870–1905*, by Jeremy W. Kilar, 1990

Detroit Kids Catalog: The Hometown Tourist, by Ellyce Field, 1990

Waiting for the News, by Leo Litwak, 1990 (reprint)

Detroit Perspectives, edited by Wilma Wood Henrickson, 1991

Life on the Great Lakes: A Wheelsman's Story, by Fred W. Dutton, edited by
William Donohue Ellis, 1991

*Copper Country Journal: The Diary of Schoolmaster Henry Hobart, 1863–
1864*, by Henry Hobart, edited by Philip P. Mason, 1991

John Jacob Astor: Business and Finance in the Early Republic, by John Denis
Haeger, 1991

Survival and Regeneration: Detroit's American Indian Community, by Edmund
J. Danziger, Jr., 1991

Steamboats and Sailors of the Great Lakes, by Mark L. Thompson, 1991

Cobb Would Have Caught It: The Golden Age of Baseball in Detroit, by Richard
Bak, 1991

Michigan in Literature, by Clarence Andrews, 1992

Under the Influence of Water: Poems, Essays, and Stories, by Michael Delp,
1992

The Country Kitchen, by Della T. Lutes, 1992 (reprint)

The Making of a Mining District: Keweenaw Native Copper 1500–1870, by David J. Krause, 1992

Kids Catalog of Michigan Adventures, by Ellyce Field, 1993

Henry's Lieutenants, by Ford R. Bryan, 1993

Historic Highway Bridges of Michigan, by Charles K. Hyde, 1993

Lake Erie and Lake St. Clair Handbook, by Stanley J. Bolsenga and Charles E. Herndendorf, 1993

Queen of the Lakes, by Mark Thompson, 1994

Iron Fleet: The Great Lakes in World War II, by George J. Joachim, 1994

Turkey Stearnes and the Detroit Stars: The Negro Leagues in Detroit, 1919–1933, by Richard Bak, 1994

Pontiac and the Indian Uprising, by Howard H. Peckham, 1994 (reprint)

Charting the Inland Seas: A History of the U.S. Lake Survey, by Arthur M. Woodford, 1994 (reprint)

Ojibwa Narratives of Charles and Charlotte Kawbawgam and Jacques LePique, 1893–1895. Recorded with Notes by Homer H. Kidder, edited by Arthur P. Bourgeois, 1994, co-published with the Marquette County Historical Society

Strangers and Sojourners: A History of Michigan's Keweenaw Peninsula, by Arthur W. Thurner, 1994

Win Some, Lose Some: G. Mennen Williams and the New Democrats, by Helen Washburn Berthelot, 1995

Sarkis, by Gordon and Elizabeth Orear, 1995

The Northern Lights: Lighthouses of the Upper Great Lakes, by Charles K. Hyde, 1995 (reprint)

Kids Catalog of Michigan Adventures, second edition, by Ellyce Field, 1995

Rumrunning and the Roaring Twenties: Prohibition on the Michigan-Ontario Waterway, by Philip P. Mason, 1995

In the Wilderness with the Red Indians, by E. R. Baierlein, translated by Anita Z. Boldt, edited by Harold W. Moll, 1996

Elmwood Endures: History of a Detroit Cemetery, by Michael Franck, 1996

Master of Precision: Henry M. Leland, by Mrs. Wilfred C. Leland with Minnie Dubbs Millbrook, 1996 (reprint)

Haul-Out: New and Selected Poems, by Stephen Tudor, 1996

Kids Catalog of Michigan Adventures, third edition, by Ellyce Field, 1997

Beyond the Model T: The Other Ventures of Henry Ford, revised edition, by Ford R. Bryan, 1997

Young Henry Ford: A Picture History of the First Forty Years, by Sidney Olson, 1997 (reprint)

The Coast of Nowhere: Meditations on Rivers, Lakes and Streams, by Michael Delp, 1997

From Saginaw Valley to Tin Pan Alley: Saginaw's Contribution to American

Popular Music, 1890–1955, by R. Grant Smith, 1998

The Long Winter Ends, by Newton G. Thomas, 1998 (reprint)

Bridging the River of Hatred: The Pioneering Efforts of Detroit Police Commissioner George Edwards, 1962–1963, by Mary M. Stolberg, 1998

Toast of the Town: The Life and Times of Sunnie Wilson, by Sunnie Wilson with John Cohassey, 1998

These Men Have Seen Hard Service: The First Michigan Sharpshooters in the Civil War, by Raymond J. Herek, 1998

A Place for Summer: One Hundred Years at Michigan and Trumbull, by Richard Bak, 1998

Early Midwestern Travel Narratives: An Annotated Bibliography, 1634–1850, by Robert R. Hubach, 1998 (reprint)

All-American Anarchist: Joseph A. Labadie and the Labor Movement, by Carlotta R. Anderson, 1998

Michigan in the Novel, 1816–1996: An Annotated Bibliography, by Robert Beasecker, 1998

"Time by Moments Steals Away": The 1848 Journal of Ruth Douglass, by Robert L. Root, Jr., 1998

The Detroit Tigers: A Pictorial Celebration of the Greatest Players and Moments in Tigers' History, updated edition, by William M. Anderson, 1999

Father Abraham's Children: Michigan Episodes in the Civil War, by Frank B. Woodford, 1999 (reprint)

Letter from Washington, 1863–1865, by Lois Bryan Adams, edited and with an introduction by Evelyn Leasher, 1999

Wonderful Power: The Story of Ancient Copper Working in the Lake Superior Basin, by Susan R. Martin, 1999

A Sailor's Logbook: A Season aboard Great Lakes Freighters, by Mark L. Thompson, 1999

Huron: The Seasons of a Great Lake, by Napier Shelton, 1999

Tin Stackers: The History of the Pittsburgh Steamship Company, by Al Miller, 1999

Art in Detroit Public Places, revised edition, text by Dennis Nawrocki, photographs by David Clements, 1999

Brewed in Detroit: Breweries and Beers Since 1830, by Peter H. Blum, 1999

Detroit Kids Catalog: A Family Guide for the 21st Century, by Ellyce Field, 2000

"Expanding the Frontiers of Civil Rights": Michigan, 1948–1968, by Sidney Fine, 2000

Graveyard of the Lakes, by Mark L. Thompson, 2000

Enterprising Images: The Goodridge Brothers, African American Photographers, 1847–1922, by John Vincent Jezierski, 2000